DISCARD

This book is drawn from Robert Prechter's media interviews (1977-2000), selected excerpts from *The Elliott Wave Theorist*, *The Elliott Wave Financial Forecast* and other sources. With a contrary yet common-sense approach to markets and a straightforward style, Prechter tells us what modern investors go out of their way to ignore: the market is layered with complexity. An added bonus is that much of his commentary on markets, investing and social events is timeless. In displaying the full bounty of the Wave Principle, Bob paints a compelling and highly readable portrait of both the structure and the irony behind the social activities of man.

"In the biggest imaginable picture," says Prechter, "the trend is always up, according to the Wave Principle. Mankind is on an upward path, with corrections along the way as he moves through history." Beyond this heartening message, the Wave Principle's true value is the way in which it accounts for those "corrections along the way." In doing so better than any other tool, it has an accomplished record of forecasting success. Bob has extended this success to forecasting changes in the culture at large, which he covers in the final chapter.

Join me on an enjoyable journey through *Prechter's Perspective*.

Peter Kendall, Editor

D1512230

DISCARD

WESTCHESTER PUBLIC LIBRARY

Donated By

Jim Wagner

PRECHTER'S PERSPECTIVE

Conversations with Bob Prechter
Legendary Market Theorist

Edited by
Peter Kendall

New Classics Library

PRECHTER'S PERSPECTIVE

Copyright © 1996/2004 by
Robert R. Prechter, Jr.

Cover photo copyright © 2002 Barry Williams

Printed in the United States of America

For information, address the publishers:
New Classics Library
Post Office Box 1618
Gainesville, Georgia 30503
USA
or visit our website:
www.elliottwave.com

The material in this volume may be moderately excerpted without written permission of the publisher provided that the source
is acknowledged. The publisher would greatly appreciate being
informed in writing of the use of any such quotation or reference. Otherwise all rights are reserved.

ISBN: 978-0-932750-61-7

Library of Congress Control Number: 2004101826

Acknowledgments

This "interviews" book has been in the making since the earliest days of Elliott Wave International. Quotations from various publications were originally assembled by Stephanie White, who also handled proofreading, and Sally Webb, who with Karen Latvala prepared the manuscript for printing. Leigh Tipton and Rachel Webb prepared the charts and graphs, and Marc Benejan designed the cover graphic.

We also owe thanks to the many financial journalists who took the time to look past the immediate prospects for the markets and recognized that the Elliott Wave Principle itself warranted a deeper look.

Contents

Foreword

If you do not rest on the good foundation of nature, you will labour with little honour and less profit.

—Leonardo Da Vinci

Robert Prechter has said many times that the outstanding characteristic of the Wave Principle is the perspective it brings. In the broadest sense of the word, perspective is a mental view where all the relevant data are assimilated into a meaningful relationship.

Leonardo Da Vinci understood the importance of perspective. To illustrate a three-dimensional world on a two-dimensional surface, Da Vinci used methods that came to be known as projective geometry. Similarly, the main thrust of Prechter's work over the last 25 years has been to articulate the tremendous extent to which the three-dimensional world of our everyday lives applies to the financial markets, and vice versa. Da Vinci and the Renaissance painters brought natural images to canvas. Prechter introduced depth to a flat investment world.

Applying the Wave Principle is similar to the artistic technique of perspective because the analyst uses mathematical and visual relationships that are best applied by someone with an artistic mind. The classical definition of art that reigned over the work of Leonardo Da Vinci and his contemporaries is, as Umberto Eco has explained, a practice in which art is one with craftsmanship. Originally, art reflected the opposite of the superficial. It pertained to activities that give man the ability to realize possibilities inherent in nature. Art was knowledge of the rules for making things. The rules were given, objective. "It was a capacity for making something, and thus, a *virtus operativa*, a power of the practical intellect." The Elliott Wave Principle is a result and a tool of this power.

As Bob explains in the following pages, there are two aspects to the Wave Principle's construction that are set deeply in the dictates of natural law. First, there is Elliott's discovery that the patterns in the market repeat themselves at different degrees of trend. Long after Elliott made this discovery in the 1930s, chaos theorists confirmed the existence of fractals throughout the natural realm. The deeper we dig, the more "amazing coincidences" we find. Another trait that sets the Wave Principle on a higher plane of analysis is Elliott's discovery that the number of waves he observed across degrees of trend comprised the Fibonacci sequence. This numerical sequence was presented to the western world by Leonardo Fibonacci in the *Liber Abaci* (1202) or *Book of the Abacus.*

Mathematical historians are sometimes baffled by the long "dull" passages that make up large segments of Fibonacci's book. They cannot understand why the great mathematician who actually introduced Arabic numerals to Europe and was three hundred years ahead of his time wasted so much parchment on currency conversions. "The *Liber Abaci* is not a rewarding book for the modern reader...it stresses problems in commercial transactions, using a complicated system of fractions in computing exchanges of currency," complains one. Undoubtedly, this portion of his book is the "power of the practical intellect" at work. Fibonacci's deep interest in exchange shows that he and Elliott were driven by the same passion for practical application.

Fibonacci says on page 1 of the *Liber Abaci*, "Knowledge of the art very soon pleased me above all else." He refers to his craft as the "school of accounting." Elliott was an accountant as well, one who also took great pride in his work and viewed it as a higher calling. In a 1924 article, he wrote bemusedly of finding that others were not similarly enthralled. "When I introduced myself to one young lady and opened the subject of accounting, she said that the very word 'accounting' made her sick at her stomach." He then explained, "Now, I do not like accounting, but *I do like the work I am doing.*" What to Elliott was the work? As he noted in the same article, "The question is whether you are making money, and if not, WHY. In order to know why, you must know where the difficulty lies."

While practicality is widespread in Western culture, for many, difficulty with the Wave Principle lies in seeing the beauty it offers, or perhaps, in accepting it. It is a beauty so sublime that it is concealed beneath a veneer of high practicality and hard work. We know, however, that it is worth the effort because we owe its very discovery and passage down through the last half century to an underlying appreciation of the Wave Principle's aesthetic. In 1978, when Frost and Prechter were striking up their partnership to co-author *Elliott Wave Principle*, Frost put it this way in a letter to Prechter: "Truth stands so tall in a garden, the galaxies, mathematics and so many other facets of life that it is somewhat of a revelation to find it in such mundane parts of life as the stock market...." Frost goes on to say, "Besides, it is a great way to make money."

Bob's thoughts on the matter appear in the final paragraph of this book. Here he reveals the secret behind his long fascination with Elliott. Readers don't have to read through to the last word on the subject to realize, however, that Prechter's not in it just for the money. Yet, like Elliott, Frost and Fibonacci, he wholeheartedly embraces the practical value of his studies.

From my own experience, I think the Wave Principle brings pleasure because it prompts discovery. Indeed, in compiling these quotations and pursuing historical perspective for this foreword, I made a couple of small discoveries myself. For instance, I "met" Jakob Bernoulli, the 17th century mathematician who is the father of probability analysis. In Section 2, Bob says that "the practical application of the Wave Principle is an exercise in ranking probabilities." Bernoulli, a champion and master of the "practical intellect," was also the first Western observer to recognize the importance of the Fibonacci ratio in nature. By the end of his life, historians say he was very nearly obsessed with its amazing properties. On his tombstone, Bernoulli placed this inscription alongside an etching of the Fibonacci spiral: "The same transformed I shall rise again." Bob notes herein that it is not usually the Fibonacci numbers per se that the Elliott wave analyst makes use of; it's the ratio between the numbers: .618. So, centuries after Bernoulli first recognized its vital importance, Elliott realized that it was one of the essential aspects of the Wave Principle. By observing that aggregate stock prices reflect proportions found throughout nature, he put more distance between his method and all other tools of financial analysis.

As it happens, Elliott's other discovery, the existence of fractal geometry in financial markets, was also foreshadowed by Bernoulli and his brother, Johann. At the dawn of our current understanding, Jakob penned this verse in words as poetic as they are prescient:

So the soul of immensity dwells in minutia
And in narrowest limits no limits inhere
What joy to discern the minute in infinity
The vast to perceive in the small what divinity!

Joy is the emotional reward for the balance and insight that the Wave Principle provides. After all, it binds us together and to nature itself. Bob explains in the pages that follow how Elliott brought this reality to light and how disciplined students can use the rhythm and implications of the Wave Principle to enrich themselves, both financially and intellectually.

—Peter Kendall
1996/2000

Publisher's Note:
The final interviews for this second edition were conducted late in 2000. Now that the first edition has sold out, we are proceeding with publication. The most important expansion of Bob's thinking since that time is the further development of his theories of finance as distinct from those applicable to economics. We will be videotaping his up-coming presentation to the London School of Economics and will perhaps make it available on the web. He is currently planning a third book on socionomics that will address the theoretical framework of this new field. Some of Bob's observations herein about coming bear-market events have already become manifest, but glancing references to a major top in the stock market are still timely here in the first quarter of 2004, as optimism is once again breaking records.

Prechter Meets Elliott

You graduated in 1971 with a degree in psychology from Yale University. How did you get from there to technical market analysis?

Well, at first I thought it was more of a leap than a transition. I had been peripherally interested in markets for a long time starting in high school and continuing in college, mostly because my father was a student of finance and the markets. He was a stock market investor and subscribed to market letters back in the '50s and '60s, which was less common back then. He had a small library on the stock market, and a few of the books were on technical analysis. I would say that is where my interest began. I majored in psychology, but didn't want to be a psychologist, so I thought for awhile that I had wasted my education. Shortly after I decided to make markets a career, I realized that mass psychology is what they're all about. So my training was very useful in the field I finally chose. It wasn't such a leap, after all.

Why didn't you study economics in school?

My freshman year economics prof was a Marxist. I couldn't imagine wasting my time with that kind of mindset. We studied the standard textbook all year, and the idea that the economy was some kind of machine where physics formulas worked was anathema to my understanding of microeconomics. Are we dealing with people or machines? I just thought the whole approach was bogus. The economics I know I learned myself, from great books and studying markets.

You have said that you came into the markets *tabula rasa*, as a blank slate. What do you mean by that?

Just that I didn't learn a lot of theories before going head-to-head with the real thing. I didn't major in economics or finance.

A lot of theories of market behavior that I think are fallacious were started by someone who dreamed up a concept and then tried to force stock market movements into it. If you come to the markets with that kind of bias, you have to unlearn a lot of stuff. My discovery of what Elliott had postulated came after my initial interest in technical analysis, which was generated from an interest in what made markets tick and ultimately how one went about making money in the market.

You found the methods to which you were predisposed, but you didn't make a beeline for Wall Street. You took a few years off to be a drummer in a rock and roll band, but your days in the music industry were numbered — so to speak — when you started carrying stock charts to your engagements. What was it that finally pulled you into the markets?

Quintupling my money in 16 months in South African gold stocks in the early 1970s on my father's advice. In 1972, I purchased shares of West Rand and Orange Free State and sold out with a 400% gain. Even after that, the long term gold rise still had over five years left in it. So despite a limited experience with investments, I figured one thing out early: that was a bull market. Needless to say, to this day, I haven't bettered that rate of gain in unleveraged investments. But at the time, it got my attention.

You had the bug from that point forward?

Yes. Then I started doing a little bit of trading for myself, and I think anybody who wants to do market timing is forced to turn to studying market behavior, because otherwise, you'll go bankrupt. You might go bankrupt anyway, but at least it will not be assured. Once I started studying technical methods, I investigated every one out there.

Along the way, there was naturally some exposure to the other side of stock market study, fundamental analysis. What do you see as the essential difference between technical and fundamental approaches?

Fundamental analysts use data generated outside the market to come to their conclusions. Fundamentalists assess events and situations apart from market behavior, considering them the cause of market movements. They forecast where markets are likely to go in response to those background events or conditions that they feel are significant. For example, they will study the managers of a corporation and the trend of its earnings to decide on such bases whether the company's stock is worth buying. In a macro sense, they will study the political environment, interest rates, the trade deficit and all kinds of outside factors and then will try to predict — I would use the word "guess" — where the market is going.

Since you chose to base your market analysis almost entirely on technical considerations, you've obviously become very comfortable with them. What was it about being a technician that drew you in?

The technician looks at the data generated by the market itself, the construction of patterns within the market, the psychology of the players in the market, the speed and breadth of price change, and so on. He studies past patterns of market behavior and decides from that data which way the market is likely to go next.

You mentioned psychology. How do you *measure* psychology?

We can determine, for example, how many people are short and how many shares are held short. We can calculate the volume of put buying vs. call buying, which are bets on a decline versus an advance. We poll money managers and ask, "Do you think the market is going up or down?" to determine aggregate sentiment. We study reports of the long and short commitments of various types of speculators, both the typically sophisticated and the typically unsophisticated. The latter more easily succumb to fear and hope.

Hope is a bad thing?

Hope is a four-letter word in the world of investment. Only a cold reading of the pertinent factors can keep you on track for more time than you're off.

What other aspects are there to technical analysis?

The speed and breadth of price movement is observed through what are called momentum indicators. Is the market rising with the same internal strength or declining with the same power as it was before? Momentum also considers leadership — that is, which groups of stocks are doing best in an uptrend or falling fastest in a downtrend. We study the breadth of the market — how many stocks or subgroups are rising vs. falling as compared to recent history. All of these have implications with regard to where the market is likely to go next because the market has styles of behavior in this regard.

So history repeats?

I would not say that, no. The tenor of history is patterned, which is a different formulation. Thus, the tapestry of past market behavior often provides valuable information with respect to the most likely direction and extent of future price movement.

Can a novice come in and employ some basic tools and expect to have success?

A friend of mine likes to say that "a kid with a ruler" can sometimes outwit the computers, so restricting yourself to using easily recognizable chart patterns is not too bad an idea. I realized early that with just a ten-day moving average of the net advances and declines, I could make money in the stock market. But by definition, market turns are not "easily recognizable" to the majority. So, while simple technical analysis will make money, using a comprehensive pattern recognition approach gets the most out of technical analysis and has the added benefit of opening your eyes to a good deal of truth about human nature.

Is there a basic secret to market behavior?

The single most important insight is the fact that markets act paradoxically from what novices typically expect.

Why are investor expectations so important?

The principle of investor expectations is one of the most important and least understood of all technical market concepts. To form a bullish opinion on gold, for instance, it is not enough to know that the inflation rate is rising. What is important is how much it is rising relative to what people expected to see. If it is anything equal to or less than what they expected, the price of gold will not rise, since those expectations would already be built into the price. Measuring investor expectations is difficult business, but it's business worth conducting. Ignoring that factor can result in an incorrect conclusion and a costly decision.

An interesting example, outside our field, of the importance of expectations was this headline: "[U.S. Olympic] Hockey Team Completes Collapse With a 3-3 Tie." It's from the 1984 winter Olympics. The actual chain of events was that the team lost its first two games, then tied the third. In other words, the tie was their best result yet. What's more, the team was not supposed to win any medal in the first place! *Sports Illustrated* had already rated Russia, Czechoslovakia, Sweden and West Germany as the best teams. So what, in reality, "collapsed?" Simply the fans' expectations, unrealistically based upon the "miracle" performance of the 1980 Olympic hockey team, a completely different group of players who won against terrible odds, but odds that were probably less than those for the 1984 team. The news writers and commentators pummeled a team that didn't deserve it with outpourings of despair, all because their own expectations had been unrealistically high. To relate this to a market, when in the 1980s inflation failed to provide another "miracle" performance, i.e., an unexpected rate of rise such as occurred in the last major cycle, investor expectations were dashed and the price of gold fell, *even though the money supply continued to be inflated every year since 1980*.

On the other hand, just because you mention "investor expectations" doesn't mean you've said anything sensible. Read this headline, then look below and to the right at the date it appeared:

Heating-Oil Plunges As Warmer Weather Is Seen for Northeast

— April 26, 1984

Doesn't late April normally coincide with the approach of "warmer weather?" I doubt that its arrival was a big jolt to investor expectations. And people wonder how another good but far more complicated concept like the Wave Principle can be misapplied!

For the most part, people don't take the relatively simple first step of measuring a system or indicator against random chance. Most see an indicator or system work once, and believe in it until one time it doesn't work.

Yes. That's the fallacy of expected perfection in a field where success can be measured only by *percentages* of perfection, like a batting average.

Did you investigate any technical approaches that didn't work?

Sure. There are some widely followed theories on Wall Street that I've delved into quite deeply and decided are complete fantasies. It was only the Wave Principle that really stopped me cold and said take a deeper look.

What was it about Elliott that captured your attention?

I had seen some mentions of the Wave Principle in a few market newsletters and a couple of obscure books, and I decided that either this was someone's elaborate fantasy or it was an amazing discovery. I wanted to reject it from what evidence I could find or include it as part of my growing arsenal of technical analytical methods.

How long did it take you to develop your "eye" for discerning these waves?

About 30 minutes — when I plotted my first hourly chart covering a few months. Apparently, there is such a thing as an eye for patterns. One person told me he had trouble finding the fives and threes. The key is to keep a chart. Most people have no trouble seeing the Principle at work.

You accepted it just like that?

When you begin to see the five-wave impulses and the three-wave corrections unfold over and over, it does not take long for you to say either "I see, but I refuse to believe it," or "This is obviously what's happening; let's see how far it continues." It took about a year and a half of applying it until I knew that Elliott was absolutely right. I'm pretty hard-headed, and it takes substantial reason for me to accept a new idea. By that time, I decided I had seen what amounted to proof. I then said to myself, "This is unbelievable. How come no one is commenting on this? The market is pulling back to points he said it should pull back to in the patterns. It is rising up to levels he said it should, in ways he said it should."

What was it that convinced you?

The Wave Principle proves itself when you merely keep a chart. Once I did that, I recognized what was going on rather quickly. The wave patterns are repetitive and at times, over protracted periods, they are easily discernible.

Is it possible that you were simply projecting the patterns you read about in Elliott's work onto the market?

No. For instance, I have used cycles for many years as well, and in that field, I am more of the opinion that some projection is required for the theory to maintain itself. Certainly fundamental analysts project their biases and unfounded conclusions into the market without realizing it and without checking historical correlations that would dissuade them from the effort. I didn't waste any time doing that because I recognized the invalidity of the process from the outset. Elliott is a different story. I observed and forecasted the market in light of the theory, and the results convinced me.

When did you first put it to work?

After I bought those gold stocks, I started to keep charts. I also kept up with A.J. Frost's wave counts in Richard Russell's *Dow Theory Letters*. In December 1974, The Dow made its final low that month. Gold topped in a "B" wave, I called the high at $200 within one day and sold my gold. I turned bullish on the overall stock market and bought shares of six different companies in January 1975. The market blasted higher for six months. Over the next year and a half, gold dropped by one-third.

Sounds like you gave Elliott a road test and liked the way it handled.

Definitely. My next very specific forecast on the market also came to pass. Then I began to make more forecasts and decisions based on it.

They were all good calls?

Some were right and some were wrong, but the more I memorized the patterns and guidelines and became accomplished, the better things got.

Tell us about your first Elliott wave prediction.

This was fun. One day, after learning the simplest aspect of the Wave Principle, that a "five" is followed by a correction, I was talking to my broker, who happened to be at Merrill Lynch, as most beginning investors' brokers are. I said, "Over the next few weeks, the Dow Jones Industrial Average is going to move to a new high, while the Dow Transports will not confirm." I was basically being a wise guy, but my broker said, "Well, O.K., we'll keep an eye on it."

About a month later, in July 1975, my broker called one morning to say that I was going to lose that bet I made. I said, "What bet?" "You know," he said, "about the Transports and the Industrials. The Industrials have been going higher and higher for the past few weeks to post new highs, just like you said, but the Transports are finally catching up, and today they're just points away from making a new high." So with mock confidence, I said, "Call me back at the close."

Just before 3 o'clock, he called back and said, "*How did you know?* The market is falling apart! And the Transports didn't make a new high!" In fact, the market began a rather large correction that very day. The only reason I made that forecast originally was that the Transportation Index had already completed five waves up, a typical Elliott wave pattern, while the Industrials had not. So the Industrials then completed their five waves, while the Transports failed to make a new high in their "B" wave.

A bit later I tried several other forecasts with my limited knowledge, but they did not work out so neatly. For instance, "B" waves sometimes do make new highs, under certain circumstances. So, I decided that either the theory was invalid or there was more to it than had been revealed in the bits and pieces I had read. And that's what turned out to be the case.

In those days, there were no comprehensive books on the subject. In fact, among the few Elliott wave practitioners, there wasn't even agreement as to exactly what Elliott wave was. Where did you turn for the true description?

A friend at Merrill Lynch gave me a barely readable photocopy of Bolton's 1960 book on Elliott. Hamilton Bolton wrote the *Bank Credit Analyst.* He pioneered the studies of bank credit and its relationship to stock prices. He also was the one man who kept Elliott's theories alive from Elliott's death in 1947 until 1967 when Bolton himself died. However, his book still wasn't the original source. So I tracked down R.N. Elliott's original books. They weren't even in the Library of Congress. But I finally dug around in the New York Public Library and found a catalog card listing of a copy on microfilm and had photocopies made. In studying them, I was amazed to find that there was a wealth of information that had been lost to Wall Street. Elliott had actually formulated, in a few short years, a complete and all-encompassing theory of stock market behavior.

So your forecasts got better?

Oh, yeah. I'll never forget seeing the next leg up begin to develop in December 1975. It had an odd beginning, but by the end of the month, I could see that a third of a third wave was about to explode upward. I bought a bunch of calls. And that's back when they were ridiculously cheap. I made more than ten times my money in a few months. I started agreeing with Elliott: It was the secret of the universe! Later I found out that not all waves are so clear.

If the Wave Principle can be that powerful, why was it so obscure at the time you rediscovered it?

Because applying it is a complex task. Few people continued to use it after his death, probably for that reason. A lot of people describe Bolton as a genius. You don't have to be a genius to apply it, but you can't be lazy, that's for sure.

Was Elliott's original work your main source of instruction, or did you have to search out other people who understood the mechanics of it?

I learned entirely from Elliott's original work. In fact, I found that most practitioners of the time were screwing it up by trying to take shortcuts or from lacking the full explanation. No one since Elliott has added anything to his observations of pattern mechanics, except for two pattern variations that I identified in the early 1980s. But they are so minor as to hardly be worth mentioning.* None of the literature following Elliott's death has added anything important to the principle. So even though I did seek out everything written about the Wave Principle, there wasn't anything to learn other than what was in Elliott's work in the first place. However, I believe I have advanced the *implications* of the Wave Principle substantially. [See Section 3. — Ed.]

----

*Note for 2004: Since then, Prechter has added a third pattern variation as well as a host of additional observations in *Market Analysis for the New Millennium*, *View from the Top* and *Beautiful Pictures*.

And this brought you in contact with Frost?

In a roundabout way, yes. Frost had been an associate of Bolton's, and I got to know him when the Market Technicians Association asked me to get him to speak for their annual conference. I didn't know him, but because I was writing Elliott wave reports for Merrill Lynch, they figured I had an "in." Everything worked out, and we met in May 1977. It was at that time we agreed to write a book together, which was certainly a good thing for me.

Your rediscovery of the Wave Principle is, at the very least, a historically significant stock market event. The theory has since become widely followed by analysts the world over. *Elliott Wave Principle* **by Frost and Prechter, the product of this archeological dig, is in its tenth edition and has been translated into a dozen different languages. The method has also attracted notoriety for allowing its most prominent practitioners to predict every historically important turn since its discovery. In your opinion,** *Elliott Wave Principle* **was a definitive restatement of an immutable natural law. Did you realize what you were onto at the time?**

I realized I had found something that dwarfed every other approach I had seen in terms of importance because it was all-encompassing, not only giving you the broad perspective on what markets do but also allowing you to analyze down to the smallest detail. Having a strong handle on the one or two high-probability outcomes over the next day, week or year is extremely comforting. Without that anchor and perspective, I wouldn't be involved in this business. Even more important, though, is its implications about human behavior, human progress and perhaps even the progress of life forms and life itself through time. That is another subject, but it's what has kept me fascinated.

Your interest in markets and technical analysis took you to Merrill Lynch in 1975, where you worked as a technical analyst. In 1979, you started *The Elliott Wave Theorist.* **It's been published continuously since then, initially from New York and more recently from near the shores of Lake Lanier in Gainesville, Georgia. Did your Elliott wave outlook for the markets influence your choice of location?**

Yes, I did have the coming economic debacle in mind. We have a spot on Lake Lanier where I will at least be able to catch fish for dinner if circumstances leave me high and dry someday.

In the 1980s, you gained a measure of renown on Wall Street and eventually Main Street by making a number of accurate long term calls — first catching the tops in gold and silver in 1980 and then the bottom in stocks in 1982. By 1985, your letter was on its way to becoming the premier investment "must read" on the Street — as more than just a market letter. Your commentary extends to a wide range of topics, many of which are beyond the scope of money and markets. How did you accomplish that?

After I had published for five years, word-of-mouth interest was pretty strong. I was interested in getting some notice so that I could get to a wider audience. The way I did it was to enter the U.S. Trading Championship in 1984 in the options trading division. And I poured myself into it. The account was up 444% at the end of the four-month period. At the time, it was the highest score in the history of the contest. That got some attention from the media, and they said "This guy must be for real," and that started, I suppose, what you would call some national attention.

So a lot of people jumped on board?

Frankly, out of all the people who have ever been exposed to the message, probably 2% or 3% ever took it to heart, but that's a large number of people. They stayed interested not just because the Wave Principle has been pretty successful, but because it is so darn fascinating. You are even reading the paper in a completely different light. You are not saying "What does this article *say?*", but "What does it *imply?*"

The great thing is the people who write joyous letters and say, "This is wonderful. It has changed my life, not just financially, but the way I look at everything, my understanding of what's going on in world events, social events and even when I go out and buy a different kind of tie. Or why I like certain kinds of music." That's been the great satisfaction of it. All I can ever do is present the evidence. If someone picks it up and wants to use it, great! The people who don't are the ones who create the trends from which Wave Principle users profit. If you don't have someone who is willing to sell at the bottom of a bear market because they just heard some more bad news, you will not have cheap stocks to buy. If you don't have a bunch of people willing to buy when the dividend yield on stocks is 2% and the trend's been up for 60 years, you're not going to make money, because those are the people who bring values to an extreme and let you profit.

Who are your subscribers?

From the indications I've gotten, the people who subscribe to my letter are generally people who've been around the markets for a while — money managers, traders and students of the market. In some cases, they have subscribed to 15 other market letters first. They are looking for something that satisfies them after going through the ones that are very basic — the ones that say, "Well, we're bullish because we think interest rates are coming down." They want to get into more detail about how the market works.

That is the kind of people I get, and I think a reflection of that is that even when I have been wrong in a market, I have a pretty high renewal rate. When you have a number of general public-type subscribers, as soon as you make an error — which everyone does — they cancel in droves and don't come back. They are searching for unerring perfection, and they go from advisor to advisor, hoping to find what does not exist. But my people have been around enough to know that somebody batting .700 is someone they want to listen to.

Do you expect subscribers to do exactly as you say?

Most take my input, add input from one or two other people, and ultimately make up their own minds. That's all I really want to provide: an adjunct to someone's thinking. All I do is take Elliott's observations and, using those patterns and guidelines, rank the probabilities for the likely paths of the markets. It's just a matter of memorizing the patterns and their implications and having the discipline to apply them without letting your emotions or extraneous information cloud your judgment. And I'm not perfect at avoiding those pitfalls, either. Every now and then I get stubborn, and it's counterproductive.

For a lot of the investors who are familiar with Robert Prechter, the story begins and ends in the 1980s. Throughout the first part of the 1980s, you predicted that the great bull market would be followed by a stock market crash, but you were nonetheless surprised by the events of October 19, 1987. Is that right?

Near term, yes. No one, including me, forecast that big of a drop. Near the top early that month, I was looking for about 300 points down, which according to Mansfield Chart Service was about 700 points more than most advisors, who were then calling for 3000 by year end.

So you were still on the side of the correctly bearish minority. Was that a plus?

Oh, yes. In fact, the crash of 1987 gave us our biggest sub-scription month ever in November 1987 because I got a lot of publicity for the "sell" recommendation of October 5. After hold-ing "long" for over three years from the 1984 low, that advice was on the front page in capital letters just before the Dow fell 900 points. That caused the biggest flood of subscriptions I ever had.

But it was what happened next that compromised your guru status?

Yeah, it wiped it out. After the crash, I didn't say to buy stocks back again. We rode the broadest wave of the bull mar-ket — right up to the 1987 high — and kept all the profits. 1988 was one of my best trading years ever, and I saved subscribers from many debacles in 1990. At the 1987 high, 80 percent of the bull market was over in terms of the Value Line Composite index, which tracks the average stock, but the blue chips and the NASDAQ were just gearing up for glory. So I was too cau-tious for wave five, which developed into the biggest fifth-wave extension in history.

What happened in the other markets that you follow?

We shorted the Nikkei well. We made 100% in silver mining stocks in 1993. We were short for the entire bond collapse of 1994 and covered at the low. We stayed even with the stock market through 1994 just holding T-bills but fell behind in 1995. The stock market had been making the heroes, and my time was up. My first task is to make sure you don't lose money, and I felt that the stock market held too much risk to tell people to get back in. We've made money in other markets since then, but it was just in the wrong markets for the guru image to be maintained.

Where did you go in 1989? You weren't in the papers anymore. It seems like you went into hibernation or something.

After the crash of 1987, investors soon split into two camps. One camp said, "I'll never own stocks again the rest of my life," and the other camp said, "I'll give all my money to professionals to manage through mutual funds, and I won't have to think about it anymore." So the newsletter industry went into a steep decline because either way, people weren't timing the market or picking their own stocks. They didn't even want to hear about it. After about a year, I decided the public was no longer the place to focus my emphasis. There was no use beating the bushes if there was no one in them. So I took a sabbatical in terms of the media. I decided that the right place to focus was on institutional money managers and currency traders. First, professionals understand that market analysis is a task involving probability. Obviously no practitioner can be perfect. The question is, who is among the best? I knew I could satisfy that criterion. Second, I knew they would need good technical analysis when markets change direction. When their fundamental analysts and economists fail them, which means at every major turn, they need our work.

Have you had any forecasting success in recent years?

In 1998, we got back on track again, as *The Elliott Wave Theorist* began identifying a long term topping process that started with a peak in the NYSE advance/decline line. In March this year, the NASDAQ topped out, and there is a long way down to go on that one! We've forecasted gold and silver better than anyone else for over twenty years. You can make a lot of money being on the right side of a bear market, particularly when you can call the rallies along the way. The next bull market in the metals will be a whopper, too.

You also handed off the day-to-day management of the company, Elliott Wave International.

Yes, to concentrate on building the long range vision of the business and write books. But I am now back to my role as CEO.

Over the years, the media seemed to dwell upon the fact that you don't work out of an urban setting. I guess it was an obvious story line because your woodsy location was so far from Wall Street. But by the time the media crescendo reached a peak in October 1987, your two-story home on the outskirts of Atlanta was a "cabin in the woods," according to one foreign press account. Just to set the record straight, you live and work much of the time in an office building in a large, relatively well-populated recreational area about 60 miles from Atlanta.

That's right, and I love this environment. It's an advantage in my opinion to be away from the storm of mass psychology that exists in the financial centers. I have purposely distanced myself from New York to avoid the overload of superfluous information that you are exposed to there. I am an observer of crowd behavior. I think it is extremely difficult to shield yourself from the crowd's influence when you are part of it. In New York, people are always rushing around and panicking because prices are lower or higher for the moment. People are bursting in and out your door every two minutes to holler about some company or some movement in the market. Pretty soon you are so caught up in the whirlwind that it's difficult to focus on the larger picture and calmly do your work.

The same thing applies to quote machines, which are tools of an addiction, like gambling tables. A gesturing hand comes out and it draws you into the short term maelstrom. I used to have the stock market TV station on in the office with the sound off, but I got rid of the TV ten years ago.

But you're still paying pretty close attention. Is it true that you didn't take a vacation for something like 20 years?

Yeah. I was afraid the very week I took off something important might happen in the market, and I would miss it. In fact, that happened in 1981, the week we moved to Georgia. I had seen a little movement in the market that indicated a change in outlook. But my computer and my mailing list were packed in the trailer, and there was no way to get the word out. So I took some flak for missing a market decline. On another occasion, I was around watching the market like a hawk, and made a good call that a close friend of mine, who was neck-and-neck with me in the rankings at the time, missed because he was on vacation. That little thing made a big difference. In the marketing sense, there is a huge gulf between being #1 and #2.

It seems like a delicate balance between paying close attention and keeping your mind from being drawn into the mob. How do you keep from getting dragged into the emotion you're supposed to describe?

Sometimes I still fail at it, although the instances have become fewer over the years. The best antidote is a cold reading of the patterns and indicators. When they do not provide a clear message, the emotional pressure rises. The same thing happens when you have too much money at stake, which is always a prescription for disaster.

What happens when circumstances keep you away?

Back when I traveled a lot, I always tried to arrange to fly when the market was closed. Or if I had to fly when it was open, I would check the market before I left and then immediately after touchdown.

But, rather than leave the impression that the market can all of a sudden change its message, it's pretty rare for that to happen. The market is a *process*. That's why I don't need to put out a letter every week. Once a month is plenty. Novices in the market analysis game can quickly become frustrated because they feel they must know exactly where the market is going every minute. While I personally have to deal with that problem daily because it's my business, for most people it's unnecessary. The market usually gives many warnings before it changes direction.

But there are periods of uncertainty when each day might resolve the picture.

Yes. And in that case, the only thing that's necessary is keeping up your charts. No matter how difficult the pattern is to read sometimes, it always resolves satisfactorily into a classic pattern. As each day or hour is plotted, one after another, as you ponder the probabilities without satisfaction, there will come a point, as in a revelation, when the picture suddenly falls into place, and you can say, "Aha!" In my experience, it has never failed to happen. While a good Elliottician will rarely be completely surprised, the resolution to your train of thought may occasionally be one that you did not expect to find. Either way, it's always a pleasure when you arrive.

What is the greatest reward you derive from your daily work?

Watching the market operate. It is phenomenal how precisely it moves, how cleanly it advances and declines in channels and well-defined triangle patterns with boundaries, how well it reflects mathematical relationships over and over again. What it says is that human beings in the aggregate are acting a little bit as if they're conducting a concert. It's very, very precise, not just a random walk from day to day. Things are very orderly, even the panics. It's quite beautiful to watch.

What are your goals going forward?

If I have a goal as yet unrealized, it is to have R.N. Elliott receive the worldwide recognition he deserves for his pioneering work. He discovered what I think is the greatest breakthrough in sociology ever. The Wave Principle is on par with the discovery of some of the first laws of the physical sciences. I think the social sciences have been operating in a dark age ever since they began. They are in a position similar to where the physical sciences were 400 years ago, just before some of the great discoveries and advances were made.

Interest in Elliott runs deeper on Wall Street than it ever has, but he's still a long way from the history books. If he ever makes it, what will it be for?

In my opinion, all of history flows from the truth that the human mind has an impulsive aspect, that this aspect produces patterns of interaction, and that these patterns of interaction produce results. Elliott broke major ground in the field of sociology when he showed that behavioral patterns inherent in human interaction shape financial events. I would add that they shape *all* collective events and trends. I'm sure that given time and attention, the Wave Principle will ultimately save sociology from the realm of meandering speculation and place it firmly in the sphere of science. Anything that's *true* and this profound ultimately wins.

Is it a natural phenomenon that occurs everywhere? How do you account for its existence?

A short answer is that it results from the unconscious herding impulse that all humans inherit from their evolutionary ancestors. So yes, it is natural. What's more, it's extremely powerful, being an impulse of the primitive pre-rational portion of the brain. *The Wave Principle of Human Social Behavior* has a lot more on the subject.

Why did Elliott remain virtually unknown for so long outside of a relatively small circle of rogue stock market analysts?

Elliott was 50 years ahead of his time, for one thing. History is replete with examples of innovators and discoverers, men years or even centuries before their time, whose ideas reached so far ahead of their contemporaries' that they were ignored by the professional establishment of their day. While Elliott was not ignored, he most certainly was not afforded the recognition he deserved. But that will change. In fact, it already *is* changing. I'm developing a new website, www.socionomics.org, that I hope will help spread the word.

Elliott left behind no estate and few followers. His work is admired far more now than it ever was when he was alive, a fate more like that of a great artist than a great financier. You really had to dig to find out something about him.

Most of it I got from Charles Collins' files and Elliott's market letters. I had good help from three other people, who investigated some obscure government records.

You and your team were eventually able to uncover a rather extensive biography, which appears in *R.N. Elliott's Masterworks*. What was his life like?

Elliott was a fascinating guy. In 1925, he was selected by the U.S. State Department to rearrange the financial affairs of Nicaragua. That's when the U.S. basically ran that country. Previously, he had become well known as a corporate re-organizer. He wrote magazine articles. He wrote books. He traveled much of the world. Basically, he was an efficiency expert who would go into one company after another and reorganize its entire financial base, putting it on sound ground.

Why was he the particular person who discovered the Wave Principle?

Precisely why, no one can know. But his accounting profession certainly made him suited to discover the Wave Principle. In fact, he billed himself as an "expert organizer." Over his entire working life, he took various details, time after time, and examined them to come up with an overall corporate plan. In other words, he took detail and turned it into a whole. And that is what led to his discovery — he took millions of bits of data on price action, recognized the previously hidden pattern and came up with a comprehensive theory on what it was all about.

* * * * * * * * * * * * * *

From R.N. Elliott's Masterworks

"A Biography of R.N. Elliott"

While serving with the Central American railway system in his last corporate executive position, R.N. Elliott wrote a comprehensive book titled *Tea Room and Cafeteria Management*. The first favorable reviews appeared in *The New York Herald-Tribune* and *The New York Times Book Review*, which commented "Mr. Elliott writes with authority upon all these matters because of his wide and varied business experience and observation." Ads referred to Elliott as "an expert organizer," an ability which was later manifest in his exposition of the Wave Principle. In the book, Elliott referred to business cycles as "the ebb and flow of circumstance," a phrase that uses the liquid metaphor he later called "waves."

* * * * * * * * * * * * * *

Is there anyone around who knew him in the late 1930s and early 1940s when he was on Wall Street?

I've talked with three people who had met him personally.

What was Elliott like as a person?

They all described him as being rather professorial. He liked to expound. He was rather impatient, particularly with people who disagreed with him. Apparently, late in his life, he was uninterested in anything other than the discovery that he had made. That makes him sound overly focused, but I think anyone who discovers anything as vitally new and important as he did, knowing also that he was at the end of his life, would probably feel the same way. He was obviously likable, as before his discovery, he had made friends in high places — such as Charles Collins and Jeremiah Jenks — and wrote for a magazine.

Elliott was not a Wall Street person. In the latter days of his career, when he was in his 50s, he was employed in South America as an accountant for several major railroads. What brought him back to the U.S.?

Elliott's lifestyle had been adventurous for decades, and he had a hardy build. But time and chance caught up with him. He contracted anemia in South America. In 1927, Elliott returned to Los Angeles to adopt a more settled lifestyle after 36 years of intense work, travel and hotel living. But instead of recovering, he relapsed. Several times over the next five years he came close to death. His photograph in *Financial World* magazine a decade later shows that the relentless affliction had taken its toll, leaving Elliott much thinner than in earlier years.

If Elliott was a stock market investor at the time, he probably endured a lot of financial pain like everyone else.

It is possible, although there are no records, that he had some money in the U.S. stock market, which was considered safe for widows and orphans in 1928. All I can surmise is that following the 1929-32 crash, Elliott was virtually broke, either from investments or from the expense of his illness. Although he was physically debilitated, he was mentally alert. A guy who had traveled as much as he had was not content to stare at the walls. He got interested in markets. After all, it was one of the most dramatic scenes of the day, not only in the late 1920s but into the early 1930s. He began following some market letters and soon decided to dedicate the remainder of his life to discovering whether there was any way to predict movements in the stock market.

Then in May 1934, two months after his last brush with death, his observations began coming together into a general set of principles that applied to all degrees of price change in the stock averages. Today's scientific term for this part of Elliott's observation about markets is a "fractal." He described these component parts and how they linked together. So the former "expert organizer" of businesses had uncovered the organizational principles behind the movement of markets.

His stock market data must have covered a limited time span — about a century?

Not even. The data available to him was from 1857 until 1938, when his first book was published. He died in 1948. But the patterns he saw in that span of time had implications about the future and the past for decades in both directions.

What was he looking for in the data? Did he have a model or theory about price behavior that he was trying to establish or deny when he first observed his waves?

Elliott had no basic premises, just a mind that was open to the idea that the market might be patterned, which he may have adopted from the then relatively new Dow Theory, which was a set of very few and far more general observations about market behavior. Though the Dow Theorists formed only very rough concepts, they broke ground, tremendous ground, in merely coming up with their observations that market behavior was non-random and tied to investor psychology. That was probably the germ of the idea that kicked off Elliott's research. He read Robert Rhea's 1932 book, *Dow Theory*, and became one of the first subscribers to Rhea's stock market service, *Dow Theory Comment*. Other than that, the Wave Principle was developed entirely empirically, without any preconceived formulations.

What was his procedure?

He did what every good researcher must do. First, he recorded the data that reality provided. He looked at the movements on chart paper and wondered, "Can I find forms that occur over and over again?" His answer was "Yes." He found that they occurred on hourly moves, daily moves, weekly, yearly. He even plotted moves that were decades long and noticed they were following the same form. Likewise, the specific market did not matter. It could be the stock market, the gold price, interest rates or any other market. Then he organized the data, which was his talent. He began recognizing recurrences in the data, so it became clear that there were indeed repetitive patterns, which he ultimately organized into concepts. It was years later that these concepts jelled into his grand theory.

What exactly is Dow Theory and how does it relate to the Wave Principle?

The Dow Theory was developed by Charles Dow in the late 1800s. One of the tenets of Dow Theory is that, in general, a primary bull market runs in three upward phases. In the initial phase there is a lot of disbelief, and the markets are at very depressed levels. The middle phase is a kind of recognition phase when people begin to realize that the fundamentals are improving, and the markets are rising in harmony with them. The final stage is when the euphoria and the gambling come in. Elliott discovered that this basic formula of three steps up, separated by two intervening corrections, making five waves, was applicable not just to a primary bull market but to any degree of advance. He then observed that corrections take a different path: a three-wave shape or variation thereof. Then he observed that these cycles were not independent of each other but part of the market's larger structure, which in turn developed according to these principles.

Obviously, Elliott was the first to put his observation to the acid test. What happened when he applied what he saw in past markets to real time stock market activity?

As he later put it, he felt "something like the inventor who is trying to become proficient as an operator of a machine of his own design." As he got more proficient and corrected errors in his initial formulation, he made more and more accurate forecasts.

* * * * * * * * * * * * * *

From R.N. Elliott's Masterworks
"A Biography of R.N. Elliott"

Collins had put off the numerous correspondents who continually offered him systems for beating the market by asking them to forecast the market. Any truly worthwhile system would stand out when applied in current time. Not surprisingly, the vast majority of these systems proved to be dismal failures. Elliott's principle, however, was another story.

The Dow Jones average had been declining throughout early 1935, and Elliott had pinpointed hourly turns by telegram with a fair degree of accuracy. In the second week of February, the Dow Jones Rail Average, as Elliott had predicted, broke below its 1934 low of 33.19. Advisors were turning negative and memories of the 1929-32 crash were rekindled as bearish pronouncements about the future course of the economy proliferated. The Dow Industrials had fallen about 11% and were approaching the 96 level, while the rails had fallen 50% from their 1933 peak to the 27 level.

On March 13, 1935, just after the close of trading, with the Dow Jones averages finishing near the lows for the day, Elliott sent this famous telegram to Collins: "NOTWITHSTANDING BEARISH (DOW) IMPLICATIONS ALL AVERAGES ARE MAKING FINAL BOTTOM."

Collins read the telegram on the morning of the next day, the day of the closing low for the Dow Industrial that year. The day prior to the telegram, March 12, marked the 1935 closing low for the Dow Jones Rails. The 13-month corrective wave was over, and the market immediately turned to the upside.

* * * * * * * * * * * * * *

It is through Collins that we know about the genesis of the theory. He more or less sponsored Elliott's introduction to Wall Street and helped him think through various aspects of becoming professional. In fact, he was the ghostwriter of a good deal of Elliott's first important book, *The Wave Principle*, which came out in 1938. Did Collins make any contribution to the theory itself?

Yes. The catalyst for tying the Principle to grander natural forces was Collins' discovery that the number of waves in Elliott's idealized pattern reflected the Fibonacci sequence. Collins wrote Elliott during the development of the theory and said in essence, "You ought to read this book by Jay Hambidge on Fibonacci ratios and spirals because I noticed that when you count the waves through lower and lower degrees of trend, you find the Fibonacci sequence." That sent Elliott off on the track to his grand conclusion. It is comforting to know that he did not *start* with the Fibonacci sequence or a theory based on it and then force nature to it. Nature showed its law, and these two men observed it.

We'll talk about Fibonacci some more later, but is it really that crucial to the theory?

It is not crucial to the what, but it is crucial to the why. First, Elliott observed the Wave Principle operate. Then he took the next step and asked, "*Why* does it exist?" He concluded that there must be some progression that human beings go through as they move overall from a state of deep pessimism to extreme optimism and back again, because they continue to trace out these patterns. His eventual conclusion was that it was a natural law of human behavior, that human beings were part of the natural world, and just like trees and wolves and lemmings and anything else you can name, they have certain ways of acting. It shows up in the charts vividly, making it clear that mass psychology is structured. The unifying conclusion, that mankind's progress follows a law of nature exhibited by countless forms of life, is a profound and reasonable explanation that fits the facts.

Were other analysts working with Elliott, or along the same lines as Elliott, at the time he published his theory?

No. Since I have all of Elliott's early correspondence with Charles Collins, I know he had no collaborators. And there is no evidence that any other analyst was working on any idea of the sort, except to a far lesser degree the Dow Theorists who preceded him. Neither did Elliott ever mention any other theory. In poring over the research from that time, I don't find anyone else's research to be remotely similar prior to Elliott's first publication date. His achievement was a leap in understanding, to put it modestly.

* * * * * * * * * * * * * *

From the Foreword to Elliott Wave Principle
by Charles J. Collins

Human nature does not change, nor does its pattern. Four men in our generation have built their reputations in the economic field on this truth: Arthur Pigou, Charles H. Dow, Bernard Baruch and Ralph Nelson Elliott.

Pigou, the English economist, reduced it to the human equation. The upward and downward swings in business, Pigou said, are caused by excesses of optimism followed by excesses of pessimism. An excess in one direction breeds an excess in the other and so on, diastole and systole in never ending succession.

Charles H. Dow, one of America's most profound students of stock market movements, noted a certain repetition in the market's continuing gyrations. Out of this seeming confusion, Dow observed that the market was not like a balloon plunging aimlessly hither and thither in the wind but moved through orderly sequence. Dow enunciated two principles that stood the test of time. His first was that the market in its primary uptrend was characterized by three upward swings. Dow's second principle was that at some point in every market swing, whether up or down, there would be a reverse movement canceling three-eighths or more of such swing.

Baruch, a multi-millionaire through stock market operation and adviser to American presidents, hit the nail on the head in just a few words. "What actually registers in the stock market's fluctuations are not events themselves, but the human reactions to the events. In short, how millions of individual men and women feel these happenings may affect their future. Above all else, the stock market is people. It is people trying to read the future."

Now we come to Ralph N. Elliott, who at the time he evolved his theory had probably never heard of Pigou. Elliott had been working down in Mexico but due to a physical malady – I think he said it was anemia – had graduated to a rocking chair on a front porch in California. With time on his hands, as he endeavored to throw off his difficulty, Elliott turned to a study of the stock market as reflected by the history and movement of the Dow Jones averages. Elliott, in developing his theory through observation, study and thought, incorporated what Dow had discovered but went well beyond Dow's theory in comprehensiveness and exactitude. Both men had sensed the involutions of the human equation that dominated market movements, but Dow painted with broad strokes of the brush and Elliott in detail.

* * * * * * * * * * * * * * *

Was Elliott a trader?

There is no evidence that he traded. Nor should he have. He probably didn't have money to invest in the first place. But consider also that he was already 65 years old by the time he began to research the stock market. By the time he had fully developed the theory and moved to Wall Street, he was nearly 70. And he had no children, no heirs. The idea of making a million dollars couldn't possibly have had much appeal to him. I think it was much more important to him, at that time in his life, to be remembered in history as someone who made a great discovery.

Was most of his analysis directed toward the stock market?

Yes. He took a look at some commodity markets and economic data and made some occasional comments, but for the most part, his focus was the stock market. In fact, I think it was fortunate, because his entire idea that mankind as a whole is traveling along a natural growth pattern is particularly reflected by the stock market. The stock market is essentially a record of the valuation of mankind's productive capacity, which has been in a growth pattern since caveman days.

Why do you say the stock market is a "record" of human progress?

What is the stock market? It is an arena in which people are valuing their fellows' progress every minute it is open. It is a wonderful coincidence that people are so interested in money, because it means that for quite a long time, human beings have kept intricate records of their valuation of productive enterprise. It's the one area of social mood where we have intricate data. You can plot it and see the fractal patterns. The market is not a perfect reflection of overall social mood, but it is a good one.

Implying what?

Since aggregate stock prices are a sensitive valuation of humanity's productive capacity, and by extension, our emotional and psychological feelings of well-being, the fluctuations in those prices are a direct and sensitive record of changes in mankind's feeling of self-worth, which weaves itself into an overall pattern of progress and regress.

You say the best representation of that pattern is the Dow Jones Industrial Average. Why is an average of 30 somewhat randomly chosen stocks so reliable in exhibiting over and over again these phenomena of construction?

I think that part of the answer to the Dow's precision lies in the concept of biofeedback. The Dow Industrial Average is the most widely followed market index in the world. It not only *reflects* the pulse of investors, it *affects* the pulse of investors. Not only do our investment decisions force the Dow to go in a certain direction, but the direction of the Dow often causes us to make those very investment decisions. There is a complex emotional involvement there of which we're quite aware but which we don't fully understand. How else can we explain the fact, for instance, that even though 3M was substituted for Anaconda in the Dow in 1976, the 1976-78 decline still managed to fall exactly to the level which retraced a Fibonacci ratio .618 of the 1974-76 advance?

But the academics say the relationship is not there. The view on campus is that the market is a random walk with an upward bias.

Yes, but that view is rapidly being discredited. I have kept a file on Random Walk for years with plans to refute it. That's no longer necessary. Mathematically speaking, it is much more implausible to argue that the patterns reflected by the market are random or coincidence than it is to accept that changes in mass emotions, as reflected by the stock market and most especially the Dow Jones Industrial Average, have a certain form to them.

Maybe so, but other than the mania-era success of the college pension funds and various student-led investment clubs, academia has very little to show for the holes that have been blown in the efficient market theory. And random walk's cheerleaders clearly have yet to yield. The November 2000 issue of *Money* magazine says, for instance, that "rats and pigeons might make better investors than people do" because they are better at predicting random events. Random still rules the roost.

Not really. The leading-edge people have already laughed it out of town. A Yale professor called it the biggest error in the history of finance.

But if the market is not rational, if it is not controlled by the combined intellect of the people in the marketplace, how can you predict what is going to happen to it?

The unconscious mind is not rational, but *it is not random*, either. It is greatly patterned, and therefore, to a degree, pre-dictable. The truly rational investor must study how that part of the mind operates to gain both an understanding of the dynamic at work and an edge. The Wave Principle is a description of the emotional crowd dynamic, and therein lies its value.

How Markets Behave

What does the fact that the stock market is patterned *mean*?

My addition to the theory is that the stock market is a direct reflection of mass psychological change, which in turn shapes events. If you study the patterns produced by the averages, you must conclude that mankind goes through natural and rhythmic sociological changes. In other words, such changes are not reactions to events, as is popularly assumed, but are natural and occur ahead of related events, which are the results. This is a profound conclusion, and contrary to what everyone has always believed about history. My book, *The Wave Principle of Human Social Behavior* (1999, New Classics Library) is an effort to develop and present this idea more fully.

That sounds like determinism.

It's almost incomprehensible to consider that there could be a mathematical expression that explains mass human behavior. That is the most fascinating aspect of the Wave Principle. People are a long way from accepting it as a possibility in the social sciences. Still, this is not determinism. As individuals, we can unquestionably exert free will. But the style of behavior of the crowd is entirely different from that of an individual. It is based upon unconscious mental processes, not reason, and that is why most people do not understand them, do not accept the possibility, and go on participating in it day after day, year after year!

I'm not sure I see. Is human psychological response the Wave Principle's causal agent?

Not exactly. My opinion is more radical than that. Market psychology is not responsive. It is not the result of events outside the market. Collective psychology is impulsive, self-generating, self-sustaining and self-reversing. The dynamics of social psychology operate by the same dynamics over and over again, regardless of different attendant historical or cultural specifics. Events that make history are the result of the mass mental states that take time to develop. This is the only possible explanation for the constancy of structure and consistency of pattern that markets reveal. Unconscious minds are participating, I would say, as opposed to responding.

The fact that markets follow the Wave Principle, as opposed to some other law, provides the added insight that social mood, and its result, history, follow the same law of pattern found throughout nature in other processes of growth and decay. That is what makes the subject more engaging than, say, the put/call ratio.

You said "markets" and not just "the market." Do you apply it to a lot of different trading arenas?

Yes. And while this is another of the properties that make the Wave Principle attractive, it can also hurt the reputation of the theory if it is applied where it doesn't belong.

Such as?

The Wave Principle works best with markets that are the most heavily influenced by mass psychology. An individual stock may have a lot of reasons for going up or down according to the various investors involved. When you're discussing the entire market, or an average of blue-chip stocks, the bottom line — after all the individual decisions about whether to buy or sell stock A, B or C — is the answer to the question, "As a whole, are people putting money into or taking money out of the stock market?" The answer to that question depends upon their collective emotional state.

Gold in particular follows the Wave Principle impeccably, at least in a world of fiat paper currencies. Gold is a wonderful reflector of the Wave Principle because unlike, say, pork bellies, it is traded by people around the globe, so the prime mover is the psychology of human beings at the most shared and basic level. I think that's one reason the wave structure has been so perfect. If you trade gold or silver, think about using Elliott. It will keep you on track much of the time.

I thought gold went up and down with inflation.

That's not quite it. Gold reflects a psychological orientation to *rates* of inflation as they relate to investor expectations, which is quite a different thing.

But there is some connection?

Sure, but understand what it is. Gold's price relative to currencies certainly reflects the inflationary and deflationary forces in the various states' money supplies, which is made up mostly of promissory notes called bonds, notes, bills and currency. Now, most people respond that this observation proves that markets are mechanical responses, which is utterly false. After all, *inflation and deflation are at root primarily psychological phenomena as well.* They derive mostly from the expansion and contraction of credit, and the other side of the transaction, debt, which is based upon the waxing and waning of aggregate confidence in the financial future. So it still comes back to social psychology, which is the driving force behind change in the rates of debt accumulation and dissolution, and thus of inflation and deflation. For that reason, interest rates reflect the Wave Principle almost as well as gold.

Can't a big fundamental change shake psychology and therefore interest rates or the gold market?

The gold price is not a function of fundamentals but of market dynamics. No sudden event can change those dynamics. Social events are the result of forces that take time to build. The market is not blind to them. It is part and parcel of them.

I just can't shake the idea that inflation caused gold to go up. Or maybe I should say a rising rate of inflation.

Go ahead and say that, if it makes you believe you understand the phenomenon. Then say that disinflation made it stop. Now ask, *what caused the changes in the rate of inflation?* Maybe you will answer, "The Fed created too much credit, and then cut back." Fine, *why did it create too much credit and then cut back?* Keep going, and you keep arriving right back where you started; the question remains the same. What *caused* it? The train of causality is infinite until it ends at one point, which is that *people*, acting in concert, created the phenomenon. If people caused it, then study the behavior of people to answer the original question without taking any intermediate steps. What's actually happening becomes even more compelling when you notice that the market's trends often precede changes in the supposed cause.

* * * * * * * * * * * * * * *

The Atlanta Journal / The Atlanta Constitution
March 5, 1989

The Wave Principle reveals that social psychology is patterned, and to a great degree predictable. The nature of man has within it the seeds, the desire and the requirement of and for change. It's the way people are.

* * * * * * * * * * * * * * *

I think I get it now, so let's switch gears. You have made dramatic forecasts in gold, for instance. But a lot of analysts have looked at the production and demand for gold and reasoned that it would be very difficult for gold to get above $390 or below $250 based on its economic value alone.

I have two responses. First, I do not think you can compute the economic value of gold very well. A lot of people do it based on what it costs to bring it out of the ground, which is irrelevant, or on what industry is willing to pay today, which doesn't reflect what they will pay tomorrow. Prices are a current market mechanism. There is no such thing as so-called intrinsic value. Value is what people are willing to pay for something at a particular moment in time, and that's all.

How about interest rates, where we have the tremendous effect of and control by the Federal Reserve Board?

When I first started following interest rates, I figured, "I'm not going to see wave structures in here, because to a great degree, they are manipulated." I started in 1979, and that was two years into Jimmy Carter's administration. Chaos reigned in the bond market, and upon examination, it was unbelievable how closely the price of money was following typical Elliott wave structures. When the anchor of gold was kicked away by Nixon in the early 1970s, the bond market became a boiling pit of mass psychology. It has been a mixing bowl of confidence, anxiety, hope and fear, shifting back and forth as the players try to guess what the government will do and the government tries to guess what the voters want. That is a terrific background for clear Elliott wave patterns. As for the Fed, today the bond market is bigger than the Fed. The Fed cannot do whatever it wants anymore. If it acts, the market will make a judgment, and depending upon the psychology of bond investors, they can support, neutralize and reverse whatever the Fed attempts to do to affect the money supply. The market is in charge, and the Fed knows it. Why do you think the Chairman keeps going on TV to explain what he's doing? He doesn't want bondholders to panic. Most of the time, though, the Fed doesn't *act*. It *reacts* to what the market has already signaled. Watch closely and you can see it. The idea that these people are masterminds pulling the strings is ridiculous.

O.K., so the Wave Principle is applicable to the stock averages, precious metals, and interest rates.

And currencies, many commodities, and even to hot stocks that reveal powerful psychological forces at work.

Does it also apply to economic trends, such as those in money supply, federal deficits, trade imbalances and the inflation rate?

Yes, but to a lesser degree, because these trends are less direct reflections of the social psychology at work. Still, they are not *that* far removed, so they often show Wave Principle patterns.

It works on orange juice, too. But only to a "lesser degree." How come?

The Wave Principle cannot forecast freezes in Florida. It will reflect the psychology of the players *about* such an event, but it cannot anticipate the event itself.

* * * * * * * * * * * * *

What is the Elliott Wave Principle?

Over the years, the Wave Principle has been described in a lot of different ways by journalists and financial writers. Here is a short representation of how the basic idea has been expressed by a host of publications since 1977:

Financial World
October 15, 1977

Market watchers have long felt intuitively that price changes were wavelike. But until 1938, nobody had formulated these intuitions into a cohesive principle that made counting feasible. In that year, Ralph N. Elliott, a retired accountant, published a monograph that established an entirely new way of looking at the stock market. He not only detected systems of waves in price charts of the DJI but discovered ways of counting them and measuring them that proved to have significant predictive value.

Financial World
September 15, 1979

The Elliott Wave is a statistician's delight – though for others, following its swoops and wiggles can be daunting. Basically, Elliotticians predict the Dow on the theory that mass psychology reacts to and feeds on itself in a swelling pattern known as the Fibonacci ratio.

The (New York) Daily News
May 25, 1981

Prechter closely follows such indicators as trading volume on the Big Board, advance-decline figures, activities of corporate insiders and advisory service sentiment. But the backbone is the Elliott Wave Principle. A brainchild of the late R.N. Elliott, it's based on the theory – developed from massive research – that all bull markets are based on five up-and-down moves; in other words, up, down, up, down, up. The most important and vigorous of these – the one, says Prechter, "where just about everyone makes money"– is the third stage.

Barron's

February 28, 1983

Elliott's axiom was that there is form and pattern in human action no less than there is in physics. In the market there is a regular pattern of building up and tearing down. In a bull market, for instance, there are five waves, three up and two down. Waves one, three and five are up, and two and four are down. Two and four "correct" one and three. Just why there are five, said Elliott, "is one of the secrets of nature."

Financial Planning

October 1984

With an accountant's quiet, methodical zeal, Elliott began watching the market – keeping daily, hourly, and even half-hourly charts of price movements. Only after several years of intense study did he begin to draw conclusions about the patterns he observed. What he found formed the basis of his Elliott Wave Theory, which posits that price movements are the results of mass investor psychology that swings from pessimism to optimism and back in a natural sequence, creating specific, and predictable, patterns.

Wealth

Winter 1985

[The Elliott Wave Principle] is not a cycle theory, for it is not based on the assumption that history repeats itself in a cyclical pattern over and over again, without progressing. On the contrary, Elliott's Wave Principle is a spiral theory, based on his belief in growth through time on a path that is ever upward, with corrections along the way.

Business Week

March 24, 1986

The Elliott wave theory is based on a simple idea: investor psychology – not earnings, interest rates or OPEC – is the driving force behind the stock market. This mass psychology swings from pessimism to optimism in a more or less rhythmic fashion, much like such natural phenomena as the tides. Elliott's work describes the structure of market waves in great detail.

Newsweek

January 17, 1987

How does Prechter know so much? He sees it in the waves, that's how. If it sounds a little weird, take note: Prechter is one of the most accurate market forecasters in America. And he does it using waves – Elliott waves. Prechter is the foremost practitioner of Elliott wave theory, an arcane method of stock market analysis originated by Depression-era accountant R.N. Elliott. Prechter has used the theory to predict every major ebb and flow of the stock market since 1982. Just who is Robert Prechter – and what is his secret formula? Prechter's theory maintains that predictable waves of investor psychology – not interest rates, earnings or oil prices – are the driving force behind stock market cycles. It further holds that such patterns repeat themselves in a complicated numerical sequence first discovered by 13th century mathematician Leonardo Fibonacci. While many analysts find the theory mystical, to say the least, Prechter defends its logic. "It simply says that human beings have a nature and they follow that nature," he says. "People do not act randomly."

The Wall Street Journal
March 18, 1987

The idea behind the Elliott Principle is that stock prices are a barometer of the national mood and that the mood moves in predictable waves between optimism and pessimism. The waves, which are based on stock market data, unfold in specific sequences. For example, the wave in a bull market rally will go up, down, up, down and up, followed by a correction in which waves will go down, up, down. Each wave contains smaller series of waves so that, for example, between January and July of 1984, the market was in a second wave on one scale and a fifth wave on another. A single large wave can last as long as several centuries; one that occurs within other waves can last as short a time as an hour.

The Economist
April 18, 1987

Elliott wave theory teaches that the market moves in a predictable pattern. Such is his confidence in the tenets of Mr. Elliott that Mr. Prechter had been waiting for the bull market of the 1980s ever since 1975. That was when he recognized the market would soon be entering, in Elliott wave-speak, the "fifth wave" of a bullish five wave trend that began in 1932. In Elliott's theory, each upward move is characterized by three up waves and two down (and each downward move by two down and one up). The final fifth up-wave cycle from 1932 began in August 1982.

The Atlanta Journal / The Atlanta Constitution
March 5, 1989

The Wave Principle reveals that social psychology is patterned and to a great degree predictable. More simply put, its key tenet holds that people, being part of nature react [collectively] according to mathematically precise natural laws, the same ones that make it possible for scientists using geometric equations to calculate the rate of growth of plants and animals. The stock market acts according to these laws because it is a creation of man.

Citicorp Futures
November 1995

CFC: Mr. Prechter, in your original book, *Elliott Wave Principle*, you described how "crowd behavior trends and reverses in recognizable patterns." Can you elaborate a little more on what you believe the source of these constant patterns may be?

RP: Sure. People have often accepted the evidence that markets unfold in patterns, but no one has suggested a mechanism for them. It is my opinion that the desire among many individuals to belong to and be accepted by the group, as well as letting others think for them in intel-lectually difficult fields, make their unconscious minds dominate their conscious minds in emotionally charged social settings. When the market panics, for instance, investors are not panicking individually in isolation but in response to the panic of others. The same is true of their buying, but that is a slower process and therefore less obvious. Now, when the unconscious mind dominates, it does not do so randomly (as that would mean no thought at all), but in patterns peculiar to it. Those patterns show up in price movement.

* * * * * * * * * * * * * * *

What is the Wave Principle?

The Wave Principle is, first and foremost, a detailed description of how markets behave. Now, there's probably more that is not in that sentence than is in that sentence. For instance, a detailed description of how markets behave does not refer to what outside events are occurring, such as in the fields of economics, politics, or social trends. It's strictly a study of how human beings behave collectively in the trading arena.

What specifically did Elliott discover?

Elliott's most important discovery is that the patterns that develop in the stock market occur at all degrees of trend. The larger patterns are made up of components that are themselves composed of smaller ones. The same patterns on a smaller scale combine to create any one of those patterns on a larger scale. The larger pattern will combine with several others of the same degree to create an even larger pattern, and so on. He described in detail exactly what those patterns look like. He identified 13 of them. Only recently has data been available for general stock prices back to the late 1700s, and the patterns are there as well.

How did he label the "degrees" of trend?

Elliott began by naming a particular structure with an arbitrary label, Primary degree, a term borrowed from Dow Theory. The next larger degree he called Cycle, and the next larger Supercycle. The lower degrees he named Intermediate, Minor, and so on. We therefore have a way to refer to the degrees of trend that we are talking about.

What was the biggest degree trend he talked about?

Grand Supercycle, which he guessed dated back to the founding of the United States. Since then, more detailed stock market data has confirmed that he was right. That's not the biggest degree, though, as all waves are components of larger ones.

You once referred to the Wave Principle as the "purest form of technical analysis." Why?

For a hundred years, investors have noticed that events external to the market often seem to have no effect on the market's progress. With the knowledge that the market continuously unfolds in waves that are related to each other through form and ratio, we can see why there is little connection. The market has a life of its own. It is mass psychology that is registering. Changes in feelings show up directly as price changes in the register known as the DJIA. The Wave Principle is a catalog of the ways that the crowd goes from the extreme point of pessimism at the bottom to the extreme point of optimism at the top. It is a description of the steps human beings go through when they are part of the investment crowd, to change their psychological orientation from bullish to bearish and vice versa. That description fits the movement of any market, as long as human beings are involved, rather than Martians, who may have a differently operating unconscious mind. Since this aspect of people doesn't change, the path they follow in moving from extreme pessimism to extreme optimism and back again is essentially the same over and over and over, regardless of news and extraneous events.

What is the basic path?

Very simply, Elliott recognized that movement in the direction of the one larger trend subdivides into five waves. Movement against the trend subdivides into a three-wave pattern or some variation involving several three-wave patterns. In rising markets, true bull markets, the subdivisions occur in five waves up, an up-down-up-down-up sequence. Bear markets tend to occur in three wave sequences, down-up-down. Each one of those movements has a shape and a personality. As long as you can recognize the shapes that are occurring, you have a handle on what might happen next.

But the five-wave form does occur on the downside.

Yes, but only as a component of a larger three-wave pattern. The essence of the Wave Principle is that the moves in the direction of the one larger trend are five-wave structures, while moves against the one larger trend are three-wave structures. From that, you can tell what the underlying trend is and invest accordingly.

You just go on Elliott's description alone. Does that mean you must act without knowing what's causing the pattern?

On the contrary, I know what is causing the patterns: human nature as it relates to a person interacting with his fellows. When you ask what outside force is "causing" the patterns, you are asking the wrong question, so you are already on the wrong path. Elliott's description of how markets behave forces you to a conclusion about cause and effect in social events. All of the causes most people assume to be operative are not, such as the latest political speeches or the latest numbers on the economy. They are simply results of the patterns of mass human psychology.

Is Elliott's a mechanical system?

Not really. What we're dealing with here is the behavior of people. If the tools you work with measure something other than the behavior of people, you'll be removed from the reality of what's going on. One of the biggest failures, in terms of approaching the stock market, is to assume that the market is mechanical in the sense that outside action causes market reaction, such as the idea that the market "responds" to Fed policy or the trade balance or political decisions. Others have tried to reduce it to a sum of periodic sine waves, but they always find that it cannot be done, because the market is not a time-repetitive machine in its essence.

From the standpoint of theory, market behavior is tied to a mathematical law, but it is just not the same type of law found in the physical sciences. From the standpoint of practical application, the Wave Principle is tracking a living system, which is allowed variation in its forms, in fact, infinite variation, but limited by an essential form. A rigid system with numbers, strict mechanical numbers, never works.

Doesn't infinite variation imply that anything goes?

Not at all. Trees vary infinitely, but they all look like trees, don't they? And you can tell them apart from clouds, which also vary infinitely, and buildings as well. In fact, despite infinite variability, they are amazingly similar. The same is true of market patterns.

* * * * * * * * * * * * * *

Elliott Wave Principle

The Wave Principle reveals that the market reflects more the properties of a spiral than a circle, more the properties of nature than a machine.

* * * * * * * * * * * * * *

Does knowing Elliott guarantee profits?

Only the most trained and experienced market participants can act contrarily to their natural tendencies. I have yet to meet a man who invested or traded with a completely rational program based on reasonable probabilities without allowing his greed, his fear, his extraneous opinions or his irrelevant judgments to interfere. It is man's emotional side, particularly his social dependency, that makes him think the way his fellows do, and when he does that, he loses money in the markets. At least using Elliott, you have a basis that makes winning possible.

Most users are more interested in how it works than why it works. Is there any one thing people need to remember to make it work for them?

The key to Elliott wave patterns is that the market goes three steps forward for every two steps back. If you do not get scared by the two steps back, and if you are not euphorically confident after the third step forward, you're light-years ahead of the pack. Even then, I would add that it is one easy thing to recognize that the Wave Principle governs stock prices, while it is quite another to predict the next wave, and still another to profit from the exercise. There is no substitute for experience, so that you can learn what you feel and when you feel it, with respect to market behavior.

Is it possible for a machine to recognize Elliott waves, thereby eliminating subjectivity?

Maybe. On the plus side, it could deal with many degrees of data at once. On the minus side, human minds are designed to recognize shapes, and defining them to a computer is not easy.

Along those lines, Jack Frost describes the Wave Principle as something that has to be seen to be believed. Is that what you're saying?

Essentially. The principle is complicated to express in words. With the Wave Principle, you are dealing with a phenomenon that reveals itself visually. Try describing the concept and variations of "tree" in detail to someone who's never seen one and you'll see that it can be a complex task. Saying, "Look! There's one," is a lot easier. The human brain is very good at recognizing a pattern visually. If a computer must be programmed to recognize shapes in the sky, it would be difficult to teach it the difference between a cloud, a bird and an airplane. Once you have that programmed, of course, a blimp floats by and the computer is in trouble. The human brain works differently and is extremely efficient at pattern recognition. If you draw out the Principle, it is much more quickly grasped. Then when you compare actual market pictures with the model, you can accept the truth more readily. It is at the *perceptual* level that it is best presented. Then you can move to the conceptual.

Can you really teach it?

Sure. Video is an excellent approach, for instance. A lot of people have learned how to apply it that way. Some have trouble at first, but then say "Once I saw your video tape, I understood it." After all, waves are pictures.

What do you advise people to do who want to learn to use the Wave Principle?

The first thing to do is to start watching market plots closely. Label and channel the movements according to the Wave Principle. You'll gain confidence immediately if the market is in an impulse rather than a correction. That is when I was fortunate enough to begin, so I saw what was happening quickly. Corrections are more varied and difficult, but as they are always components of larger impulse waves, and because they also *contain* impulse waves, you always can find them at some degree.

Where should I start looking at past data to get the big picture?

You should go back as far as possible, as far back as the data exist.

What are the Wave Principle's key strengths?

Frost liked to say, "Its most striking characteristics are its generality and its accuracy." Its generality gives market perspective most of the time, and its accuracy in pointing out changes in direction is at times almost unbelievable.

Why does the Wave Principle work so well?

Because it is 100% technical. No armchair theorizing from economics and politics is required.

What are its biggest shortcomings?

There is one main weakness, and this accounts for just about all the problems. There are eleven different patterns for corrections. When a correction starts, it is impossible to tell in advance which pattern has begun, so you do not know how it is going to unfold. Therefore, the best that you can do is apply some of Elliott's observations as guidelines in making an intelligent guess as to what it is.

Another problem is duration. Corrections can do what Elliott called "double" or "triple" — that is, repeat several times. Triple corrections are the largest formations possible, so at least there is a limit. These repetitions can be frustrating because they can last decades. For example, we had a 16-year sideways correction in the Dow Jones Industrial Average from 1966 to 1982. A.J. Frost and I thought it was over in 1974 and that the market was ready for another bull wave. To be sure, most stocks rose from that point forward, but the Dow went sideways for another eight years in a doubling of the time element, which caused some frustrations before the next bull wave finally began on August 12, 1982. Another problem is that in rare cases, a wave will contain no extension, such as the advance in November-December 1976, or two extensions, such as the bull market from 1974 to 2000. Those rarities can be frustrating.

It sounds like a chess game. The number of possibilities, and therefore the probabilities of success, vary at certain junctures.

Chess provides an excellent analogy. The market can do whatever it wants, except that it will always do it in an Elliott wave structure. Similarly, your opponent can move chess pieces wherever he wants, except that he must follow basic rules. On the other side of the board, you still have a lot of hard thinking to do despite your absolute knowledge that pieces must move according to those rules.

Are there situations where the Wave Principle does not hold true?

No, it always holds true. But of course, it is one thing to say the markets will follow the Wave Principle and another thing entirely to forecast the future based on that knowledge. It is always a question of probabilities. Once you have hands-on experience with it, once you understand all the rules and guidelines, it is a lot like becoming Sherlock Holmes. There are many possible outcomes, but guidelines force you along certain paths of thinking. You finally reach a point where the evidence becomes overwhelming for a certain conclusion.

Have you ever had a case where you thought the probability of a certain outcome was high, say 90%, but the market went otherwise from your expectation? What did you do then?

Of course it happens. But you should never be wrong for long relative to the degree that you are trying to assess. One of the terrific things about the approach is that it's price that tips you off. With other approaches, price can go a long way before the reason behind your opinion changes, if it ever does. No matter how difficult the pattern is to read sometimes, it always resolves satisfactorily into a classic pattern.

Can you illustrate how knowledge of "wave structure" comes into play when trading?

For instance, the bottom of the fourth wave, which is a pullback, cannot overlap the peak of the first rally. If it does, then it's not a fourth wave. The fourth wave is still ahead of you, and the third wave is subdividing. Knowing this tenet can keep you out of a lot of trouble that an armchair wave analyst would encounter. Another basic tenet is that wave three is never the shortest. It is usually the longest. Wave three is the recognition stage when the majority changes its orientation from bearish to bullish or vice versa.

* * * * * * * * * * * * * * *

R.N. Elliott

(in a letter to Charles Collins)

February 19, 1935

Waves do not make errors, but my version may be defective.

* * * * * * * * * * * * * *

But if there is always a correct pattern, and it is only a matter of seeing it, why aren't accuracy levels higher than the 40%, 50%, 60% or even the 80% ratios of hits to misses?

First, just because R.N. Elliott discerned that the market follows rules as in a chess game doesn't mean you can predict the market's next move. All you can give are probabilities. But the psychological difficulties are at least an equal impediment. Hamilton Bolton once said that the hardest thing he had to learn when using Elliott was to believe what he saw. Despite all I know, I have fallen prey to that problem more than once. The fact that even perfect analysis only results in the best probability provides the uncertainty that feeds the psychological unease. As Frost is fond of saying, "The market always leaves its options open." So when you combine human weakness with a game of probability, the result is many errors in judgment. Nevertheless, I must stress that the ratio of success with Elliott is better than that with other approaches, and that is the only rational basis for judging its value. Besides, the inestimable value of the Wave Principle is not so much that it provides a high percentage of correct "calls" on the market, but that it always gives you a sense of perspective.

Is it possible that the system merely takes into account every possible pattern and thus allows the practitioner to force things into a satisfactory wave count retrospectively — but not prospectively?

No, for two reasons. First, if that were true, then there would be no record of success such as the Wave Principle has over the decades. There are numerological approaches to the market, ones based on fantasy that may as well be dealing with a random walk, and they produce worthless results, as they should. As Paul Montgomery likes to say, a good test of a theory is whether it can predict. Second, there are many non-Elliott patterns that the market *could* trace out if it were a random walk, but it has never done it. I have never seen a market unfold in other than an Elliott wave pattern.

That's the way it often worked throughout your career. I recall another time that you were incorrectly bearish on bonds for a number of months and shorted them continually on your Hotline, but ended up actually making a point and a half of profit.

Yeah, I was proud of that. The near term patterns kept telling me exactly where to sell short. When the market pulled back, I placed the stops properly. All of them were hit, but some were below entry points, so we made money. Well, actually we probably broke even after commissions. But that's better than losing the fifteen points that an unhedged bear using "fundamentals" would have done.

But there has been one big exception. In the 1990s, you shorted the stock indexes a few times and lost money at it. Why is that?

If I could answer that question, maybe I would never lose money again! One reason is that the market provided subnormal corrections from 1987 through 1999. Twice I was ready to cover at a profit and buy if only the market had corrected a bit further, but it didn't. Probably the overriding reason, though, has been my certainty about the degree of the coming trend change. In 1982 and 1983, I described the coming mania, which would be "like 1929, 1968 and 1973 combined...indicators will give sell signal after sell signal, and the market will just keep on going." It was an insight only "Elliott" could provide. Unfortunately, I thought we would reach that point in no more than 8 years, which is actually on the long side for most of history's manias. But it lasted nearly two decades. It was frustrating. If

I weren't such an optimist, I would think that this means that the top is even bigger than Grand Supercycle. Calling the top of a one-year trend within fifteen trading days would be a great call. Calling the top of a 216-year uptrend within 13 years is an equally good call, and I think I've done that. In money terms, I have been wrong for only five years, from 1995 through 1999. So I have been on the wrong side for a relatively short period, though it has been a very long time in terms of people's market experience. I know the biggest bear market in nearly 300 years is upon us, and what we lost over the past few years will be recovered at a fast rate.

What about the opportunity cost?

The idea of "opportunity cost" is valid only if someone gets out at a higher level. Most people won't. The gunslingers who have ignored historic overvaluation to "make money" in the past decade don't understand market cycles, so they will be holding on throughout the down move.

That won't be fun for the person who stays in.

No kidding. His financial dreams will dissolve. Would you rather be that person, or the one who cashed out early and avoided getting caught up in the mania?

Have you ever had a sure thing — a case where the market absolutely had to go up or down?

All Elliott can do is order the probabilities, and they are never 100%. But there have definitely been times when my own mind *felt* that the probability was 100%. I get so excited I can barely contain myself when that happens. I'm usually right then, but not always!

Keep in mind that while one can never say that a certain event must happen, there are times when one can say that a particular market event is impossible. There's always an alternate count, but there are certain things that can't happen under Elliott, which is a very useful fact.

The calls you made on stocks, bonds and gold helped you to establish yourself as a media presence in the 1980s. But one response to the record is to say that the Wave Principle is not behind your success. Some say it is gut feel or instinct, rather than the method. In other

words, it's not the theory, it's the theorist. You've always insisted that it is the Wave Principle. How can you be sure it's giving you the edge and not the other way around?

Gut feel and instinct will get you clobbered in the market. The market *is* the collective gut, which means you have to be counter-instinctual to beat it. The only way to do that is with a method that takes that reality into account.

Looking in more detail at an Elliott wave, what is the progression that takes place over the course of an "impulse," which is Elliott's term for the classic five-wave pattern?

If you watch any of these wave structures, whether over the last 40 weeks, 40 years or 40 minutes, you see the same progression recurring. After a market reaches its low, so-called strong hands — people who have been around a long time, do some buying. Psychology has passed its low point. News remains scary because it is the tangible result of the prior downtrend in psychology. That is the first wave up.

Then the second wave, the correction of the first move, takes place. The vast majority of investors are convinced that wave 1 was merely a bounce in the previous bear market and that wave 2 is the beginning of the next phase of decline. Usually, the fears that were around at the actual bottom recur at the bottom of wave 2. Again, news is very dark, but the prices are ahead of news. They do not fall to a new low.

From that base, wave 3 begins, which is the middle portion of the larger advance, and that third wave is almost always accompanied by increasingly positive news and "fundamentals." Those better fundamentals are the result of the preceding increase in optimism, and they reinforce the psychological upturn. That is why wave 3, as Elliott noted, is most often the longest, strongest and broadest in the sequence. Every day, there is reason to be more optimistic. All of those people who thought during waves 1 and 2 that the long term trend was down finally become convinced that the long term trend is up.

That change persists all the way to the top of wave 3. Then comes wave 4, which is a correction of that long third. Most people have finally become convinced by the top of wave 3 that the long term trend is up. Wave 4 is a surprising disappointment.

From the fourth wave correction low, the market stages the final wave up. The fifth wave is generally easy to recognize because the psychology tends to be more speculative and euphoric, while at the same time, the internal strength, the breadth and usually the momentum of the market are not as strong as they were during wave 3. The psychology goes through its final binge in the fifth wave. That's when, figuratively speaking, the last guy puts his last nickel in, and that's the end of the sequence.

Let's examine one of these waves — the fifth wave — since, by your wave count, the Dow Jones Industrial Average has been in a fifth wave of Grand Supercycle, Supercycle *and* Cycle degree for the better part of many people's lives. What is the profile?

The market is usually quite selective and rotational in a fifth, creating a weak upward trend or even a sideways trend in the advance-decline line. You will often see huge rises in certain individual issues, while many lag significantly. Usually in fifth waves, the general speculation is concentrated heavily in the blue chip sector. You also generally see the market attracting new players, unsophisticated players who have been watching the bull market year after year and finally became convinced that they should be involved.

That is one reason why the market, or at least large segments of the market, becomes extremely overvalued. It is attracting new players who have no concept of value and are willing to buy just because they think someone else will be buying from them tomorrow. In other words, it's an engine that is running on increasingly available fuel — which is more people with money — with its forward movement as it own end. The situation creates a speculative bubble, a chasing of paper value for quick profit. Often it is a craze that sinks very deeply into the society. We had this style of advance in the 1920s, for instance.

In this most recent fifth wave, mechanisms were put in place that fostered terrific speculation. There was the development of the stock index futures market and the very intricate options markets, with options on stocks, options on futures indexes, and so forth. There has been an increased media coverage as well. In fact, it's an incalculable increase. Television, for instance, didn't report on business or markets prior to the 1981 launch of Financial News Network, which is now CNBC. It has been so successful that more all-business news networks have recently been launched. It's a great major top signal.

* * * * * * * * * * * * * *

Money Maker

August/September 1986

Let's take a look at the big picture...From extreme pessimism of the depression lows of 1932, we traced out a textbook five-wave upward stock structure according to Elliott's observations, forming wave I to 1937. We have wave II, a downward correction of that first wave up, which lasted into 1942. We have wave III, a middle upward movement, ending in 1966. Then occurred a fourth wave lasting all the way into 1982, with the Dow Jones Industrial Average moving sideways for 16 years. In inflation-adjusted terms, of course, stock prices during those years were getting killed.

From August of 1982, we have been in the fifth wave. At least it has all the earmarks of a fifth wave, both on a fundamental and a technical basis.

Now that fifth wave, in turn, can also be expected to subdivide into five waves. From the extremes of pessimism in August 1982, we should reach a corresponding stage of optimism at the top. And we have indeed had a first wave up ending in January 1984 with a 500-point rally. We had that 200-point decline in July of 1984, ending phase two. We have been enjoying wave ③ ever since, as I interpret it.

And how high will wave ③ go?

There's no good way to be certain about that. The third wave is not particularly forecastable. However, the later we get into the third wave — in other words, into the fifth intermediate wave within it — the higher we go and the closer we get, the more I'll be able to say it's likely we're going to a particular level. But just from the typical shape of third waves, which tend to be quite long, I estimated at the beginning of this year we would see a minimum of 2700 and a maximum of 3200 in the third leg. And probably, we'll know more later if my prediction for this year holds up.

Before asking what happens next, let's clarify: In addition to the two uptrends you mentioned, are we also in a third larger trend?

Yes, we are talking about the uptrend from 1982, the uptrend from 1932 and the uptrend from the late 1700s. Each one is clearly tracing a five-wave upward structure. The largest has lasted 200 years. History shows that when any five-wave pattern is finished, there is a correspondingly severe correction, or bear market. And we are in the extremely late stages of this 200-year trend.

In effect, all three of these trends will end at the same time. Is that true?

Oh yeah. Each one is a component of another. They will all end at the same instant in time.

Then what?

We will have the largest bear market in the history of the United States.

And an attendant depression?

The world hasn't experienced a major stock market collapse without a severe economic problem following it.

How far down will the Dow go?

Well, based on Elliott's guidelines, it should fall, I would say, at least 90%. This century has already given us one instance where this has happened. So we know this kind of drop occurs; it is merely a matter of deciding when.

* * * * * * * * * * * * * *

What is the relationship between a Kondratieff "long wave" cycle and an Elliott wave Supercycle?

The Elliott Wave Principle and the Kondratieff cycle are entirely different concepts. The Wave Principle is a behavioral pattern that is not tied to periodicity. The Kondratieff is an economic cycle of inflation and deflation that lasts approximately 54 years. The Kondratieff cycle is an interpretation of the data that says that the economy has a recognizable rhythm by which expansion and inflation generally move together until inflation becomes overwhelming and the inflationary side of the cycle peaks. There is then a recessionary period when the increase in inflation stops. Then comes what is called the "plateau" period, during which time inflation is not severe and financial assets boom in value. That is followed ultimately by the "secondary" depression, a severely deflationary period during which prices fall precipitously and economic activity contracts substantially. Today, the "plateau" period is ending. In 1982, I concluded that the last Kondratieff cycle low was in 1949, not back in the 1930s, as most practitioners think, or even in 1942. 1982 to the present has been the "plateau" period, which followed the recession of 1982. The "secondary depression" is due next and should end this decade. And that fits the outlook on the Elliott Wave Principle although they are two different approaches. I explain all this in detail in Appendix B of *At the Crest of the Tidal Wave*.

You've never been timid about making forecasts. But for much of the bull market, you declined to go into great detail about an even larger degree of trend: the Grand Supercycle, which is now the focus of your commentary. Where does the Grand Supercycle begin and end and why the earlier unwillingness?

I didn't discuss that degree much in public because people are not willing to accept that trends and patterns can express themselves over centuries. However, Frost and I certainly made that point in our book, and that is the entire focus of my recent writing. To summarize, the Grand Supercycle is one degree larger trend than the Supercycle, and the Supercycle advance from 1932 to 1995 was the fifth and final phase of a two-century-long period of progress that began in the late 1700s, suggesting even more powerfully that the coming bear market is going to be one for the history books.

But now you're talking about it. Why?

I believe that we are near the cusp of the trend change. If so, then the result will be obvious in half a dozen years, and the Wave Principle will have shown its incalculable worth once again.

We'll talk about those results when we get to the implications of your work in Section 3. For now, let's figure out where the boundaries are in terms of time. How far back in history does the Elliott wave apply?

If man's actions are patterned over five days, five weeks, five years and fifty years, they are probably patterned over 500 years and 5000 years. In applying wave analysis to historical trends and events, it is my contention that all of history can be understood from the standpoint of wave patterns, and in fact at the deepest level *only* from that standpoint. The same patterns appear to be in force back to the start of the Bronze Age.

So the degrees of trend don't stop at Grand Supercycle, big as that is, do they? There's Submillennium, Millennium and Supermillennium degree beyond that. How can you possibly get data across such expansive time frames?

For the last 200 years, data available for researching investment price trends is not especially difficult to obtain. But prior to that time, we have to rely on less exact statistics for perspective. In *Elliott Wave Principle*, we used a long term market price index for a simple "basket of human needs" beginning

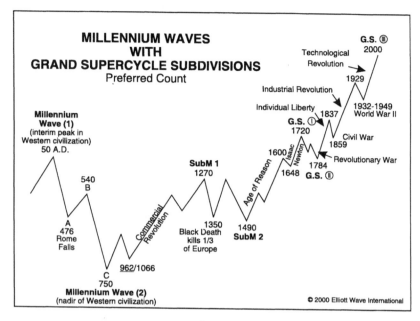

Figure 1-1

in 950 A.D. Strangely enough, this diagram, while only a very rough indication of general price trends, produced an unmistakable five-wave Elliott pattern. To get the picture of social progress, however, I have to work "backwards." That is, I have to assess the social events and make an assumption about where the waves were in their patterns that they would have produced such events. On that basis, a Millennium degree bull market began at the low or the end of the Dark Ages, in either the 700s or the 900s. We've been in a bull market of that degree ever since (see Figure 1-1).

History should show that this 1000-year advance was preceded by a long bear market which was preceded by a bull and so on ad infinitum. Of course, we have no data to capture the wave form, but does the broad outline of history actually show such a pattern?

Rome, whose cultural peak probably coincided with the top of the previous Millennium wave, began to deteriorate shortly after the time of Jesus. The rot continued for a few hundred years until 476 A.D., when Rome fell to the Germans. The next three centuries were dismal. Population was stagnant. Disease ran rampant. Mass slaughters occurred. Progress and the search for knowledge became almost extinct. So that was a bear market all right, and it was of Millennium degree.

What happened next?

The Commercial Revolution from 962/1066 to 1270 or so was behind Submillennium wave 1, an expansion that ushered in the Middle Ages. The leveling of prices from 1270 to 1490 forms wave 2 and represents a "correction" of the progress made during the Commercial Revolution.

The next phase of rising prices began Submillennium wave 3, which is extending. It has been coinciding with the great period of exploration, expansion and cultural advancement. In Grand Supercycle wave ①, business expanded and prices rose during this period of artistic brilliance and increasing luxury. We may not see the likes of it again until the start of the next third wave of Millennium degree. By 1720, prices had reached a peak. The correction that followed, and ended in the late 1700s, was Grand Supercycle wave ② of an extended Submillennium wave 3. The advance from 1784 until now has been Grand Supercycle wave ③. Its center took place from 1859 to 1929, the most rapid period of material progress the world has ever known. Recall that technically speaking, third waves in the stock market have the greatest momentum, and you can see that it's true at the cultural level at large degree.

Those who are skeptical of Grand Supercycles are less likely to accept the concept of Millennium and Supermillennium wave patterns. On the other hand, a lot of people have the idea that the Wave Principle should only be applied to long term averages. Are such restrictions appropriate?

The Wave Principle is better suited to long term study than any other approach I know, but it is also perfectly well suited to assessing trends that last only minutes or hours. As long as you are following the averages, and as long as you can record those trends as the market is moving, you'll find that the same patterns of psychological change occur over and over at the smallest measurable degree as well as the largest. In fact, for one period of time, I kept a computer generated tick-by-tick chart of gold trading. Even on that basis, where mass psychology is getting down to a very small measurement, the patterns persisted. It was a little more erratic, but the basic outline repeated even at that level, which means that some players in the market, those closest to it, are reflecting the smallest fluctuations in aggregate psychology.

In following in Elliott's footsteps, you moved out onto some relatively unexplored intellectual terrain. Your idea that history reflects the Wave Principle is one of them. Your identification of cultural trends as reflective of the overall mood is another. Regardless of the subfield you discuss, though, you reiterate that "mass psychology is structured" and that Elliott identified the structure. After witnessing this movement in the stock market data and its apparent constancy, both you and Elliott have concluded that collective human mood is not random but travels a path as if following a law of nature, like gravity or thermodynamics. If this is true, then science, the study of nature, should supply some corroborating testimony. Is there anything going on in science to support you on this?

During the past 20 years, Benoit Mandelbrot has introduced the idea of the fractal geometry of nature. His computer studies revealed that many processes in nature, while at first appearing chaotic, are actually structured, but in ways most people have never considered. The component structures are not simple geometric forms like circles and squares; they may be very jagged constructs. But the components of the jagged pattern are jagged to the same degree as the larger pattern itself. If you take a stalk of broccoli as a common example, and you break off a piece near the top, the piece you break off looks exactly like a stalk of broccoli. If you break off a smaller piece from it, it also looks exactly like a stalk of broccoli — just smaller. The components take the shape of the whole. What's exciting to me is that Elliott noticed the same thing about stock market prices half a century before Mandelbrot.

It was back in the 1960s that Mandelbrot discovered fractals in a time series for cotton prices.

Re-discovered would be more accurate because we know he was not the first to see layers of self-similar prices patterns in market prices. In his 1938 monograph and 1940 papers, R.N. Elliott described a progression that repeated at different scales and was nothing if not fractal. As a matter of fact, cotton was specifically identified by Elliott as one such market. Mandelbrot's genius was in working out the mathematics and extending the discovery to a whole host of natural systems.

Have the resulting breakthroughs strengthened the link to Elliott?

Scientists have recently observed that people's nervous systems create fractal patterns unconsciously in such things as heart beats and striding. The nervous system is a branching fractal. Elliott waves show that people's collective emotions produce fractal patterns as well.

What about market-specific verification by the scientific community? Considering the potential financial return that could come with an understanding grounded in natural law and the fact that Mandelbrot observed the phenomenon in price data, it seems like something should have come of it by now.

Cutting edge scientific work is definitely converging toward the Wave Principle. Physicist Didier Sornette of the Department of Earth and Space Science at UCLA and his colleague Anders Johansen have presented several studies that analyze past market data to get information on the future. They say the pattern they found "bears some similarity with the 'Elliott waves' of technical analysis." In one paper that appeared in France's *Journal de Physique*, Sornette concluded, "We speculate that the 'Elliott waves'...could be a signature of an underlying critical structure.'" If you want the references, they're in *The Wave Principle of Human Social Behavior*.

Wow! That's great.

I think it's just the beginning. I think some scientists will want credit for re-discovering the Wave Principle. In February 1999, *Scientific American* presented a cover story entitled, "A Fractal Walk Down Wall Street." It was written by none other than Benoit Mandelbrot. In the article, Mandelbrot presented the "new" idea that financial market patterns display multi-fractality. My response to this claim appeared in a special May 21, 1999 issue of *The Elliott Wave Theorist* ("Credit Where It Is Due"), and I'm going to reprint it in a book I'm working on called *Pioneering Studies in Socionomics*. While the article contains important knowledge, I said Mandelbrot had omitted properly crediting most of the ideas in it to Elliott, who put them in his book more accurately with respect to real-world markets sixty-one years before the *Scientific American* article appeared. Comparing the illustrations from the article and from Elliott's works (see Figures 1-2 and 1-3), one cannot help but consider the idea that Elliott was ripped off. And denigrated at the same time, by the way, which is hypocritical.

ELLIOTT'S FRACTAL GENERATOR MODEL (1938)

Wave 1, Wave 2, Wave 3, Wave 4, Wave 5

MANDELBROT'S FRACTAL GENERATOR DEPICTION (1999)

TREND LINE, Piece 1, Piece 2, Piece 3, GENERATOR, INTERPOLATED GENERATOR

Figure 1-2

ELLIOTT'S DRAWING (1940)

MANDELBROT'S DRAWING (1999)

Figure 1-3

* * * * * * * * * * * * * * *

Speech to the Market Technicians Association
May 1986

Benoit Mandelbrot discovered that most patterns that scientists had assumed were chaotic in nature were not. In looking at clouds, seacoasts and mountain ranges, for instance, the typical conclusion was that they were chaotic, governed by no specific geometry. Mandelbrot said that's not true. They follow a relational form that scientists hadn't thought of.

I just want to read some excerpts from an article about his ideas on the way nature develops: "He has invented a new way of describing, calculating and thinking about shapes that are irregular and fragmented, jagged and broken. They turn out to be nature's own...The interesting feature of a lightning bolt's path, for example, is not the straight line direction, but rather the distribution of its zigs and zags...A new kind of symmetry has emerged, not of left to right or front to back, but of small scale patterns to patterns on larger and larger scales — the self-similarity of a broccoli floret whose tiny bifurcations echo the branching of the stalk as a whole...Oddly...the mathematical description of them seemed to apply just as well to very different problems, from fluctuating cotton prices since the 19th century to the rising and falling of the Nile River through two millenniums...In unexpectedly orderly fashion, they have self-similarity on different scales." This description echoes Elliott's observation that stock market movements trace out five waves in the direction of the one larger trend and three waves against that trend *at all degrees, or sizes, of trend*, producing *self-similarity on different scales*...The article continues, "When you zoom in, looking closer and closer, the irregularities don't smooth out. Rather, they tend to look exactly as irregular as before. Some of Mandelbrot's fractal patterns looked indistinguishable from records of stock market prices. Economists needed to understand the heretical idea that prices don't change in a smooth, continuous flow. They can change abruptly in instantaneous jumps. Dam builders and risk insurers of all kinds need to understand that traditional notions of probability lead them to underestimate the likelihood of the rarest, most catastrophic events." Similarly, Elliott recognized that big bear markets are no different in shape from short term reactions. They're just on a larger scale and thus occur less often. They do not, however, occur less often relative to the scale of advances that precede them. A headline making market "crash," for instance, is merely a large version of what happens all the time on smaller scales.

* * * * * * * * * * * * * * *

It is important to note, however, that the personality of wave structures will vary somewhat for different markets. With respect to stocks and commodities, for instance, you've noted some critical differences. Give us an example of how a fifth wave plays differently in stocks than commodities.

When stock markets move into their fifth wave, it's on rising optimism. When commodities move into their fifth wave it's on rising *fear* — fear of inflation, fear of crop shortages, fear of deficits. That's why commodity tops look like stock market bottoms.

From an Elliott wave perspective, there are also differences within the same market. Advances and declines, bull and bear markets, take different shapes. Is this also true of the psychology in bull and bear markets?

The problem with declines is that they can follow a lot more paths, because there are numerous corrective patterns. At the start of a bear market, all you have are hints. You have little certainty about which one of the shapes is going to take place. All you can say is it is going to be rough for a while. Bob Farrell says that a bear market goes from caution to concern to capitulation. In most patterns, that's true, but in contracting triangles, it goes the opposite way: capitulation, concern, then caution, or at least complete disregard.

Bear markets tend to bring bad news in one form or another, regardless of their shape. Triangles, for instance, are seemingly moderate sideways patterns. Yet there is almost always a scary event or point of focus in wave e, the last wave, that keeps you out of the next advance. In a large bear market, wave e of an upward triangle correction usually features a bullish event that gets people to buy just before the rug is pulled. However, the worst news — the news that turns out making the history books — usually awaits the end of a large bear market. Bull markets do it again, only the other way around; they save the best news for last. Just look at the amazing world news of the 1990s: Communists giving up power, old enemies signing peace pacts, the implications of the computer revolution.

Do the different psychologies of bull and bear markets show up in other non-Elliott areas, like momentum indicators?

Oh, yes. For instance, extreme overbought conditions generally indicate further advance until the overboughts become milder. By contrast, extreme oversold conditions often accompany the price low of a decline. Fear does not need a period of dissipation as does hope.

So, a technically strengthening upward thrust in stock prices is usually closer to a bottom than a top?

Acceleration into a top is typical of commodities but not of stocks. The stock market has always given plenty of warning from a momentum standpoint that a top was in the making. From December 1985 to March of 1986, when the bull market of the 1980s was at its epicenter, all the talk of a "blowoff" was coming from the commodity futures traders who have less experience with the stock market than with commodities. Stocks just don't blow off. If you throw a ball into the air, it has to slow down before it comes down. The market doesn't exactly follow the laws of physics, but its action does seem to reflect this one.

Even the 1929 high was accompanied by "top building," i.e., a glaring divergence in the 6-month percentage rate of change. As the great Dow Theorist Richard Russell says, "A blowoff is when the market goes up big, and you were bearish the whole rise." In other words, in the stock market, the idea is a psychological feeling more than a true description of a stock market chart formation. The market slowed into the 2000 top, too. The a/d line topped in April '98, and the corrections of 1997 and 1998 set up momentum divergences in the first quarter of 2000.

Does this slow topping process serve any function?

Many manias in history have outlasted the Cassandras to the end of devastating the finances of the largest possible number of people.

The crowd is buying fantasies. That is why the professional who can measure the amount of emotional activity in a market and relate it to the degree of the wave in progress is going to make money. When fantasies get far out of line with reality, you've been presented with the opportunity to make money, whether it's on the downside or the upside.

Yet you see something more complex underlying the market that can't be discerned with standard momentum and moving average analysis, right?

Momentum is important. Investor sentiment is important. But they are not nearly so valuable alone as they are when used in conjunction with the Wave Principle, because only with a knowledge of the developing patterns can you anticipate the *degree* of an approaching trend change, and therefore the extents that momentum and sentiment indicators should reach at a particular market juncture.

So even a contrary stance can't be rewarding unless one is following the Wave Principle?

Precisely. The problem again is that contrarianism is only a one-way comment. The observation made by contrarians is that at the top of a market, there will be a substantially greater number of bulls than bears. This is a fact, but it doesn't tell you how far the pendulum can swing in one or the other direction. That is why the Wave Principle is necessary. It provides a background for knowing when to go with a trend and when to go against it.

In real time, the Wave Principle is a lot more complicated than it sounds when you simply describe the types of waves. Dealing with corrections is particularly difficult. What makes it so much more difficult to pinpoint your position in a corrective wave than an impulse wave?

Five-stage movements are generally uniform, with very few exceptions to the rule. When prices are moving with the trend, they are moving very freely, and you get the full five-wave structure. In that case, analysis is not that much harder than it sounds on paper. But when the short term trend is fighting the intermediate term trend, it is going against the tide. Corrective processes by their very nature are fighting the larger flow of price movement. When the market is fighting the flow, it can only go so far. It never develops the five waves. In nearly 30 years of studying the market, I've never seen an exception.

Is this also why there are several different ways that corrections can unfold?

Corrections are the point at which the outflowing river meets the incoming tide. The jumble that results is far less uniform than the river's flow or the tidal force. The analyst knows that moves against the larger trend never develop into a full five waves, but he does not know precisely which non-five-wave structure will develop out of this turmoil. Nevertheless, R.N. Elliott's compilation of the list of countertrend patterns is the product of brilliance. Though there are a number of them, he described them clearly, and that is of substantial value in practical application.

Is there a simple guideline that a novice can follow to help him weather corrective Elliott wave patterns?

Sure. During these periods in which Elliott wave analysis is the most difficult, do nothing. It is not necessary to forecast all the time unless you are in the business, like I am. So just wait for the pattern to clear and then take action.

Some analysts get annoyed at this. They say, "That's the problem with the Wave Principle. It doesn't work in bear markets."

Well, tough break! Bear markets are what they are. If someone objects to what the market *is*, then he is arguing with nature and the reality of markets. "Less predictable" does not mean impossible, indecipherable, disorderly or random, either. You can form *some* useful opinions about corrections. The ultimate price goal of a fourth wave correction, for instance, can be forecast with more accuracy than most impulses. What's more, it is the Wave Principle that tells the analyst when to expect less predictability. One of the greatest services a method can provide is to tell you when to stand aside. So your overheard "objection" is not a problem with the Wave Principle or a revelation of where the Wave Principle cannot be applied. That the Wave Principle recognizes and identifies the differences in market behavior is one of its greatest strengths.

What about those who say investing with impulse waves, or in the direction of the trend, isn't that hard anyway?

Tell that to 83% of the professional money managers who underperformed the Standard & Poor's or the Dow Jones Industrial Average for three years in the heart of the bull market of the 1980s. Tell it to the 98% of money managers who couldn't identify the end of an impulse in 1966 and got killed in the last bear market. Tell that to the 99% of public investors, who lose money in their investments over the long run. I, for one, recognize the fact that successful investing is extremely difficult. Anyone who tells you it is not is headed for a fall.

Can Elliott save you from a fall?

It can save you from a catastrophic loss. It is one of the few approaches that allows the investor to get out of a losing position with a small loss for an objective reason. The alternatives are to ride it out or simply get out because an arbitrary "stop" level has been reached, which usually has the nasty result of getting you out just before the big gains are due.

Sometimes a corrective process can take the form of what Elliott called a triangle. Are those difficult?

To the novice, they are bugaboos. But once you get used to them, they are a great blessing. They are not just movements within the shape of two converging lines. They are a specific number of moves within it and specific subdivisions within those. There are several rules about triangles, but simply finding out that you are in one can help you make a lot of forecasts about what is going to happen next. You can often recognize the end of an "E" wave and take quite a large position with a very close stop, which is paradise for a speculator.

Fibonacci Rules

Another useful aspect is the way in which the extents of the waves relate to one another within a given sequence. For instance, you used one such guideline in your first book to predict the Dow's rise to 2722. Explain how you did that.

In our 1978 book, *Elliott Wave Principle*, A. J. Frost and I maintained our conclusion that the Cycle wave IV bear market had ended in 1974, since it had met Frost's downside target to the point. We then used Elliott's guideline of "equality" to project the ultimate high. Stated simply, we said that Cycle wave V should produce the same percentage gain as Cycle wave I from 1932 to 1937. Applying the 4.716x multiple of wave I to the 1974 closing low at 577.60 projected a peak close at 2724. In the book, we rounded the expected gain to a 5x multiple, since the guideline was stated as a *tendency*, not a precise relationship. Subsequent events, however, showed an exact equality, as the 1987 closing high occurred at 2722. It wasn't the final high, but it was an important one.

Didn't you raise the ultimate target a lot higher back when the Dow was still in triple digits?

Yes, and here's why. While the *low price* occurred in 1974, Cycle wave IV can be labeled as continuing for eight years beyond 1974, finally completing a complex bear market pattern called a "double three" in August 1982. This pattern produced a critical fact that was terrifically exciting at the time: the higher price at which wave IV finally ended raised the upside target for wave V. The guideline of equality still applied, so the essential forecast was exactly the same, that wave V would equal the percentage gain of wave I from 1932 to 1937. However, the 4.716x multiple now applied to the 1982 low at 776.92, thus projecting a peak at 3664. I forecasted intraday highs as high as 3885 and rounded off the forecast to 3500-4000.

A good call in 1982. But the market went well past even that target.

It sure did. Stock speculation developed into a full-blown Grand Supercycle mania, surpassing normal wave development at lower degrees. Still, you have to realize that after 16 years of sideways action, the Wave Principle said the Dow would go up five times in value from the 1982 low, which no one believed. I think the fact that the market made it is quite a testimony to the value of long term forecasting using the Wave Principle. Not only that, but from the nearly 4000 target level, despite all the fanfare, it certainly hasn't quintupled·a second time. That shows how radical my forecast was.

O.K., we've gotten back to Fibonacci here. Who was Fibonacci?

Leonardo of Pisa was the son of a successful merchant named Bonacci, thus Fi for "son of" Bonacci. Fibonacci introduced the Arabic number system to the Western world and was the most famous mathematician of his time. In the 13th century, he would entertain royal courts with mathematical problems. One of those problems was the famous rabbit problem, the answer to which is the sequence that is now named after him. The Fibonacci sequence is a self-generated sequence obtained by adding two adjacent figures to obtain the next. Start at the number 1 and add the preceding number. There isn't any, so you get another 1. Add the preceding number, 1, to that 1 and you get 2; take 2 and add the preceding number, which is 1, and you get 3: take 3 and add the preceding number, which is 2, and you get 5; take 5 and add the preceding number, which is 3, and you get 8, and so on to 13, 21, 34, 55, etc. Actually, Fibonacci *re*-discovered the sequence and the ratio which governs it, which had been known by the Greeks and as far back as the ancient Egyptians. It has been treated as a very special thing by mathematicians and scientists that far back, and to this day.

How does this sequence relate to the market?

As Collins pointed out, Fibonacci mathematics are the main determinant of all of the constructs Elliott observed. In the stock market, the simplest description of a bear market is a straight line down, one wave. The simplest description of a bull market is a straight line up. Elliott found that bear markets most often subdivide into three waves: down, up, down. Bull markets subdivide into five: up, down, up, down, up. It takes one complete bear market and one bull market to make a cycle. At the simplest level, that is 1 rise and 1 fall, for a total of 2 waves. The bear market subdivides into 3 waves, the bull market into 5, and the total is 8. When you drop to the next subdivision, you find that a bear market has 13 waves, a bull market has 21, and the total is 34. And so on to infinity; each new number is the sum of the previous two. That is the Fibonacci sequence.

In addition to the revelation that stock price patterns are self-similar at different degrees of trend, Elliott made another important contribution which is critical to his theory and represents an important breakthrough in the field. He discovered the existence of, and guidelines for the application of, the Fibonacci ratio in markets. Can you explain what the Fibonacci ratio is?

As the Fibonacci sequence progresses, the ratio between adjacent numbers is always 0.618, called *phi*, which has an inverse of 1.618. I.e., .618 times 1.618 equals 1. It is the only ratio whose inverse is itself plus 1. This ratio governs all additive progressions of this type, no matter what number you begin with.

Wait a minute. Start with three instead of one.

Sure. The result is 3, 3, 6, 9, 15, 24, 39, 63, 102, and so on to infinity. What always remains constant? The Golden Ratio *between* the numbers after the first few terms. Let's hit the calculator and see. In this example, 63/102=.61765.

So, in essence, nine is a Fibonacci number, also.

While the specific numbers making up the Fibonacci sequence may be more natural in that they begin with the number 1, they are not essential to the ratio, which governs a basic law of geometric progression.

What's the significance? Why is this relationship so critical?

The fact that the ratio governs all additive sequences derived by adding a term to the previous to get the next makes it ideal mathematics for growth patterns. That is undoubtedly why it is found in growth and decay patterns and in expansion and contraction patterns throughout nature. Many things — plants, animals, spiraling galaxies, cloud formations, hurricanes — display characteristics of motion, growth, and, in some rare cases, decay in ways that reflect the workings of the Fibonacci ratio. As a result, this ratio has fascinated scientists and mathematicians for centuries.

Why should it be *this* particular ratio?

Phi, or 1.618..., governs spirals, such as those seen from the nautilus shell to galaxies. In contrast, *pi*, or 3.1416..., another irrational number, governs the geometric shape known as the circle. The circle is a *static* shape. It doesn't imply motion; it implies stasis. A spiral, on the other hand, implies expansion and contraction, *progress and regress*. The stock market, as a direct reflection of the popular valuation of mankind's productive enterprise, is a record of man's progress or regress in that regard. Like other things in nature, then, human history seems to be following a pattern that conforms to a natural law based upon the same ratio. That mankind is producing a natural, spiral growth pattern throughout history may be a grand concept, but it is hardly fantastic.

So how do you use the ratio in markets?

One example of the use of the Fibonacci ratio in the Elliott Wave Principle is to establish targets based upon common relationships among waves. Elliott pointed out one example of when an impulse was likely to display a Fibonacci relationship among its components. I have catalogued a whole lot more.

You and a lot of other traders have made profitable use of such targets. In many cases, historic turns have conformed to Fibonacci multiples. Give us a good example.

Well, let's take a look at the 1930-1939 period in Fibonacci terms, for starters. It was one of the most amazing periods for Fibonacci relationships in stock market history. Figure 1-4 illustrates the price lengths of the eight swings. The prices quoted are daily closing prices. Having observed hourly readings for the past 20 years, I would be willing to bet that the true intraday turning points were even closer to the ideal .618 ratio. Even so, the average of the eight closing turning points is .613, less than 1% error.

As in this example, it is my opinion that it is not the numbers per se that guide the Fibonacci relationships most often, but the ratios between them. Fibonacci numbers do not mark index turning points or determine price lengths often enough to rely on any such expectations.

It is definitely there in the price action, but what about time?

I have found ways that durations fit into precise Fibonacci relationships, just like price swings, which I'm writing about now for another book called *Beautiful Pictures*. Aside from that, durations of waves do often last a Fibonacci number of time units. The distances between the turning points we just dis-

Dow Jones Industrial Average -- 1926-1943								
Eight consecutive turning points, 1930-1939								
Date:	Apr. 17 1930	July 8 1932	Mar. 10 1937	Mar. 31 1938	Nov. 12 1938	Apr. 8 1939	July 22 1939	Aug. 24 1939
Level:	294.07	41.22	194.40	98.95	158.41	121.44	144.71	131.33 (apex)
Distance:	252.85	153.18	95.45	59.46	36.97	23.27	13.38	
Ratio:	.606 (1.651)	.623 (1.605)	.623 (1.605)	.622 (1.608)	.629 (1.589)	.575 (1.739)	(avg. .613) (avg. 1.63)	

Figure 1-4

cussed, for instance if we start from 1929 high (rather than 1930, when the price relationships begin), correspond to the Fibonacci sequence. The time periods from peak to trough of these swings, in months, give or take a few weeks, was 34, 55, 13, 8, 5, 3, and 1 month — all Fibonacci numbers.

Does the Fibonacci ratio govern every degree all the time?

Not that I can determine. But relationships at two degrees are often fulfilled simultaneously, so with enough effort, we might find that it does govern every wave. My studies show that there are many times — such as retracements — when one should not expect a Fibonacci relationship. Knowing when to look for one is the key to successful application, and I have spent a lot of time standardizing my expectations in that regard.

* * * * * * * * * * * * * * *

Barton Biggs
Morgan Stanley Strategy Memorandum
February 1986

Over the years I have been sent a multitude of weird and wonderful treatises on systems for forecasting the stock market ranging from relative strength to astrology. Technical analysis does not intrigue me, and I ignore the occult. Kondratieff waves are about as metaphysical as I get, but for years I have been fascinated with the Fibonacci numbers and their possible application to the stock market in the Elliott Wave Theory.

Fibonacci found the sequence had many strange and intriguing characteristics. But most cosmic, if you divide a Fibonacci by the next highest number, you will discover that it is precisely .618034 times as large as the number that follows. And .618034 is the magic number. The "golden proportion" of .618034 to 1 is the mathematic basis of the Parthenon, sunflowers, snail shells, Greek vases, the great spiral galaxies of outer space and playing cards. It is the most pleasing shape, whether in rectangular or spiral form, in the universe.

The golden proportion has been and is everywhere. The great Pyramid of Gizeh has an elevation to its base of 61.8%. The Greeks also were aware of the .618034 and called it the "golden mean." They based much of their art and architecture on its dynamic symmetry, "whirling squares that seemed to vibrate with intense energy." The secret was lost with the fall of Greece until Fibonacci discovered it again, and in the 17th century, Jakob Bernoulli transposed the golden rectangle into a golden spiral and linked it to nature.

Fibonacci numbers and both the golden rectangle and spiral are broadcast throughout nature. *Science Magazine* has published several scholarly articles on the subject, and my summary is that the numbers are found in everything from daisy petals and sunflower spirals (55 counterclockwise and 89 clockwise) to phyllotaxis, which is the arrangement of leaves on the stalk of a plant. The golden spiral appears in horns, claws, teeth, shells and even the web of a spider. Bacteria multiply at a Fibonacci sequence, and the examples go on and on. The human body has five extremities, five fingers and five toes, and in music the octave has 13 keys with 8 white and 5 black. The musical chord that gives the greatest satisfaction is the major sixth, and the note E vibrates at a ratio of .625 to the note C. The ear itself is a golden spiral.

There are no real good explanations of why the sequence exists. One response is that God was a mathematician; others say it is all pure coincidence and the humbug of feverish minds. Some scientists argue that the Fibonacci sequence and the golden spiral are so widespread that they must be part of some recurring growth pattern. Others speculate that it is nature's way of building quantity without sacrificing quality.

As you would expect, attempts have been made to apply Fibonacci to the stock market, most notably by R.N. Elliott in the early 1930s. The Elliott wave theorists have been saying for some time that the fourth Supercycle wave ran from 1966 to 1982 and that U.S. equities are now in the fifth wave of the Supercycle. A killer three-wave downer will follow. Maybe God is a technician.

* * * * * * * * * * * * * * *

Now that we have all the parts in place, give an example of how Elliott works in real time. How about one where it kept you right on the money? Or one of those cases where Elliott helped you stay on the right side even though your interpretation was not exactly right?

O.K., here's a good story that includes both. Gold staged a blowoff in January 1980. It was clear that an ideal Elliott scenario for the next year or two would be an A wave down to $477 because of wave structure and Fibonacci relationships, then a strong rally forming B, followed by a declining wave C down to final target of $388. $388 was a 61.8% retracement of the advance that had occurred from August 1976 to the January 1980 high. On April 6, 1980, gold declined to a low of $474, a normal first stop, and the decline was a five wave structure. That's all I had to know: Wave A was over. In EWT, I said, "The first important phase of reaction is almost over and should lead to the best rally since the highs." On May 12, a month later, after prices started to build a base for awhile, I got a little more comfortable. I wrote, "A 61.8% retracement of the decline to just over $700 should be the maximum potential of any intermediate rally." The reason I said that was when wave A starts in five waves, it's in a formation known as a zigzag. The typical maximum retracement within zigzags is 61.8%. So, it was easy to say the maximum retracement 61.8% should bring gold to $710.

Keep in mind that in 1980, all the way through to the end of that year, finding somebody who thought gold would go under $400 was very difficult. I spoke in Montreal for Jim Blanchard in June 1980, and every speaker was bullish except yours truly. Although the audience was polite, it was like talking to a brick wall in terms of changing opinions. No one wanted to hear any such thing. So at the time, I was nervous and sweating. It was my first major speech, after all. I was thinking, "Am I crazy? I'm talking about this stuff going down another 45% in value from the next rally high. There are all sorts of things to think about. I mean, Jimmy Carter's in office!" The whole bit. I stuck to my guns, though. That is what Charles Collins did in 1966 when he called the top in the stock market. You can't buckle under the pressure. Besides, by this time, I had followed gold enough to be quite confident about it. Maybe too confident. I'll get to that in a minute.

On September 23rd, which was the exact day of the high, the rally finished a 5-3-5 structure, which is a typical wave B, subdividing a-b-c. So the wave structure said, "We are close to a top in this B wave." Gold opened up that morning with an a.m. fix in London of $720. The p.m. fix was $710. So at the close, I put out a one-page Special Report calling the top of the rally. From that day forward, gold underwent a relentless decline, which is typical of C waves. My downside target was still $388, so on August 2, 1981, I was sure we were close to the final bottom. The wave structure looked acceptable, so I said, "$388 should be met this week. Cover all shorts and buy." Two days later, on August 4, the exact low of London gold from the Bank of Nova Scotia was $388.00. Gold started to rally. I was certain we had caught the low. In the next letter, I said to put a stop at $388 and let the profits ride. I thought gold was going much higher, beyond the 1980 high. But I had a close stop, and its level was objectively determined. Gold had met a Fibonacci retracement, the structure was acceptable, and if gold was going to continue making higher highs in a long term bull market, it had to have turned from there.

The rally took a three wave shape and lasted only a matter of weeks. It went up, down, up and stopped. It never made a fifth wave. As I was watching the chart in November, gold started pulling back. It came under the high of the first wave. I said, "We don't have a five wave rally. This is not a bull market. It was just a bear market rally."

So in early January, as gold had just come under $400 again, I said, "A break of the $388 level is now extremely likely. I suggest reinstating your short position." That was strictly from wave structure. I was unhappy that my bullish forecast didn't work out, but it was irrelevant financially. Not only did we not lose any money during that period, but we were also all set up to go short again as if we had never covered in the first place. And that's what we did. So there is a description of how you can be both perfectly right and very wrong with Elliott wave based forecasts, yet make money in the first instance and not lose money in the second.

Your story demonstrates the utility of the theory. But as theories for making money in the stock market go, you've really staked out some high ground here, with Fibonacci mathematics, fractal geometry and a mass psychological condition that guides all of history. From both the practical and intellectual standpoints, how come more people aren't aware of it and rushing to embrace it?

Well, some have. But the majority doesn't realize they need it. The bull market is being mistaken for good forecasting. That illusion is temporary, so we will have many more adherents in coming years.

There should be legions of people expanding upon it with related concepts.

Well, I'm doing it, so that's a start.

But there are many more on Wall Street who won't have any truck with it.

Some people reject such ideas out of hand. They will not expend the energy required to find out if it is true because they have decided it cannot be true.

In the old days, those who used the theory did their best to keep it secret. Early on, I was asked several times by students of the Wave Principle to refrain from publishing any material at all on it for fear that "too many" people would start using the Wave Principle in their investment timing, thus diluting its utility. But human nature being what it is, there is no way it will be overused.

Will the Wave Principle win out over those people and become an accepted part of financial science?

Yes, because it's true. It has already won out over obscurity in finance. The new science of chaos will prime even more people to give it the time of day. And we shouldn't forget the *incentive* to do so. After all, the Wave Principle may be nature's way of giving us a peek at the future. Of course, that is only a peek, not the full panorama. Foretelling the future with exactitude all the time is not one of the blessings available to man, and likely never will be. But what an advantage some of us now have over everyone else in that endeavor! As in so many fields, all it takes is an edge over the competition, and you win the game.

Does your Wave Principle analysis have its own waves of popular acceptance and non-acceptance?

I find that my services do go in and out of popularity. If I've just called a big rally, people love it. When the inevitable error occurs, even if those errors average only 30% of the time, people give up on the approach. Then they miss its next string of successes, which attracts new people. Its popularity also ebbs and flows with people's perception of whether they need it. As trends mature, few people think they need guidance. As they develop, the psychological stress is high and people desire input. So it goes back and forth, just like the market. Of course, some people are knowledgeable enough to know that market forecasting is a task involving probability. If you have a high percentage of success, you are doing the best that can be done. Batting 1.000 is not possible. Yet most new stock market fans don't get that fact, and they fire every batter who doesn't do it, which means everyone. And each time, they wonder what the *advisor's* problem is!

What would happen if your accuracy rate increased to 90% or 95%, resulting in a proportional increase in the number of people who accept your forecasts and act upon them. In other words, if your track record encouraged more people to follow your forecasts and stick to them, would your forecasting ability lead to its own destruction? And would the market become so influenced by your forecasts that it would behave in reaction to them?

Theoretically speaking, if everyone felt that Bob Prechter was correct, there would be no difference of opinion and therefore, by definition, no market. But the question is impractical and contradicts itself. You're asking, if I become very successful, must I therefore become unsuccessful? The converse certainly isn't true. If a forecaster is unsuccessful, it doesn't mean he must become successful, does it? Nor is the question necessarily a reflection of causality. If someone is more successful than normal, he will have a period to balance it, to return to whatever his norm is. If a baseball player bats .560 for two weeks, you can be sure he will not maintain that level.

Truly, questions like this are not uncommon, but they are primarily a reflection of the human trait of skepticism. It's a good trait in that it aids survival in many ways, but it is counterproductive in areas where success is a matter of probability. That trait is why I could be right three out of four times and still be met by skepticism. Your question proves my point. You're saying, in essence, that no matter how good my forecasting, you will believe that the whole thing could turn worthless overnight. When my forecasting is bad, you will simply walk away; you won't take the other side of the argument and say it's time to follow my advice because it is due for a period of success. So opposite actions on my part lead to the same conclusion on your part.

So skepticism is unavoidable.

Right. One thing that you and I both know is that I will never be right 100% of the time. There will be errors. In such a case, not only do the errors generate skepticism, but the periods of success do, too, because everyone knows, consciously or otherwise, that 100% success is impossible. This is as it should be. When the market is selling off against the trend, the standard conclusion I hear is: "The Elliott outlook has failed; it doesn't work." On the other side of the coin is the standard objection in my best years that "Now Elliott has worked so perfectly, it must be attracting attention, so it can't work from here." People say, "Why should I follow you? You've been right so long, you're due for a fall." People always find a reason for not doing what the Wave Principle suggests doing. I never fail to hear these objections, over and over, at seminars and conferences.

The mere fact that people ask the question, "If you or Elliott wave become too popular, won't that destroy the theory?" provides the answer to the question. As I said, it is normal human behavior to be skeptical, doubting and cautious. It's a good trait. It is one of the tools by which the species has kept itself alive for so many millennia. It's just that in the market arena, it can prevent you from making money. You have to apply caution correctly.

* * * * * * * * * * * * * *

The Elliott Wave Theorist
August 12, 1991

> Long term forecasts that indicate a change in trend at the right time will always fail to achieve widespread acceptance. One reason that such forecasting is dismissed is that by nature, human beings project the future linearly, not cyclically. If you think about the consequences of this trait, you will realize that it is precisely that trait which causes the social excesses which produce the cyclicality. A good deal of study and practice (and for most, experience) is required to unlearn the natural tendency and adopt the correct orientation. The Wave Principle is a tool for anticipating trend changes and events; it doesn't merely reflect them. By definition, it cannot be popularly accepted until the forecasted trend is well past its centerpoint. When the superbullish *Elliott Wave Principle* was published in 1978, almost nobody bought it. Eight years later, deep into the bull market, tens of thousands of copies were being sold.

* * * * * * * * * * * * * *

In your business, is it success that breeds failure?

One thing that I did not fully appreciate when I began in this profession was the irony of selling financial market advice. A.J. Frost and I wrote a very bullish book in 1978 with the Dow at about 800. We sold very few copies, at least for the first several years. In the mid-90s I wrote a book called *At the Crest of the Tidal Wave*, which is long-term bearish. Once again, I could not get people to buy it. On the other hand, people who wrote books about how to survive the big depression sold millions of copies in 1979 and 1982, and today people writing books about a never-ending bull market are also selling millions of copies. So the irony is, the more responsible you try to be, the less money you will make. Even if I had the chance to start over, though, I would not change styles.

But your own experience can be instructive, can it not? In the early 1980s, your following increased rapidly because you were one of the

few bulls anticipating the great rise of the 1980s. By 1986, your public image was entwined in that middle phase of the bull market. You were actually being credited and/or blamed with movements in the marketplace. Massive media coverage of your work reached a feverish peak with the crash in 1987.

Of all of the forecasts I've been right on, the one I'm most proud of is knowing when my own trend was going to peak in terms of social acceptance. In fact, on October 9, 1987 there was an article on the front page of the Money section of *USA Today*, if you ever want to dig it out. In the last paragraph, I said people are going to start focusing on my failures and errors when the trend of my image changes to down and enters its own bear market.

How did you figure that out?

I had studied pop music stars, movie actors, the kind of trends they were popular in and what happened when the popularity waned. Television shows are another example. Go back and check and see how many of the family sitcoms and so forth went off the air in 1966 at the end of a bull market, as an example. So I was one of those. I was a family sitcom. My image was a bull market with a certain shelf life. I may be the only beneficiary of a guru image who *knew it*.

You could predict that your star was going to go out, but you couldn't change it?

No, but I tried to alleviate the coming damage. When I did interviews during 1987, I'd say, "I want you to point out the fact that I've made errors on markets. I don't want people to get the wrong opinion and think I'm always right, because they'll risk their money and could lose it."

They never paid attention to that.

Not during the uptrend in the image. It didn't fit. One article did, as I recall. The one in *The Wall Street Journal* in March, 1987. So at least it's on the record that I said it.

Didn't their later stories objectively reflect an actual change in your performance?

I had made errors previously, and I had successes during the negative blitz. For instance, in 1988, I was among the top three timers for all three markets I cover: stocks, bonds and gold, in *Commodity Traders Consumer Report*. Despite that record, I got the worst coverage that year. Some implied that I was the worst market forecaster that ever hit the pike. I'd say, "Call the independent rating services; they'll give you the real numbers." Well, they wouldn't bother, because they were writing an article or doing a TV show for the downside of my image. It wasn't emotionally easy to accept, but intellectually I knew exactly what was going on. The key is that the media writes success stories when the trend of a person's public image is up, and when it turns down, they write failure stories. It's that simple. And no, theirs is not an objective approach.

You predicted the change. Did you do anything about it?

I sure did. When 1988 was over, I retired from all media exposure, public speaking, you name it. I knew from plotting my own professional success by way of subscriptions that I had begun a bear market. My worst forecasting years, which occurred in the 1990s, *followed* the media's change of focus, which shows that they were not objective and that I got out of the limelight at the right time.

* * * * * * * * * * * * * *

The (Gainesville, GA) *Times*
September 5, 1990

An entertaining rumor that flitted around Gainesville for a few days has finally been squelched.

Word was that Gainesville's Bob Prechter, nationally-known stock market analyst, was seen talking in the lobby of a local financial institution with Ed Bradley, a reporter for the CBS television show "60 Minutes."

And very quickly, the rumor was enhanced to say that Prechter was going to be on a segment of "60 Minutes" to make a dire prediction of another stock market crash, as he correctly did in his newsletter back in 1987.

When asked about the rumor, Prechter inserted a bit of humor into his denial when he said, "No, that was Bob Bradley, Ed Bradley's brother, who has a television show called 'Six Minutes,' which is longer than than anyone would want me to be on television."

* * * * * * * * * * * * * *

What if you had stayed in the limelight, or tried to?

If you are foolish enough to fight a public image in transition, you will be destroyed. Several former gurus tried to do it. All it did was make things worse for them. The media can't stand someone opposing their image of him. They will just bash you with it until you acknowledge their view or quit. So I used the time productively. I built an international business. Now my trend is about to turn up again, and it's time to take advantage of that.

So it's your time again. Are you going back on the circuit?

No way. I don't have the stamina for that any more. But you'll see it on our website and in our subscription base. And I'll do some media.

But you're not concerned that you could become too powerful? If your forecast about the next big move works out, a lot of people could bail out and cause the kind of deep decline you been anticipating.

The "power" of advisors is a myth. Advisors have almost no power to move markets. People used to say that Joe Granville could move the market. Baloney. He was merely making great calls. The proof of that is his last major call, which he made in 1982. The market didn't do what he said it would, and supposedly he was at the height of his power. But of course, that "power" just does not exist. Markets are bigger than anybody.

A lot of other people aren't so sure. In fact, in the wake of the crash, some that are pretty knowledgeable about the market, like the internationally famous hedge fund manager George Soros, said that your views had actually pushed the market over the edge that day. And someone else may have believed in your power as well. Is it true that one of your appearances on the Financial News Network right after the crash was actually blacked out?

There is no question that I was blacked out, because it happened twice, across the entire country, on live hookups about an hour apart. On Thursday, two days after the crash ended, FNN called for my weekly commentary, as usual. I gave the whole commentary twice over the telephone, not being able to tell that a nationwide blackout was in effect. As soon as I finished talking, FNN returned on-air. They couldn't explain it, but they knew it had happened, calling back both times to reschedule. The third time, an hour later, I was broadcast, so whoever did it must have decided I was not making alarming statements. It was my only exposure to the kind of event that makes the conspiracy theorists look as if they are onto something. The only organizations with the motive and potential means to accomplish such a thing are the government and the Fed, unless you believe in the power of the Trilateral Commission.

So, what if everyone all at once became more accepting, not of your opinion, perhaps, but suppose everyone agreed, "It's not always right, but the Wave Principle really is *the* answer?"

Well, let me begin my answer with a quote from a national financial magazine dated October 1977, 23 years ago. "Over the last few years, the Wave Principle has gathered too much of a following and, therefore, it has less value today. Almost invariably, you can write off a technique when it gets too much of a following." How does that statement look in light of the decade that followed it? "Elliott" had one of its greatest successes. Like the Energizer Bunny, it keeps going and going. And I believe its next success will be its biggest ever. The Principle itself is undoubtedly on an upward spiral of acceptance: three steps forward and two steps back.

Now let's suppose that a large number of educated people accepted the Wave Principle, which is not an impossible idea for say, a thousand years from now. There would still be room for differences of opinion on the market and the future. And there are countless other factors. Even people who practice the craft don't necessarily take action when they get a signal. Unconscious doubt and worry often foil people's actions. Very few traders have the emotional strength to turn even good analysis into profits. So the whole line of questioning is in a theoretical realm that does not conform to reality.

The Wave Principle is intrinsically contrarian. Does it have some built-in defense against becoming the consensus?

I think so. The Wave Principle is a description of natural human behavior. This is what human beings are; this is part of their nature — how they behave. In order for markets to continue to go through these stages, a part of human nature must be to believe that such theories of mass psychology are incapable of being true — that is, something not worth examining. They must be primed to accept bullish arguments at tops and bearish arguments at bottoms. That means they have to be ever open to bogus theories of market behavior. How else will they create the patterns that fear, greed and hope produce?

* * * * * * * * * * * * * *

An Elliott Wave Wave

In the late 1970s and early 1980s, The Elliott Wave Theorist's *success in forecasting the gold and stock markets made the Elliott Wave Principle known to the investment world. But the media did not immediately and wholeheartedly embrace the Wave Principle. It was generally described as "esoteric" (*Barron's, *July 16, 1984) and its primary proponent was received in friendly terms, but in such a way as to put some distance between the writer and the subject matter. In December 1984, after Prechter had accurately anticipated the first wave of the bull market, but before his call for a powerful third wave was realized, this description from* Money *was typical: "The man who believes this is neither a mystic nor a quack. In fact, Robert R. Prechter Jr., 35, is a manifestly levelheaded father of two from Gainesville, Ga." Later, after the third wave hit in September 1985, the financial press had an increasingly (and as it turned out fleetingly) tolerant view of Elliott. The tone of press clippings changed dramatically. Instead of arcane, The Wave Principle was an insightful tool which had as "its most practiced diviner," (*Newsweek *February 3, 1986) "the popular guru of this bull market" (*Christian Science Monitor, *August 10, 1987). The volume of press coverage also increased exponentially as big and small papers around the world picked up wire stories hyping the notion that Prechter's Elliott wave forecasts were somehow guiding the market. Some examples of the mania for Elliott wave that unfolded in the mid-1980s and culminated with the crash of 1987 follow.*

Business Week
March 24, 1986

Outlandish predictions? Perhaps, but nobody scoffs at Prechter's erudite monthly, *The Elliott Wave Theorist.* His stock market forecasts have been uncannily correct. Prechter's buy and sell signals carry a lot of clout these days because of his large following among the stock-index options and futures crowd. "Given the depth of his readership, Prechter definitely has an impact on the markets," says Paul Tudor Jones, a futures trader. "There are few pros who are not aware of his recommendations."

Newsday

June 14, 1986

The Minds That Move the Market

The seers who move financial markets and the rock and rollers who catapult to the top of the record charts often seem to share the evanescent life span of a May fly. After all, they are both creations of good press and often become the media's supper in the end.

Prechter attained growing stature because of consistently intelligent calls over the past four years on which way the market will turn.

Prechter, Georgia-born and 37 years old, is a bohemian by Wall Street standards, following a sociologically inspired investment strategy based on anticipating human responses to market highs and lows called the Elliott Wave Theory after its designer R.N. Elliott.

The Media General Financial Weekly

July 14, 1986

Wave Analyst Rings Warning Bell at Top

According to the saying, "Nobody rings a bell at market tops," but at least one analyst sounded a loud and clear alarm at the most recent top.

On Wednesday July 2, with the Dow Jones Industrial Average at a record high of 1909.03, Robert Prechter warned readers of his newsletter, *The Elliott Wave Theorist*, of an impending intermediate correction. Prechter had been consistently bullish since issuing a buy signal in July 1984, at a major intermediate market bottom. But two weeks ago, he recommended that traders take profits and stand aside.

His timing couldn't have been better. The market did an abrupt about face and plummeted from its peak.

Prechter bases his calls on the somewhat abstruse and controversial wave theory propounded by R.N. Elliott during the 1930s and '40s.

Some press reports on last week's market action cited Prechter's sell signal as a contributing factor in the market's sharp decline, but he disagrees strongly. "I think that's a myth," he said. "Had I come out on July 2 and said, 'I think the market's going to go up 50 points on Monday,' it would have crashed anyway. So I have no power to move the market whatsoever."

The New York Times

February 18, 1987

Yesterday, the market got an added push when word spread throughout Wall Street that Robert Prechter, editor of *The Elliott Wave Theorist*, was predicting that the Dow would advance to the 2,300 level before any correction. He made the prediction over his recorded hot-line service on Friday night.

The prediction sent futures prices moving widely ahead of the stock market, and speculators stepped in to capture the difference by selling futures and buying stocks in an arbitrage technique called program trading, setting off a buying frenzy.

The New York Times

February 19, 1987

"Enjoy the party." That succinct advice comes from Robert R. Prechter Jr., who in the past year has emerged as the market's leading guru. He believes the best is yet to come.

"Bob Prechter set out his long term case for the bull market shortly after it began in August 1982 with the Dow at 776.92 and he has stuck to his guns," said Robert S. Robbins, a strategist with the Robinson Humphrey Co. in Atlanta. "That makes him the best-known super bull in the business."

Hollywood Squares (TV show)

September 18, 1987

"Stock market analyst Robert Prechter says that as skirt heights rise, stock prices move with them. True or false?"

The Atlanta Journal / The Atlanta Constitution

October 8, 1987

Prechter Predicted Market's Tumble About a Month Ago

What did Bob Prechter say, and when did he say it?

That's the question investors were still asking Wednesday, the day after the stock market's biggest one-day point decline in history.

Forget about the prime rate being hiked, or Robert Bork's Supreme Court nomination being on the skids, or the threat of oil prices rising due to the Persian Gulf War. What investors wanted to know was what Prechter had said, if anything, to touch off the market's tumble.

Few had any idea, but rumors that he'd turned bearish cause tremors on Wall Street, and the Dow ended the day with a 91.55-point loss, its biggest one-day decline ever.

His method, and his uncannily accurate forecasts, have earned him the distinction of being ranked tops among the nation's market forecasters for several years in a row.

USA Today

October 9, 1987

A Man who Moves Markets

From his home and office in the misty foothills of north Georgia, Robert Prechter can stick out his foot, and Wall Street stumbles.

Prechter has rescued the late Ralph Nelson Elliott from obscurity and made the Long Island accountant's theory the rage of Wall Street.

Although he's now riding high, he has no illusions that it will last forever. Like the stock market travels along those waves he and Ralph Nelson Elliott made famous, Prechter knows there are some dips in store... "There will come a time that people will focus on the bad calls."

The Atlanta Journal / The Atlanta Constitution
October 23, 1987

Who is Robert Prechter and What Has He Done?

At Home, Prechter Just Another Guy
Some Unaware of His Impact on Market

The outside world knows Robert Prechter as the reigning king of the stock market gurus — so influential, some say, that when he turned bearish earlier this month, so did the market.

On Thursday Robert James, editor of Timers Digest, a Florida service that tracks and rates stock market newsletter writers, called Prechter "one of the premier market timers, now and probably for all time."

Fred Harkins, who owns a gas station less than a mile from Prechter's home, said he's tired be being asked for directions to the forecaster's obscure house.

"He's a nice guy who keeps his business to himself," Harkins said. "Press people are always asking me what he's like, but I don't pay them much mind."

The New York Times
October 28, 1987

As far as Mr. Soros is concerned, the crack came two weeks ago, when Robert Prechter, the popular market forecaster who had run at the front of the herd of bulls for five years, reversed course in mid-stride and warned his clients to pull out of the market.

"I was stunned by his comments, just as everyone else was," Mr. Soros said. Mr. Prechter had predicted for years that the Dow Jones Industrial average would crest at 3686. In his view, investors would pour into the stock market the same way they had into all sorts of markets periodically for thousands of years, indulging in a buying frenzy that would ignore underlying values in the belief that tomorrow would bring a bigger fool willing to pay even more than the ridiculous price of today.

"Mr. Prechter's reversal proved to be the crack that started the avalanche," Mr. Soros said yesterday.

The Elliott Wave Theorist
March 1, 1991

When I put together *The Major Works of R.N. Elliott* in 1979, at a time when the Wave Principle was virtually unknown, it was necessary to answer those few practitioners who thought that revealing "the secret" would cause it to stop working since so many would then be privy to the true hierarchy of probabilities for future market action. In response, I commented as follows:

Readers must realize that despite the basic simplicity of the concept itself, "Elliott" is not that easy to apply if one's goal is to do it well. On the other hand, it is very easy to apply haphazardly, and most part-time practitioners do exactly that. Even if the Wave Principle became popular, there would be so many opportunistic hacks floating about their ill-considered opinions that the truth would be lost to the investment majority in the ensuing babble.

As you can see, those were the days when my language was less tempered. However, "Elliott" has become quite popular indeed, to the point that in a single *week* on television there are more "Elliott wave" commentators than there were in any *year* up until about 1989.

* * * * * * * * * * * * * *

How big is the pool of analysts who rely on the Wave Principle?

I think there are quite a few people who are proficient in applying Elliott to past and present markets, say perhaps 1% of all technical analysts, which is a pretty good number of people, I suppose. A lot of those are my subscribers, and they learned it through studying the *Theorist.* However, as far as the number of people proficient at applying the Wave Principle for *forecasting* market turns, which is significantly more difficult than applying it in real time, I think there are very few.

This has been the basis of some criticism. To quote one critic, "relying on arcane methods does have one advantage. Interpreting the linear squiggles is left in the hands of the major heir to Elliott's work." How do you respond to those who contend the complexity of the theory is a cover that allows you to retain the Wave Principle as your personal theory?

With regard to any supposed self-serving secrecy, not only did I co-author a book on how to apply the Wave Principle, as well as reprint Elliott's writings against protest from practitioners, but also I continually go into great, some might say excruciating, detail in each issue of *The Elliott Wave Theorist* explaining exactly what I think the market has done and will do, and why I think it. If there is any market letter that has educated potential competitors, it is mine. The reason is that the study of markets is more important to me than exclusivity, secrecy or power.

Another common approach critics take when they try to dismiss Elliott as bunk is to refer to you as a mystic or a numerologist.

A mystic believes in things for which there is no evidence, only desire. I do not consider myself a mystic at all. My approach is objective. The empirical basis of Elliott's discovery speaks to that fact. So do the results of the trading competition. Not once during any month since the independent rating services have been following market timers has a timer using a numerological approach such as "Gann" analysis ever placed in the top 10 rankings. Just as would be expected, such methods don't work!

The true mystics are those who believe, for instance, that current economic performance is a basis upon which to predict stock market prices. There is no evidence for it. They just feel comfortable with the idea, so they espouse it.

So you say the challenge to validity is on the other side?

You're darn right, it is. I am no longer at the point where I feel I have to justify the objectivity of the Wave Principle. I think the results have done that. Technical analysis is entirely rational and has proven itself. If someone goes back and looks at the record of Elliott wave writers over the decades, he will find a track record of forecasting success that is well beyond a random result or chance. If you can do that, the ball is in the other guy's court. It's up to him to show that this is luck or something.

What's more, the only challenge to a theory is a better theory, and I haven't seen a contender yet.

You don't feel you have been effectively challenged by any fundamental approaches?

I think there's a place for fundamental analysis of individual companies, but I am firmly convinced that you can make a very rational argument showing that fundamental analysis applied to overall market timing is like reading the entrails of goats. In fact, I presented such a critique in *The Wave Principle of Human Social Behavior.* If you think my ideas as presented here are controversial, just read Chapter 19 of that book.

But that's not to say Elliott wave doesn't have its shortcomings. We've already talked about the problem of corrections. Another limitation is that of time. Frequently, you can say with some accuracy where the market is going, but you seem less certain about when it will get there. The bull market that began in 1982 is a good example. It took a lot longer to get there than you thought it would, and it's gone further.

Yes, but your objection is that I didn't have a perfect handle on the extent of the bull market *before it started*, which is when no one understood the coming event except Elliott wave guys! Its value was far greater than any disvalue. But to answer your question, I thought the bull market would last five years, eight at the outside. It lasted eighteen years from 1982. The time factor is the least predictable element in the Wave Principle. Form is unfailing — you have only 13 patterns. Price level is second most predictable, and even there, I called for equality with wave I and we got much more. As I said before, being right two-thirds of the time means you have to be *wrong* one-third of the time. There's no way around it.

* * * * * * * * * * * * *

The (New Orleans) *Times Picayune*
November 9, 1994

"I'll tell you right up front when I've been wrong, it has been on timing," Prechter said. Prechter understands people can be wrong. He admits his advice to people after the crash of 1987 to stay out of the stock market "killed off the image of the perfect guru that the public loves so well."

The market, he said, "was a lot smarter than I was."

* * * * * * * * * * * * *

I assume a mania carries other extenuating conditions?

Yes. For example, the majority is actually right for once. Of course, the bulls will not be right in the end, but the market has definitely tolerated unprecedented levels of bullish sentiment. In normal markets, a widely publicized forecast for another doubling of prices after they had already gone up five times would never succeed. But that is exactly what happened at Dow 4000, when the normal crop of people programmed for failure did their usual thing but this time were allowed to be right! Remember, it wasn't until 1998 that we started to see forecasts for targets of 36,000 and higher on the Dow. One famous forecaster called for 53,000 in 2020 and was heralded for "the passion with which he preaches the equities gospel." Someone else called for 100,000 on the Dow in 20 years' time. Historically, the financial markets have always punished this kind of "passion" with a prompt reversal. All markets work this way, except in manias.

So, the value of sentiment as an indicator was lost?

Not at all. While the optimistic extreme contributed to our inaccurate anticipation of a top, even in this context, its extent speaks to the *degree* of the approaching trend change. At turns of Primary and Cycle degree, extremes in sentiment can occur up to three months ahead of the actual turn. This time, the extremes have been in place for years. This persistence is a measure of the degree of the top and the size of the bear market to come.

Do you think the problem of time forecasting will be permanent?

No, someone may crack the time code some day. I have done a lot of work on time aspects of the market lately and have made some observations that I'm pretty sure will pay off.

Given that time is the most difficult element to predict, how have you attempted to predict it?

There are ways within the Wave Principle to get some pretty good ideas about time, particularly late in wave development. Elliott provided all sorts of guidelines to indicate the upcoming end of a wave sequence.

I also use time cycles, which is a concept completely outside the Wave Principle. But there is no question, having gone over the price charts, that there is often a prolonged tendency for lows in the stock market to occur at particular regular intervals. There are usually groups of cycles operating at any one time on prices. And it's quite surprising how precise these cycles can be. In other words, if a cycle is X days long, it usually falls within one day of expectation.

But they don't repeat like clockwork, I take it. One has to analyze continuously.

Yes, and that is an unavoidable aspect of market analysis. Nevertheless, I have a pretty good handle on how to determine what the important intervals are. I can also recognize *changes* in those intervals, which is the key to avoiding losses. In fact, there have been times when certain cycles became popular and I knew they would fail. [See *Futures* article below. —Ed.] However, cycles don't reflect the essence of stock market behavior, which is strictly the realm of the Wave Principle. So, many times my cyclic forecasts have just plain flopped.

Where can prospective cycle theory students go to get started?

Two cycles books I recommend are *Cycles — The Mysterious Forces that Trigger Events* by E.R. Dewey, and *The Profit Magic of Stock Market Timing* by J.M. Hurst.

* * * * * * * * * * * * * *

Riding a Cycle

In late 1985, the Dow Jones Industrial Average was stalling in the middle of a multi-year advance. Due to expectations of a peak in the four year cycle and other factors mentioned below, most observers were suggesting that the bull market was in for a decline. Even though it was past the third year in a historic bull market, Robert Prechter took the contrary view in declaring that 1986 was going to be another good year.

Futures

January 1986

1986 Stock Market Battle: Elliott Wave vs. Four-Year Cycle

The majority on Wall Street "knows" that 1986 is supposed to be a bear market year in stocks.

Fueling the fearsome forecasts are numerous fundamental negatives: The federal deficit is out of control; foreign loans are a disaster for banks; the majority of economists are predicting an economic recession.

On the technical side, institutions are said to lack cash reserves with which to buy stocks. The market is said to be "an old bull," running out of time by historical standards. The four-year cycle, which has been regular since 1934, is scheduled to be pointing down this year. Is there a dissenting voice in the house?

Some of the arguments can be dismissed easily. "Fundamentals," a misnomer for facts peripheral to the market but assumed to impact the market, have never had much predictive value. The age of a bull market per se is no case for a top, as the eight-year advance of the 1920s proved.

The "lack of money" argument ignores the billions of dollars in money market accounts, foreign money and new buying power generated by the Federal Reserve Board and by an expanding economy. A mere fraction of this total would be enough to propel the Dow Jones Industrial Average, along with the rest of market, to its lofty Elliott wave target.

What about the four-year cycle, which last bottomed in 1982? First, it should be pointed out that, although cycle lows came on schedule in 1978 and 1982, the intervening price action strayed far from the normal profile. So already the cycle was giving some evidence of irregularity.

Look at how the market performed against four-year cycle expectations in 1984 and 1985. You may recall that, based upon this popular mode, the 1984 market was supposed to be up in the first half of the year and down in the second half. The actual path of prices was exactly the opposite.

On the other hand, 1985 was definitely supposed to be a down year for the stock market, according to cycle theory. In addition to being a bearish post-election year, it was scheduled to lead prices into the four-year cycle low due in 1986. However, 1985 may, in fact, end up being more profitable on the upside than 1983.

So what is happening to this widely followed cycle? R.N. Elliott provided the answer years ago. He recognized that, when one of the three main impulse waves in a five-wave sequence is extended (that is substantially longer than the others), the other two impulse waves tend toward similarity.

Because Wave III was the extended wave in the Supercycle advance from 1932 (from 1942 to 1966), A.J. Frost and I concluded in *Elliott Wave Principle* in 1978 that "Wave V should be a simpler structure with shorter cycle lengths and could provide for the sudden contraction of the popular four-year cycle."

Relying on the four-year cycle has caused investors to lose money by holding through the sharp correction of early 1984 and missing the big rise or shorting since then. In contrast, the Elliott Wave Principle provided a reliable road map for the actual course of prices during those years. In dealing with cycles, it is imperative that an analysis be discarded whenever the market deviates significantly from expectations. In other words, if it is broke, fix it. However, the investing public is doing no such thing with the four-year cycle, and their reliance on this concept may have them walking into another trap.

1986 turned out to be one of the best years of the bull market. The Dow Jones Industrials gained 23%.

* * * * * * * * * * * * * * *

That sounds useful. But you say working with cycles can be frustrating at times.

I sometimes get letters demanding to know why I don't "throw the cycles out" because the Wave Principle is more accurate. Sure, they fail to provide turns at times, but you have to be flexible enough to deal with that fact. I can't figure out why anyone would want to throw away his second-best forecasting tool just because his best forecasting tool is better! Cycles are sometimes shockingly accurate, and the few times that they lead you astray are a small price to pay for the terrific advantage gained overall.

How do you establish that a specific cycle length exists?

I disagree with the common cycle methodologies and have developed an approach that so far has worked well. I start with a series of momentum oscillators, which are simply rates of change for a particular index. I use the New York Composite Index in the last X number of time units. I use shorter time periods for shorter cycles and longer time periods for longer cycles. Once I put all of these on graphs, I observe where the deepest oversold conditions have occurred. The bottoms of the cycles create deep oversold conditions in the oscillators, and you can pinpoint them. The same is not necessarily true of prices, because sometimes cyclic forces will cause very little movement in prices but will show up in the oscillators, clear as a bell. Even if the market has made very little progress — let's say it's gone sideways — if your oscillator has gone from an extreme reading to neutral, it could be time for a resumption of the previous trend.

That's pretty straightforward. What makes cycles so hard to deal with?

There are two things that cause cycles to be difficult. One of them is that occasionally there is a shift in one subharmonic. If you have, for instance, a 24-week cycle and it subdivides into three eight-week cycles, occasionally you find that there is a fourth eight-week cycle that you can't explain, pushing the more severe bottom out eight weeks.

The other thing, which is rarer, is a complete shift in cyclic length. One big key to good cycle work is to stay on the alert for a shift in dominance of the different length cycles. Long term subscribers will recall the shift to the 23/8/4-week complex in stocks that occurred in September 1981. Recognizing that all-important cycle change allowed EWT to forecast almost every intermediate term low in 1983 and 1984. Prior to that time, there was no clear and regular eight-week cycle. Following that crash low, all of a sudden an eight-week cycle emerged. It was just wonderful to trade. It lasted into 1986, which is a long time.

How do you know when an old cycle is going to fail or a new cycle is going to emerge?

The market starts topping and bottoming differently than what you would expect if the cycles you have identified were operating. It's that simple. Often it will give warnings before you experience any losses.

While fixed-time cycles can shorten, lengthen, and disappear at times, it never pays to *presume* a change. The probability of success in anticipating market trends is always greatest if you take each indicator at face value until proven false.

* * * * * * * * * * * * * *

The Elliott Wave Theorist
March 1992

Fixed time cycles are slippery things. There is enough repetition to prove that markets adhere to cyclicality much of the time, yet enough variation to make precise prediction impossible. So what is their value? Cycles are useful in alerting the investor to the probable, and therefore in preparing him to take action if certain market events occur. It is better to buy in an oversold condition than in an overbought one and better to buy near a cycle low than elsewhere. That cycle analysis can help you recognize such points may not guarantee profits, but it substantially increases the probability of profits. If an oversold condition is in effect within two weeks of a scheduled bottom for a 23-week cycle, then it is reasonable to conclude that the probability for a rally is higher than it was before. Conversely, if the market is in an overbought condition within 12 weeks prior to that time window, then the probability for a decline is higher than it was before.

* * * * * * * * * * * * * *

Fourier analysis is used to analyze cycles, isn't it?

Yes, and the results show that cycles do not govern stock prices. I have studied dozens of Fourier-based projections, and the empirical evidence is overwhelming: the market is *not* a result of regular periodicities. Nor is it logical that Fourier analysis should work, because it applies to processes that are mechanically periodic, not those that are of an arrhythmic yet patterned nature. Examples of things analyzable by Fourier are sound and electricity. Ask yourself this: Why in the world should the dynamics of social crowd behavior necessarily follow the laws of mechanical processes? If they did, every statistician and engineer would have figured out stock price movement years ago. But every attempt at this type of analysis has failed. The only way to approach cycles is as I described earlier. Treat them as products of a living thing, and be alert for changes.

Are there any other benefits to the observation of market cycles?

I think cycle analysis is extremely useful for a number of reasons. It trains you to be patient, waiting for possible opportune times. It orients you toward buying into market lows and selling into tops. It gives you a frame of reference for making decisions. It gives you a frame of reference for changing your opinion so you won't be "wrong too long." Finally, the mere idea of cycles puts you in a frame of mind for anticipating changes in market direction, thus consistently keeping you from joining the trend-following herd.

* * * * * * * * * * * * * *

Elliott Wave Principle

While the Wave Principle has some application to individual stocks, the count for many issues is often too fuzzy to be of great practical value. In other words, Elliott will tell you if the track is fast but not which horse is going to win.

* * * * * * * * * * * * * *

You've stated that individual stocks often reflect the Wave Principle too fuzzily to have great practical value. Why is the analyst less likely to have success trying to apply wave counts to a given stock?

The reason the Wave Principle is so clear in *aggregate* stock price indices is that the Wave Principle is a reflection of changes in mass psychology. Now, when you are dealing with an individual stock, there may be many reasons to buy or sell a particular issue, e.g., what the competition is doing, what foreigners are doing with similar products, government policy, whether the CEO is having family problems, or whether the brain behind the company has left. There are a lot of specific and individual reasons why a single stock will be going up or down on a particular day, week or month. So, if you try to follow an individual stock, it won't necessarily trace out patterns that are perfectly reflective of the Wave Principle.

On the other hand, the market *averages* show you whether people involved in the market as a whole are putting their money in or taking it out. When they are more optimistic about the future, they tend to put more in. When they are more pessimistic, they tend to take it out. Such behavior does show up in many individual stocks, but you have to act only on the clearest patterns, which indicate that crowd emotion is in charge.

Obviously, though, if the averages are headed lower, a lot of individual stocks are going down.

Yes. Despite the important distinction I have just made, many stocks tend to move more or less in harmony with the general market. An old adage says that 75% of all stocks move up with a bull market and 90% of all stocks move down with a bear market.

But individual stocks do trace out their own patterns. Under what circumstances is it worthwhile to act on the wave pattern of a stock?

The best approach seems to be to avoid trying to analyze each issue on an Elliott basis unless a clear, unmistakable wave pattern unfolds before your eyes and commands attention. Decisive action is best taken only then.

Even if your count for the overall market is headed in the opposite direction?

Regardless of the wave count for the market as a whole.

So, a stock can go its own way and act individualistically. Couldn't a couple of maverick performers upset the averages and throw the long term wave count out of whack?

No. The unique circumstances surrounding each company cancel each other out, leaving as residue a mirror of the mass mind alone. Therefore, the progress of general business activity is well reflected by the Wave Principle, while each individual area of activity has its own essence, its own life expectancy, and a set of forces which may relate to it alone. After all, many companies go out of business. That's hardly an Elliott wave, which continues progressing, is it?

I guess you could say the same thing about an individual investor vs. the group.

Absolutely. An individual's capacity to reason allows him to understand the Wave Principle, and his free will gives him the capacity to alter his own actions so as to avoid the pressures of the crowd and even take advantage of the opportunities presented. But his individual action will not change the direction of the group, just as one falling stock will not change a bull market, nor a rising stock a bear.

Money Making Rules for the Investor

What qualities do you feel contributed most to your success as an investor?

When I have been successful, it was due to discipline, which usually means taking decisive action immediately when called for. When I've lost money, it is because I did not do that.

Describe that discipline.

When I first began trading, I did what many others who start out in the markets do: I developed a list of trading rules. The list was created piecemeal, with each new rule garnered from books on trading. I would typically add a new one following the conclusion of an unsuccessful trade. I continually asked myself, what would I do differently next time to make sure this mistake would not recur? The resulting list of do's and don'ts ultimately comprised 16 statements. About six months after the completion of my carved-in-stone list of trading rules, I balled up the paper and threw it in the trash.

I'll bite. Why?

Well, after attempting to apply the "rules," I realized that I made not merely a mistake here and there in the list, but a fundamental error in compiling the list in the first place. The error was in taking aim at the *last* trade, as if the next trading situation would present a similar situation. When rules are situation-specific, you can't apply them generally. In fact, they lead to contradictions.

Like what?

O.K., here's an example of the kind of ironies that result. One of the most popular maxims is, "You can't go broke taking a profit." The brokers invented that one, which is one reason that new traders always hear it. This trading maxim appears to make wonderful sense, but only when viewed in the context of a recent trade with a specific outcome. When you have entered a trade at a good price, watched it go your way for a while, then watched it go against you and turn into a loss, the maxim is a pronouncement of divine wisdom. What you're really saying, however, is, "I should have sold when I had a small profit."

Now let's see what happens on the next trade. You enter a trade, and after just a few days of watching it go your way, you sell out, only to stare in amazement as it continues to go in the direction you had expected, racking up paper gains of several hundred percent. You ask a more experienced investor what your error was. He advises you sagely while peering over his glasses, "Remember this forever: Cut losses short; let your profits run." So you reach for your list of trading rules and write this new maxim, which means, of course, "I should not have sold when I had a small profit."

So now your trading rules #2 and #14 are in direct conflict. Is this an isolated incident? What about rule #3, which reads, "Stay cool; never let emotions rule your trading," and #8, which reads, "If a trade is obviously going against you, get out of the way before it turns into a disaster." Stripped of its fancy attire, #3 says "Don't panic," and #8 says "Go ahead and panic!" Such formulations are in the final analysis utterly useless. And believe me, this is the typical method used to generate lists of trading rules.

But there must be some steps you can advise for the average investor?

Well, my best advice to the average investor is stop being an average investor. You cannot survive as an average investor. The pros will beat the pants off of you, and the markets will, too, because what seems logical is exactly what will not happen. That is one of the first keys to understanding how not to lose money in markets. So step one is: stop being the average guy. Get a foundation. And the only way to do that is to start reading.

Can you just imagine deciding tomorrow, "I think I'm going to be a structural engineer, and I'm going to build a skyscraper. I'm going to go get some wood and some bricks and get going."

You haven't read the first thing about it. You haven't studied it. People reach the ripe old age of 60, they've worked all their lives in a business that they know inside and out. They know a competitor couldn't walk in and take over from them without knowledge and work and study and experience. But they decide to put all their money into silver futures because they're sure they'll go up. They don't study the craft. They don't realize this is work. It takes effort and study. To do it right, to be a winner, you've got to understand how the markets work and what's going on. If you want to take risks, become an expert. Otherwise, put your money in areas that have as little risk as possible and forget about investing. Before you make that decision, understand what's involved. Making money in the market requires a good deal of education, like any craft or business. If you've got the time, the drive and the right psychological makeup, you can enter that elite realm of the truly successful trader or investor.

Assuming one decides to go for it, what does it take to be a successful investor?

Well, let's define "successful investor" as someone who can profit consistently through the exchange of speculative goods for ones of higher value without himself adding value (other than liquidity to the marketplace). Now you have to gather the necessary tools to do it.

How did you proceed in your own search for an investment philosophy?

What I finally desired to create was a description not of each of the trees but of the forest. After several years of trading I came up with — guess what?— another list! But this is not a list of "trading rules." It's a list of requirements for successful trading. Most worthwhile truths are simple, and this list contains only six items. In fact, most are actually subsets of the first one.

* * * * * * * * * * * * * *

Commonly accepted Wall Street wisdom can provide plenty of reasons to buy and sell at any given time. But over the years, Robert Prechter was asked for investment guidelines over and above the Wave Principle. He developed six general rules.

The Elliott Wave Theorist
November 1986

WHAT EVERY TRADER NEEDS TO BE SUCCESSFUL

#1 **A method**. Any time you enter or exit a market, it must be for a predetermined reason that will also apply in the future.

#2 **Discipline** to follow the method. Without discipline, you really have no method in the first place.

#3 **Experience**. The School of Hard Knocks is the only school that will teach you the emotional aspects of investing, and the tuition is expensive.

#4 **Acceptance of responsibility**. Don't blame the news, "insiders," "floor traders," or "THEM" for your losses. Accept responsibility, and you will retain control of your ultimate success to the extent that the market allows.

#5 **Accommodation of losses**. The perfect trading system does not exist, so your method must deal with taking losses.

#6 **Acceptance of huge gains**. When the big winner finally comes along, you need the self-esteem and confidence in your method to take all that it promises.

* * * * * * * * * * * * * * *

What is the first requirement?

Get a method. I mean an objectively definable method — one you've thought out in its entirety, so that if someone asks how you make your decisions, you can explain it. And if he asks you again in six months, the answer will be essentially the same. It must be developed as a totality before it is implemented.

It arrives full blown?

The point is that it must be in place before you start trading. It doesn't typically "arrive" though. While a method has to reflect market reality, which is difficult enough, it also has to suit the user's psychological makeup. To that extent, it must be built.

So you build your house and then live in it.

That's a good analogy. You can redecorate; in other words, alter and improve your method from time to time. You can even move to an entirely new house. But don't move in before the roof is on or all the walls are built. Above all, don't tear down the doorway because the piano didn't fit through it. Accepting the fact that you cannot achieve a perfect trading record is prerequisite for obtaining a reliable method. People who demand it are wasting their time searching for the Holy Grail. The number of people who waste time at it is amazing, and they never get beyond this first step of obtaining a method. They spend all their time designing and rebuilding, and never move into the house.

We don't need three guesses to figure out what your method is?

Not unless you tuned into this discussion right here. In my opinion, the Wave Principle is the best way to understand the framework of a market and where prices are within that framework. Choose the degree appropriate to your trade and buy and sell according to whether the best Elliott wave interpretation is bullish or bearish. And if the odds are too closely matched, stand aside.

There are a hundred other methods that will work if successful trading is your only goal. As I have often said, a simple ten-day moving average of the daily advances minus declines, one of the first indicators that many stock market technicians learn, can be used as a trading tool when objectively defined rules are created for its use. You don't even have to understand in detail how the market works to make money with a tool like that. All you need to know is one aspect of market behavior: that the market usually stays within certain bounds of persistence as it moves up and down.

What is the first thing you must do?

Sit down and admit, "I need reasons for making my decisions." Then spell out those reasons.

I'm not sure that would be so easy.

Obtaining a method comes down to one thing: creating parameters for making decisions for entering and exiting markets. There are two areas involved: opinion generation and money management. Money management tools are techniques to allocate and protect capital.

While this step is the easiest to apply among the requirements for successful investing, it can be a huge hurdle if you have not done all that reading I mentioned earlier. It is also time consuming. Most investors don't even bother with it. So they guarantee they will lose before their first position is taken.

How about requirement #2?

You need the discipline to follow your method. Among the true professionals, this requirement is so widely understood that it's almost a cliché. Nevertheless, it is such an important cliché that it cannot be sidestepped, ignored or excepted.

Any system with a decent track record will be profitable if you apply it rigorously and honestly. As I indicated before, using the ten-day advance/decline oscillator with reasonable parameters, you can make money seven times out of ten. But very few people have the discipline to do it. Discipline is much more difficult to obtain than a method.

More often than not, a well constructed system will work, but the investor doesn't?

Well, certainly a lot of work is required. But that's not the only aspect of the task. Lots of workaholics fail at trading. What you need is the guts to do what is right when it *feels* wrong. That takes immense courage and discipline. It struck me one day that among a handful of consistently successful professional options and futures traders of my acquaintance, three of them are former Marines. In fact, the only advisor, as ranked by *Commodity Traders Consumer Report*, consistently to beat my Telephone Hotline record from 1983 to 1985 was a former Marine.

The few, the proud?

The few, for sure! Among my acquaintances anyway, this is a ratio way out of proportion to the ratio of former Marines as a percentage of the general population. This anomaly implies to me that discipline is extremely important. At some point in their lives, these guys volunteered to serve in an organization which requires discipline and stamina. These are people who asked for the opportunity to go charging through a jungle pointing a bayonet and pitching grenades, surviving on roots and bugs when necessary. That's an overdramatization perhaps, but you get the point. These people knew they were "tough" and wanted the chance to prove it. Being "tough" in this context means having the ability to suppress a host of emotions in order to act in a manner which would cause most people to shrink back in fear.

But you don't seem like the Marine type.

No, I'm not. But years ago while attending summer school with Georgia's Governor's Honors Program, I was given a psychological test and told that one of my skewed traits was "tough-mindedness." I didn't exactly know what that meant, but after trading and forecasting the markets since 1972, it is clear that without that trait I would have been forced long ago to elect another profession. The pressures are enormous, and they get to everyone, including me. If you are not disciplined, forget the markets.

Can't anyone follow rules if he puts his mind to it?

A lot of people will tell you that they have that discipline, but when it comes to actually doing it, they don't. The markets aren't merely an intellectual exercise. They're an emotional one as well. By the time the emotions have eaten away at you for several months, it's even physical. Trading is incredibly difficult to do, and it's one reason I do not like trading.

The most important factor in the market strategy is learning to stand fast if your system tells you to do so, even when the news, your friends and the tape are screaming at you to do the opposite. Outside forces don't really affect the market and never have. People hear horrible things on the news — the assassination of President Kennedy is a good example — and they panic and sell. A crisis may influence where prices go that afternoon, but not overall. You have to learn to avoid that natural human reaction to what looks catastrophic or hopeful. Stick with your system; never second-guess it; always follow it.

You've made this point clear. It doesn't pay to play the news or follow your emotions. But aren't there times when traders can use the news to gauge how strong a trend is? Let's say the news is all bad and the market holds up or only goes down a little, can that be used to say that there is underlying strength in the market?

It's sometimes said, "Because the market is holding up in the face of bad news, that's bullish." That little chestnut is a false belief. It once cost me a pile of money in my more naive days, and I've never forgotten it.

When was that mistake made exactly?

The 1979 stock market rally ended after holding up "beautifully" day after day for a month despite terrible news, heartening many an investor. The situation resolved with the "October massacre." When searching for characteristics of a major market low or a continuation of an uptrend, pervasive bearish sentiment is more important than bad news per se.

The truth is that news is virtually irrelevant to explaining and forecasting market trends. I say "virtually," because there is a relationship in that social news lags market trends. There is some forecasting utility in that fact, but only if you have a trading method that recognizes degree, such as the Wave Principle or time cycles. Then certain types of news can be a confirming indicator. In fact, some of the best analysts I know use certain types of media reports as market indicators. Paul Montgomery and Ned Davis use magazine covers, for instance. When a national general news magazine finds a trend so exciting that it makes the cover, the trend is generally one to three months from ending.

News doesn't cause any market movement?

It sometimes appears to affect the market for a few minutes, maybe up to an hour. When it moves the market in the direction you expected, it is irrelevant. If it moves it in the other direction, you can use it to your advantage by quickly increasing your position. Otherwise, news is irrelevant to trends. Sometimes it appears to fit a day's trading so perfectly that everyone "knows" what the cause of the day's move was. Other times the market does the opposite of what everyone would have expected. This unreliability proves that news is not determining the trend. There is almost always enough news to make causal claims in retrospect, which is what media people do constantly. It's occasionally funny to hear a commentator say, "Well, the market is way up today, so investors must not be focusing on the dramatic shutdown of the U.S. government and the impasse between Congress and the president; they must be focusing on the PPI figures, which were unchanged from last month...." And when they can't find a reason in all the day's news for a movement in the market, then they say the move was "technical."

You've established that news and events are not behind market movement. But if you're able to predict at all, something must be

causing the market to move the way you say it does. What is that causal agent?

The psychology of human interaction is the basic fundamental. The one thing that never changes is the dynamics of social psychology. I think it was Bernard Baruch who said that the stock market was nothing but everyone's combined hopes and fears about the future. I take it one giant step further and say that the market is the direct recording of the psychology that later *creates* the future.

Does discipline mean you should stick to one or two markets?

Not in my opinion. One of the most important characteristics of a successful commodity trader is the flexibility to go into any tradable market. If he is "married" to particular markets, he may find himself forcing a trade where none exists. The flexible trader can ignore 80% of the charts that are saying nothing and concentrate on the 20% that are calling for action. On the other hand, if one's method is market-specific to some degree, then specialization can add value.

* * * * * * * * * * * * * * *

Elliott Wave Principle

When the market rests, do the same.

* * * * * * * * * * * * * * *

What about requirement #3?

Get experience. I can't stress that enough. I don't care how much you read or how brilliant you are, you won't find out how easy it is to lose the market game until you trade with your own real money.

If you buy a computer baseball game and become a hitting expert with the joystick while sitting quietly alone on the floor of your living room, you may conclude that you are one talented baseball player. Now let the Mean Green Giant reach in, pick you up, and place you in the batter's box at the bottom of the ninth inning in the final game of the World Series with your team behind by one run, the third base coach flashing signals one after another, a fastball heading toward your face at 90 m.p.h., and 60 beer-soaked fans in the front row screaming, "Yer a bum! Yer a bum!" Guess what? You feel different! Suddenly you can't approach the task with the same cool detachment you displayed in your living room. This new situation is real, it matters, it is physical, it is dangerous, other people are watching, and you are being bombarded with stimuli. This is what your life is like when you are actually speculating. You know it is real, you know it matters, you must physically pick up the phone or click the mouse and place orders. You perform under the scrutiny of your broker or clients, your spouse and business acquaintances, and you must operate while thousands of conflicting messages are thrown at you from the financial media, the brokerage industry, analysts, the market itself, and your own inner demons. In short, trading real money successfully requires you to conquer a host of problems, most of which relate to your own inner strength in battling powerful forces and your emotional reaction to them.

Isn't requirement #3 just a reiteration or warning about #2?

Yes, this is a derivative rule, just as #2 is derivative of #1.

In essence, you're saying something is going to come into play to make following requirement #2 really hard.

Exactly. And to the extent that it ruins novices, it is worth listing separately. You must learn that if you get emotional over the market, you are immediately vulnerable. It is emotion that creates movement in the market. Of course, few people really want to admit that most of their decisions are emotionally based and emotionally driven rather than rationally based and rationally driven. There was a study that showed up in *USA Today* several years ago. They surveyed something like 200 average investors. They asked "How many of you read the annual reports before you bought your stocks?" I think they got a "yes" from three people. The rest did it on tips and reading the paper, which of course, is influence from other people. That's what it's all about: other people influencing your emotions and your decisions and, in turn, your decision influencing them until a trend is in force.

Emotions are *always* harmful?

Once you get emotional, your objectivity decreases dramatically. If it were not for that impediment, normally intelligent people would make money continually via trading. Obviously, that is not the case.

Beating the market requires a transcendence of emotional involvement. That is not to say you must deny your emotions. Quite the opposite. You must yank them out of your unconscious and view them in the cold light of reason. Then you can devise ways to deal with them.

And beat them. How is this accomplished?

The first step is to try to invert your emotions. Don't use a market rise as a reason to buy and a drop as a reason to sell. Take each move as a potential opportunity to do the opposite. That way, you're more attuned to buying low and selling high, which is the opposite of what everyone else does. Eventually it will become a habit. While this change will not solve the investment problem, it deters you from making the worst mistakes.

So when an investor is in the minority, he's often rewarded, both financially and psychologically.

An investor is, yes. He can be quite serene when everyone disagrees with him, and he's rewarded for his independence. But that doesn't go for professional market analysts. In fact, this could be the least rewarding profession imaginable in terms of psychic rewards.

How come?

When you are about to be proved right, by definition you are in the minority, so everyone shuns or ridicules you because they disagree with you. When you are about to be proved wrong, most people agree with you, so you get a burst of adulation; then you get blamed and condemned for having blown it. So most of the time, you are either ridiculed or wrong, not a great choice for people who like to be appreciated for their work.

Is it possible that the markets are evolving away from the rule of emotion? At some point, will trading be so highly computerized or so heavily hedged through derivatives trading that emotion will cease to be a significant force in the markets?

No way, ever. First, I expect most derivative stock market products to be outlawed sometime during or shortly following the next major bear market. For emotional reasons, of course. Second, and this also applies to the futures markets, a lot of computer programs have the emotional factors built in. Remember portfolio insurance? Its strategy was to sell more as the market declined, just like people in panic. Those programs participated with gusto in the 1987 crash. The same idea applies to all trading programs. To the same extent that the world of investors is divided into those who sell rallies and buy declines versus those who buy rallies and sell declines with "stop" strategies, this ratio will persist in the computer programs, which of course are designed by people. Entries and stops will all be triggered at points that the same people would presumably have chosen anyway. Even today, you can often predict "emotional" days by observing times when the market is about to break a 40-week moving average, which many computerized strategies employ as a trigger point. As new programmers try to anticipate such days by triggering action earlier or to scalp in the opposite direction, what will ultimately emerge is the same market action that would have existed otherwise.

Is there any way to ease into the experience? To take your method and discipline and put it to the test without risking your neck?

Before trading real money, satisfy yourself that your method works. Paper trading is useful for testing methodology. Some people advocate it as a learning tool, but it is of no value in learning about speculating with real money. Paper trading omits the emotional factor, which is precisely the obstacle that one must overcome to be successful. In fact, it can be detrimental by imbuing the novice with a false sense of security. He may know that he has successfully paper-traded the past six months, thus believing that the next six months with real money will be no different. In fact, nothing could be further from the truth.

Has any specific trading experience decreased your trading success?

Yes. My first trade in 1973 was wildly successful, and I was hardly wrong in my first six years at it. Then I had a big trading loss in 1979, and that taught me more than the wins. The best way to develop an optimal state of mind for trading is to fail a few times first and understand why it happened. When you start, you're better off speculating with small amounts of real money.

Using large amounts of money will bankrupt you early, which, while an excellent lesson, is rather painful. If you want to be a trader, it is good to start young. Then when you lose your first two bundles, you can gain some wisdom and rebound.

It sounds painful. Is there any way at least to *reduce* the hard knocks?

There is one shortcut to obtaining experience, and that is to find a mentor.

Did you have a mentor?

In 1979, I sat with a professional trader for about a year. The most important thing he taught me was to keep trades small relative to your capital. It reduces the emotional factor.

How would one select a mentor?

The best way to select one is to find a person who is doing exactly what you would like to do for a living, then get to know him well enough to ask if he will tutor you or at least let you watch while he works. Locate someone who has proved himself over the years to be a successful trader or investor, and go visit him. Listen to him. Sit down with him, if possible, for six months. Watch what he does. More important, watch what he doesn't do. Finding a guy who knows what he is doing is the best lesson you could ever have. You will undoubtedly find that he is very friendly as well, since his runaway ego of yesteryear, which undoubtedly got him involved in the markets in the first place, has long since been humbled, matured by the experience of trading. He will usually welcome the opportunity to tell you what he knows.

Requirement #4?

Accept responsibility. There are many evasions of responsibility that automatically disqualify millions of people from joining the ranks of successful speculators. For instance, to moan that "pools," "manipulators," "insiders," "they," "the big boys," "program trading" or Fed chairmen are to blame for one's losses is a common fault. Anyone who utters such a conviction is doomed before he starts. He has philosophically conceded that the market is random or "fixed." If he believes that, then there is no case to be made for trying to make money at it. Take every gain and loss as your due, and you will retain control of your ultimate success to the extent that the market will allow.

Requirement #5?

You need the mental fortitude to accept the fact that losses are part of the game. My observation, after twenty years in the business, is that most people's biggest obstacle to successful speculation is a failure even to recognize and accept this simple fact. Expecting, or hoping for, perfection is a guarantee of failure. Speculation is akin to developing a batting average in baseball. It will never be 1.000, but the higher it is, the better you are. A player hitting .300 is good. A player hitting .400 is great. But even the great player fails to hit successfully 60% of the time! He strikes out often. But he still earns a seven-figure salary because, although not perfect, he has approached the best that can be achieved. You don't have to be perfect to win in the markets, either; you "merely" have to be better than almost everybody else, and that's hard enough. The amazing thing is that people accept this idea with respect to baseball without a second thought, but they don't accept it in investing. When they lose, they immediately question their ability or the value of their method or advisor, even though they may have a great percentage of success overall.

* * * * * * * * * * * * * *

The Elliott Wave Theorist
January 7, 1985

Take responsibility for your own successes and failures in trading. It still makes me ill to read whining complaints. "Some game!" says one writer. "The big players bet on a sure thing and all the other investors are left to hold the bag." "A sure thing?" Give me a break. The market is very tough, but it isn't rigged. Don't sing the "loser's lament." Learn the craft, and you'll use all the market's noise to your advantage.

* * * * * * * * * * * * * *

Are there specific techniques you use for coping with losses?

The coping part should come before the loss. If you take a position large enough to inflict serious financial damage upon yourself, you are a loser going out of the gate. You should determine an appropriate amount of risk in advance. It is important to be honest with yourself. Most people cope with losses by lying to others and sometimes even to themselves. If you can't be honest, you're probably not handling losses well.

Is this where money management comes in — handling the losing trades?

Yes. Practically speaking, you must include an objective money management system when formulating your trading method in the first place. There are many ways to do it. Some methods use stops. I prefer using analysis to change opinion. Leverage is also crucial to manage. You need to decide how much of your funds to place at risk. Most people commit too much each time to futures or options and eventually get killed. After all is said and done, learning to take and handle losses will be your greatest triumph.

What about accepting gains, requirement #6? This doesn't sound like a problem. Besides, you've got a nice round Fibonacci number of rules without it.

You've got a point! And when I advocate having the mental fortitude to accept huge gains, the comment usually gets a hearty laugh. Which merely goes to show how little most people have determined it actually to be a problem. But to win the game, you have to understand why you are in it. I have seen this problem stymie lifelong traders, guys who have gained or lost one point for a living for so long that they cannot make the big money when it comes, even when they say they know what is happening. The big moves in markets only come once or twice a year. Those are the ones that will pay you for all the work, fear, sweat and aggravation of the previous 11 months or even 11 years. Don't miss them for reasons other than those required by your objectively defined method. Stay with a position during those rare times when it is hugely successful. Most people can't do it. Even though their method is telling them don't sell yet, they can't stand it. If they get double their usual profit, they get out, and they're thankful.

O.K., so once again, this is a derivative of requirement #1. But what's wrong with a 100% return?

What's wrong with it is that it may not make up for all your 15% losses. Let me give you an example of what can happen when you focus on how much money you're making instead of how it is you make it. Let's say for a full year, you trade futures contracts, making $1000 here, losing $1500 there, making $3000 here and losing $2000 there. Once again, you enter a trade because your method told you to do so. Within a week, you're up $4000. Your friend/partner/acquaintance/broker/ advisor calls you and, looking out only for your welfare, tells you to take your profit. You have guts, though, and you wait. The following week, your position is up $8000, the best gain you have ever experienced. "Get out!" says your friend. You sweat, still hoping for further gains. The next Monday, your contract opens limit against you. Your friend calls and says, "I told you so. You got greedy. But hey, you're still way up on the trade. Get out tomorrow." The next day, on the opening, you exit the trade, taking a $5000 profit. It's your biggest profit of the year, and you click your heels, smiling gratefully, proud of yourself. Then, day after day for the next six months, you watch the market continue to go in the direction of your original trade. You try to find another entry point and continue to miss. At the end of six months, your method finally, quietly, calmly says, "Get out." You check the figures and realize that your initial entry, if held, would have netted $450,000. You gave up on a trade that was going to deliver 4,000%.

So what was your problem? Simply that you had allowed yourself unconsciously to define your "normal" range of profit and loss. You looked at a job requiring the services of a Paul Bunyan and decided that you were just a Wee Willie Winkie. Who were you to shoot for such huge gains? Why should you deserve more than your best trade of the year? You then abandoned both method and discipline. In other words, it comes down to a question of self-esteem and personal limits. But perhaps more often, it is simply that you have substituted an unconscious, undisciplined observation — that the market had some kind of permanent "normal range" of fluctuation — and then superseded your method with that false idea. This is requirement #1 again, but it is such a common method of failing that I include it explicitly.

Some people, probably even a lot of people, are simply unable to accept the fact that they can earn a windfall just sitting around watching a monitor and guessing that a line on the screen is headed up instead of down.

But it's *not* a windfall. That's my point. There's no easy money on Wall Street. You earned it. By taking all those losses correctly and with the required discipline, you earned the big trade.

Doesn't the IRS categorize capital gains as "unearned income"?

Yes, but that's baloney. It's *hard* to make money in the market. You deserve your losses, don't you? Well, you richly deserve every dime you can make, too. Don't ever forget that.

What is the biggest mistake experienced futures traders make?

They're either too scared or not scared enough.

* * * * * * * * * * * * * *

The Elliott Wave Theorist
December 9, 1979

"Trading consists of long hours of boredom punctuated by moments of sheer panic." — Richard A. Trader.

* * * * * * * * * * * * * *

What percentage of success in the markets is a direct result of a good forecasting method as opposed to money management?

In one sense, it's 50/50. That is to say, you need each to be successful, in equal measure. However, a good system is far easier to come by. It is the conquest of human nature that separates the winners from the losers. Psychologically speaking, then, money management skills are 100% responsible for an investor's success.

Do you feel that close contact with the markets is necessary for success?

If you're not close to the markets, you'll lose money. If you're too close to the markets, you'll lose money twice as fast. You should be just as close to the markets as you need to be in order to monitor and protect your investments.

How often do you personally trade?

It all depends. When it comes to proving a point, like what I wanted do with the U.S. Trading Championship, I was trading pretty fiendishly. I made almost 200 trades in four months.

What was the point you were trying to prove?

I did it to advance the publicity for Elliott. But winning actually served a better purpose. If anyone declares Elliott's theories worthless, the burden of proof will be on him, not me.

What percentage of time is the Principle right for you?

The principle, I think, is operating all the time. But I'm not right all the time. I've made plenty of mistakes. As a matter of fact, one of the reasons, I think, I did well in the contest is that I took a lot of losses. That may sound counterproductive, but it's the people who emotionally can't bring themselves to take losses that always lose money. So I took losses all the time. As a matter of fact, about 50% of the trades that I made were losers. I've heard some of the best traders in the world make profits on only 10% or 15% of their trades. I think that's a good key, being able psychologically to call your broker and say, "I was a dummy, I was wrong, I blew it, get me out of my position."

Do you get out right away when you find something going wrong? I mean, the minute?

The minute I decide I'm on the wrong side of a market, for real technical, objective reasons, I get out. Sometimes it's at a profit. If you're really good at your entry, sometimes the market can go your way for a couple of days, turn around, and do something that you didn't expect. You immediately call and you find out, "Hey, I wasn't hurt after all." Other times you take a bath. With lye soap and pumice.

* * * * * * * * * * * * * *

The Elliott Wave Theorist
December 1983

If you do not take action when the opportunity presents itself, your next decision will always be an agonizing one.

* * * * * * * * * * * * * *

How did you generate your trading signals in the trading championship?

Most of the decisions were made watching the fluctuations in the hourly chart of the Dow Jones Industrial Average and buying or selling puts and calls on index options. A secondary consideration was where some short term momentum oscillators were on a short term basis. A third consideration was where the time cycles were, though that always deferred to the condition of the momentum oscillators.

So you looked for situations where these factors indicated opportunities?

Mostly, I was looking for points at which the wave structure said that a change in trend was imminent. Most of that period, February through May of 1984, was a choppy market with a downside bias, not a one-way trend, so it was tough. But it serves the purpose of precluding anyone saying it was just a lucky guess on the trend. The market overall lost ground during that period, so when I saw five waves down, which I did from time to time, I would expect a three wave rally. I would play for that, selling the top of the C wave and looking for a decline, and so forth.

Did you find ways to leverage your Elliott wave insights?

I'd say 90% of the trades I made were in OEX options. So I was trading the indexes, which is really the best basis on which to make money using Elliott.

Did you nail a couple big moves or catch a lot of smaller ones?

A lot of short term trades. No big hit or a lucky move. I think that's the way to trade options. If you go for the big hit, you usually get hit.

And were you mostly just buying and selling calls?

I was mostly buying and selling puts, because wave ② was in force, and I knew it.

What type of options were you trading — at-the-money, out-of-the-money or in-the-money?

Mostly in-the-money.

No liquidity problems?

I had to manage my money very strenuously because I started with a small amount of money, a little over $5000. The whole point was to show that you could start with a small amount of money and turn it into something. So the lack of liquidity was a very important factor, yes. It added to the pressure. I quadrupled my money from February 1 through May 31. Of course, with all those trades, I paid the broker an equal additional amount in commissions.

It must have been fun for both of you.

Frankly, it was awful. I didn't find the experience pleasant at all. It was very time consuming and emotionally draining. I had other difficulties to contend with. One of the oldest adages that traders will tell you is, don't trade when you have personal problems or when you're dealing with something important in your personal life, and I thought, "I'm stronger than this, I can handle it." Which I did, but I couldn't have continued.

Did the personal problems affect your trading?

After the first month of the contest I was up 380% in options. I thought, "This is great, if I can just keep this going, I'll reach 1000%." Right after the first month, there were extreme complications. My wife was ordered to lie flat on her back with our second child, or she would deliver prematurely. She was not allowed to get up even to eat. So I was taking care of her and our two-year-old daughter at the same time as trading. They're both in the house, I'm trying to run a business, and I'm trying to trade this account all at the same time. I'm running up and down the stairs taking care of our young daughter who regressed at the time because she thought her mother was dying. The account fell to a gain of 190% as I lost money for two months.

Talk about contractions. Then what?

One night, the phone rang. It was the doctor. He was speaking to my wife. He said, "You know you could stay on medication for another couple of weeks, but the baby is big enough now, you can come off it whenever you want." I hollered from the other end of the room because I could tell what my wife was saying on the phone. I said, "You just took the last pill." And sure enough, 48 hours later, our son was born, and the last month of the contest, I traded great and finished up 444%.

Would you want to do that again?

It's something I wouldn't want to do for a living. But I think that I could do it for a living if I had to. As long as I scheduled time off every quarter!

What did dealing with those kinds of pressures teach you about trading?

B A R R O N ' S   July 9, 1984

UNITED STATES
STOCK, OPTION & COMMODITY
TRADING CHAMPIONSHIP

FINAL STANDINGS (Feb. 1-June 1, 1984)
(185 entrants)

Stock Division		Percentage increase Feb 1-June 1	Firm holding account
1. Frankie Joe		+ 38.8%	Spear Leeds
2. Howard Harrow	(b)	+ 35.0%	Shearson
3. Henry T. Blackstock'	(a)	+ 14.9%	Bear Stearns
4. Bradford M. Johnson		+ 12.3%	Shearson

Option Division

1. Robert R. Prechter, Jr.	(w)	+ 444.4%	Spear Leeds
2. Richard H. Lehman	(b)	+ 84.2%	E.F. Hutton
3. Robert S. Gunther	(b)	+ 73.8%	L.F. Rothschild
4. Jeffrey T. Zelin	(b)	+ 67.4%	Shearson
5. Heymant J. Sampat	(b)	+ 58.2%	Merrill Lynch
6. Frankie Joe'		+ 46.5%	Spear Leeds
7. Allen G. Gelb	(b)	+ 45.6%	E.F. Hutton

Stock and/or Option Division

1. Kenneth D. Bradley		+ 46.9%	Merrill Lynch
2. Frankie Joe'		+ 45.5%	Spear Leeds
3. Richard Whitman	(b)	+ 15.2%	Oppenheimer
4. Stanley W. Angrist		+ 11.0%	Shearson

SPECIAL AWARDS

Highest percentage ever recorded in any division: Robert R. Prechter. Most money ever made in a division: Martin Schwartz. Best performance of anyone entering two or more divisions (top-all-around-trader): Frankie Joe.

Top broker, futures:	Robert A. Amato
Top broker, options:	Richard H. Lehman
Top broker, stocks:	Howard Harrow

**(a) = advisor, (b) = broker, (w) = market letter writer, '$50,000 + acct.
Above figures do not imply similar future performance.**

That the essence of trading is to be disciplined enough to fight your emotional human nature. Of course, the stock market movement and the Wave Principle are a direct reflection of natural human behavior. In other words, to be on the correct side of the trend, you must act in a way opposite to what your emotions usually tell you to do in the market. You have to be a decoding machine interpreting your indicators. To fight your emotions is very tough. I recall one afternoon when I had to go upstairs and lie down to avoid making the wrong move. My indicators were bearish and the market was rallying hour after hour. I was about to cave, and probably would have if I had stayed in front of the TV. I was in the fetal position for an hour, then came down to look at how they'd closed. Turns out, I got away from the market within about thirty minutes from the high. The really successful traders of the world have learned how to stay there in front of the screen and not flinch.

What type of investor do you feel stock index options or futures are suitable for?

If you're a hot-shot speculator and you know what you're doing, then I think stock index futures and options are ideal vehicles to be using with the Wave Principle. However, there are pitfalls outside Elliott that make these instruments difficult to use, such as the extreme leverage involved and the desperate need for a disciplined money management approach.

So you recommend trading index options?

I would never recommend options to anybody. Sometimes people will write or call and say, "What options do you recommend?" We say we don't recommend them at all. We'd be happy to give you a short term market opinion, but what you do with that is entirely up to you.

Would you advise a typical investor to stay away from highly leveraged investments?

If there is such a thing as a typical investor, he should unquestionably stay away from those vehicles, because they can separate him from his money in a flash. They provide great opportunities for true professionals, people who wish to make a living trading. If you learn how the market operates, you can have a good record of success in calling even the shortest term bottoms and tops. With reasonable stops to contain errors, you can make money with futures and options. But you must dedicate yourself to it and do it full time, as you would any other business where you expect to be successful.

Don't options sometimes fail to move with the market?

Yes. Out-of-the-money options do not necessarily move when the market goes your way. So you're betting on a whole bunch of additional factors when you play out-of-the-money options.

Don't most little guys buy out-of-the-money options?

Joe Granville used to say that he could tell the option traders because their hands would shake when they asked him what the market was going to do tomorrow. In that regard, I was willing to bet that the subscriber who called up and chewed out one of my secretaries because the Telephone Update message was twenty minutes late was an owner of out-of-the-money options. Out-of-the-money options make you angry. They make you angry because if you're wrong on the market's trend, you lose money, and 9 times out of 10, if you were *right*, you lose money. What's worse, you usually lose 100% of it! Like gambling, these vehicles offer the prospect of a huge return but only at tremendous odds. I've heard all sorts of excuses, but the bottom line is that if your option expires worthless, you weren't right, even if the stock or index upon which you bought your call is 5% higher. If the underlying stock or index doesn't cross the strike price by a sufficient margin by the expiration date, your decision to buy was wrong.

So you would never touch them?

Not precisely. Out-of-the-money options can be huge moneymakers about once a year. If you can buy them just before the onset of a powerful third wave — not four weeks early — and then sell them right at the end of that third wave at maximum momentum — not four weeks late — you reap huge rewards. But playing them as a matter of continuing preference is a road to disaster.

What about at-the-moneys?

For the short term trader, the only options to play are at-the-money because that's where the liquidity is. For the position trader, the worst options to play are at-the-money. You're paying complete premium for something that isn't worth anything.

So the best way for a position trader is...?

The safest and the most productive way to play options is to trade deep in-the-money options. They are worth what you're paying for them. They are forced to move if the market goes in the direction you expect. If you speculate with deep in-the-money options, which carry almost no premium, you will win every time you're right on market direction, lose much less when you're wrong, and lose almost nothing when you're right but early. If you're caught in the out-of-the-money option rut, just think about the mathematics, and you'll see why you keep watching them expire worthless. The time to change your tactics is now.

Can you limit your losses on options, say, to 10%?

Impossible. If you can't accommodate big percentage losses, you can't trade options. Sometimes an option can make or lose 50% in an hour. That's why you need defensive money management techniques other than stop-loss.

Should you weight your trades?

Yes. If you have three or four technical analytical indicators all calling for the same direction, you should make a heavier commitment.

Which atmosphere do you like to trade in more, a bull or a bear?

I prefer bear markets, for reasons I mentioned in *At the Crest of the Tidal Wave*. Bear markets are faster, so you get more action to trade around. Bull markets can be excruciatingly boring at times. Being on the right side of a bear market also brings satisfaction in knowing that only a small minority is capable of handling a downtrend successfully. It's professionally fulfilling to make money while the majority makes excuses and wonders when the trend will reverse to its "natural" direction.

Aren't bear markets also more dangerous?

The January 1987 issue of *Futures* magazine made a reference to turnstiles at the CBOT:

> Aisles in the CBOT Treasury bond pit were becoming jammed by two-way traffic, so the CBOT copied a CBOE idea by putting in turnstiles — two to enter the pit and one to get out.

So the physical reality at the pit represents the market reality. It's always easy to get in. As for getting out, you can exit early, like a gentleman, but if you wait until everybody wants out...well, that's why bear markets move faster. But that really doesn't mean they are more dangerous. Being on the wrong side of a bull market can be worse. The losses are potentially bigger, and they move slower, keeping your hopes up until your capital is eaten away.

Let's look closer at your method, which is first of all a technical approach. How do you sort out all the indicators that are out there? How do you decide which ones you should listen to and which ones you should ignore?

I like to use indicators that help me anticipate. I don't like indicators that make me wait until after the turn has occurred, so I've spent all of my time looking at anticipatory indicators. If I get into the common situation where there are two or sometimes three valid interpretations under the Wave Principle, I use the indicators to help me decide which is more likely. But if an indicator fails me in a big way, I throw it away. An indicator that gives a completely false signal should be discarded.

So which ones have you settled on?

I don't like stochastics or other price velocity indicators that have ceilings. Unrestricted momentum indicators — percent rates of change, for instance — are better. Take the current day's price and compute its percentage difference from its price X time units ago, and do that over a broad time spectrum. Moving averages give signals far too late, as far as I'm concerned. Your goal as a trader should be to buy weakness and sell strength. While top and bottom pickers who don't have a method get destroyed, trend followers by design buy strength and sell weakness, which is a big strike against their potential profit and loss. What's more, every computer jock on the planet uses stochastics and a moving average system, so you're often buying and selling with the crowd, at least on a short term basis. You need to use indicators that allow you to buy or sell ahead of the moving average contingent.

What about volume? Does it give you any clues as to where you are in the wave structure?

Other than price, volume is one of the most important things to watch. Generally, increasing volume on a fifth wave means that the wave will extend. Light volume in a supposed third wave means it's not a third wave. Both of these situations present invaluable information. Remember, it's happening at all degrees, so there is a lot of information to assess.

How do you weight various indicators?

The winningest formula is: (1) The Wave Principle, applied thoroughly and with discipline to price and volume activity; (2) percent rate-of-change indicators of varying lengths, from hours to years, to help confirm the wave status of the market and confirm trend change indications by divergence; (3) a few tried and true sentiment indicators.

Do your indicators as a whole affect the way you view any given indicator? Or does a certain ratio of bulls to bears or a certain divergence from a moving average always mean the same thing?

Many indicators have suffered tremendously because people treat them as absolutes instead of relating them to the rest of the market environment. It is never their *levels* that matter; it is their *relationships* to recent behavior. A momentum divergence, for instance, i.e., a lower high in a momentum indicator against a higher high in the market, is more important than the level of the oscillators.

When the markets are moving against you, what changes your mind?

I don't change my opinions based on how much the market goes up or down. If it goes up, it doesn't turn me bullish. If it goes down, it doesn't turn me bearish. Usually it's the other way around. The higher the market goes, the more negative your indicators get.

In late 1986, gold stocks started up; we had a terrific run-up, more than I thought. But at the beginning I said, "There's going to be a nice rally, but it'll be a bear market rally." Gold got up to something like $390 an ounce, and I said it looked bearish. Well, gold pushed quite a bit further than that, reaching $500 months later. But the technical figures just continued to deteriorate to the point that they were signaling a top of major significance. So it's rare that if a market goes another ten bucks, I would say, well, now I have to turn bullish. Still, there are Elliott wave patterns that require the market to stop before reaching a certain level, which, if breached, means you have to abandon your previous opinion. Sometimes that means reversing it.

* * * * * * * * * * * * * *

MTA Journal

Summer-Fall 1994

Fundamental analysts rarely appreciate the fact that they must incorporate technical thinking at some point for their analysis to have any validity. Sadly, many technicians don't know it, either. You must always, always think technically.

Let me give you some examples of what I mean.

Suppose you make a good call on the market, a sector, a group or a stock, and your clients tell you they are too afraid to follow it. The market goes your way and seven or eight weeks later you get a call congratulating you on your work. You might just say thanks and hang up the phone and be very self satisfied. Or, you might understand that the phone call has a technical meaning. If you get three more calls that day, you may want to take a good look at your indicators.

Similarly, if you are ever so fortunate and simultaneously unfortunate as to be granted a certain measure of fame...or infame...you will find that publicly distributed attacks against you for all sorts of real and imagined sins are excellent market indicators, and the more vicious and inaccurate they are, the better they are as indicators. The same is true of widespread praise. In other words, instead of taking such things at face value, see if they are a comment on the prevailing psychology.

* * * * * * * * * * * * * *

What do you think of other methods of analysis that come out from time to time?

I look at them all when they come out. Almost every one is some variation, usually very minor, on a momentum indicator. You only need two or three types, and you only need the simplest construction. Advance-decline oscillators and rates of change on the broad market are all I feel I need.

If you want to use an exponential moving average, that's O.K. If you want to have a fancy combination of volume and advance-decline numbers and 60 other things, that's O.K., too. But when you plot them on a chart, they behave in exactly the same way as the simple ones. They give you signals for the same reason — either divergence or extreme readings. So the fact that people can formulate a few new twists on the same old theme and sell them on a disk for $3000 apiece has always been a source of amazement to me.

Do hourly, daily and weekly charts work differently in different markets?

No. The market is fractal, so they all behave the same way. Of course, one degree of trend can be sideways while the other is trending. One of the most interesting comments in *R.N. Elliott's Market Letters* is his comment, "In fast markets, the daily range is essential, and the hourly useful...On the contrary, when the daily range becomes obscure due to slow speed and long duration of waves, condensation into weekly range clarifies." In other words, keep them all and trade with the clear one.

If hourly charts are sometimes useful in ways that daily or monthly charts are not, wouldn't intra-hour, say 10-minute pricing charts on the DJIA, sometimes give you an advantage in short term trading?

Sometimes. But more important, you should use what fits your style. Personally, my entries in options were better if I decided that sometime in the next forty-five minutes or hour and a half, we were going to complete a five-wave sequence and then used any further trend intra-hour to take positions. If I put my bids under the market at that time, I usually come out much better than waiting to count every last tiny little tick. This is particularly true with options. Usually by the fifth of the fifth of the fifth, the professional traders can smell the turn. They can feel momentum waning already. It's too late. The option you wanted to buy at 2⅛ is already 2⅜, 2½. You want to be there at the bid, saying, "I'll buy some at 2¼, I'll buy some at 2⅛, and I'll buy some at 2." I prefer to be there anticipating the low, buying what is coming in for sale. Once the market turns, it's too late. With futures you can sometimes buy them at a discount or sell them at a premium, which often occur right at turns.

What are the characteristics of a good technician?

One of the best that I know is Arthur Merrill. Arthur's most intriguing characteristic is his combination of open-mindedness and close-mindedness. He is open-minded in being willing to explore any idea that could be construed as reasonable, yet close-minded with regard to the fact that he requires statistical proof before relying on anyone's assumptions about the effectiveness of an indicator. Through the years, he validated numerous indicators while rejecting, for instance, the utility for stock market timing of the occurrence of full moons — a darling of the astro-

economists—and also the forecasting value of earnings — a darling of fundamentalists. He also wrote a concise exposition of
the Wave Principle as an appendix to his *Behavior of Prices On
Wall Street* book.

**What did Robert Farrell, who hired you at Merrill Lynch when you
were first starting, teach you?**

Patience, among other things. It wasn't just market-oriented
patience, but professional patience in general. Letting things
have time to take their course. And, really, this goes back to the
philosophy of the Wave Principle itself: You've got to let trends
develop to their fullest extent in their own time. What you can
do is recognize the pace and adapt to it, and that brings a lot of
peace of mind.

Putting Elliott Wave to Work in the Markets

What about the Wave Principle and the way in which you apply it to making money? Is it truly accessible to the average individual investor?

I believe that Elliott is accessible to the average investor. Two evenings with the book, and it's clear to most anyone.

Is applying it an art or a science?

The study of the market must be, and is, a science, albeit one in its early stages of development, as most social sciences are. As Charles Collins often said, application of the Wave Principle is an objective discipline. For this reason, only rigorously honest interpretations can be accepted as valid. If you want your hopes or whims fulfilled regardless of the evidence, the market will punish you for that weakness. Take it from someone who had to figure that out the hard way. The worst interpreters of the theory are those who view it as art, to be "painted" with their own impulsive or imprecise "interpretations."

Until the probabilities of the various patterns and ratios can be quantified, applying the Wave Principle will retain many of the characteristics of a craft to be mastered not only by thinking but by doing. *Webster's* defines a craft as a "skill acquired by experience or study;" a "systematic use of knowledge."

That being said, it probably takes an artistic mind to do it well, because the market draws pictures, and you must decide if they are proportioned correctly enough to call them completed. There are types of minds that are rational yet unsuited for this task.

What do the people who "grasp" Elliott wave share?

A certain visual sense — an ability to recognize an overall pattern at a glance. This can prove difficult for a person limited to a step-by-step, building block way of thinking.

What else?

What the analyst does is observe the market in real time and compare current conditions with all of Elliott's various patterns to decide which pattern is most likely in force. There are certain junctures that are extremely reliable in terms of identifying where the market is and where it's likely to go next, and much time when it is not as reliable. So it requires a good deal of patience. It also requires the ability to be decisive, because sometimes a pattern will clear up on a particular day and you must act then or forfeit the opportunity the market has given you. It also requires objectivity and a little bit of humility. If you form an opinion that a week later turns out not to fit the objective evidence of the market, you have to change your mind.

At times, the art must outweigh the science, because Elliott wave practitioners seem to reach exactly opposite conclusions about a given market. Or is it possible that the odds are just evenly split between an up outcome and down outcome?

Neither. One shouldn't confuse the fact that the practical application of the Wave Principle is an exercise in ranking probabilities with the idea that different opinions are equally valid. Two possible paths for the market are almost *never* equally likely. So, two opinions are almost never equally valid. If two possible paths *are* equally valid, then the analyst who pushes only one of them is in error anyway.

When two wave counts have opposite implications, other evidence monitored by EWT is usually so one-sided that a clear preference can be discerned. Occasionally, the less probable scenario works out, of course; that is what the word "probable" means. However, this occasional outcome does not mean, even in retrospect, that the person who champions a less probable count is or was correct. He was wrong in doing so. A system that is right 70% of the time cannot work if you try to pick the times when you can outsmart it. If you really can outsmart it, then you should be able to alter the rules and guidelines accordingly and follow the revised system.

Are some analysts making things up as they go along?

Not necessarily. They are usually just focusing on a count that by the guidelines should be given a lower probability than another one. From experience, I know that jammed counts rarely work. Twisted "interpretations" that sacrifice some crucial rule or guideline tend to crop up mostly during difficult market periods. Even Elliott did it once or twice, for that very reason. But they are always incorrect and are harmful to the reputation of the Wave Principle.

* * * * * * * * * * * * * *

Elliott Wave Principle

In *Nature's Law*, Elliott twice referred to a structure he call an "A-B base," in which after a decline had ended on a satisfactory count, the market advanced in three waves and then declined in three waves prior to the commencement of the true five wave bull market. The fact is that Elliott invented this pattern during a period in which he was trying to force his Principle into the 13-year triangle concept, which no interpreter today accepts as valid under the rules of the Wave Principle. Indeed, it is clear that such a pattern, if it existed, would have the effect of flatly invalidating the Wave Principle. The authors have never seen an "A-B base," and have every reason to believe that it cannot exist. Its invention by Elliott merely goes to show that for all his meticulous study and profound discovery, he displayed a typical investor's weakness in (at least once) allowing a prior opinion adversely to affect his objectivity in analyzing the market.

* * * * * * * * * * * * * *

There are exceptions to the rules. Elliott allowed for "extensions," "irregular" patterns, and "failures," which seem, to the untrained mind at least, to allow practitioners to count the waves in ways that fit into preconceived notions of where a market is headed.

These are *not* fudge words. They are words that relate to specific phenomena. Elliott may have chosen some unfortunate terms for naming those phenomena, but then perhaps he was not as sensitive to chronic critics and naysayers as we are forced to be today. In fact, in *Elliott Wave Principle*, I substituted better words for these, and we use them in our shop. An "irregular" flat, for instance, is better labeled an "expanded" flat, a "failure" a "truncated fifth."

You've said the Wave Principle is relatively easy to understand. How about application?

The basic idea is easy to understand. The intricacies can take a fair amount of time to learn. Once you've learned them, it becomes an easy step to recognize forms in the market. When you can recognize five wave moves, A-B-C corrections and Elliott triangles, a glance through your commodity charts will show definite buys and sells with no additional work whatsoever. It offers the best reward-for-the-effort-expended ratio I know.

On the other hand, you've also said that it is mastered by a relative few. Out of all investors, how many do you think the Elliott wave method is geared for?

Only people who want to put in the extra effort. That's frankly a very small group. I think everybody will find the idea of the Wave Principle fascinating. People who aren't even in the market find it an interesting concept. But the people who should actually apply it are only the people who want to make the market a very large part of their lives. You can't make money at something without working at it. The Wave Principle demands that much because the market demands that much. They are one and the same.

It's deceptive — a construct that is simple and easy to understand, but because of the inherent uncertainty, it demands rigorous and disciplined application.

Well, the rules of chess are simple, but winning the game is not so easy.

The essence of the task is to order the probabilities correctly. How is this accomplished on an ongoing basis?

The first thing you have to do is eliminate the impossible by applying the rules of wave analysis. At any market juncture, there are certain events that are impossible. For instance, for reasons specifically spelled out, a small five wave rally following a large five wave decline cannot possibly constitute the entire advance from the low. While a small pullback may occur, further advance is required. Therefore, calling for new lows to occur immediately must be rejected as one of the possible paths for the market. Remaining may be a formidable list of possible interpretations. However, each possible interpretation must then be judged according to its adherence to the guidelines of the Wave Principle, including alternation, channeling, Fibonacci relationships, relative sizes of waves, typical targeting methods based on wave form, and volume and breadth, if appropriate.

The interpretation that (1) satisfies the most guidelines and (2) does so the most satisfactorily is the one that must be considered as indicating the most likely path of the market. The next most satisfactory interpretation indicates the next most probable path, and so on. These are sometimes referred to as preferred and alternate interpretations.

The analyst must then monitor the market closely to determine if and when any one of the less probable interpretations becomes the most probable due to the elimination or decline in probability of other interpretations.

This sounds complicated.

Not really. Often, the best interpretation is so clearly superior that an investment decision is easy. Similarly, sometimes, the top two or three interpretations have the same implications regarding market behavior, also making an investment decision easy. At other times, interpretations with different implications carry nearly equal weight, dictating a "stand aside" posture. In the latter case, sooner or later the scales always tip in favor of one particular conclusion.

* * * * * * * * * * * * * * *

The Elliott Wave Theorist
January 7, 1985

If you're an amateur, do your own work every day. Use source material as a guide, not the commentary of an untested analyst, no matter how strongly phrased. Much of what is written today is false or lacks thoroughness.

Make sure that the internal subdivisions of your wave count fit the larger interpretation. Make sure that all degrees of trend fit all the rules and as many guidelines of the Wave Principle as possible.

You will know you have arrived when you begin experiencing time after time the deep thrill of discovery and fulfillment as the market follows the Wave Principle and your expectations.

* * * * * * * * * * * * * * *

Once you're over the fact that you're going to be just plain wrong sometimes, what contingencies do you establish to preserve your investment capital?

The key, in terms of making money, is having a plan for managing losses, which means cutting them short. Trend followers must use arbitrary rules for placing stops. The Wave Principle, on the other hand, is one of the best possible approaches for doing that because it relies entirely on price patterns, which provide a reason for placing stops at certain levels. Let's say that a forecasted weak economy is expected to hurt the stock market. The economy stays weak, but the market keeps going up. If you follow this traditional fundamental line of thinking, what is the basis for deciding you're wrong? If interest rates are high, and the market keeps going up, when are you going to bail out? But the Wave Principle has a built-in method for keeping losses small. When a price pattern that you think is unfolding isn't doing what it should for your opinion to be correct, you must change your mind — you are forced to change it, unless you evade the implications. The Wave Principle is unbeatable for determining where to place a stop-loss order. You're given an objective place to put a stop. It forces you to be disciplined, and in the long run, that is the only way you can have a good track record.

Even a technical indicator, like a put-call ratio, might give a sell signal, but if the market keeps going up, what are you going to do? A market sentiment indicator will tell you there are many bulls around and may give you, based on historical figures, a sell signal at Dow 1000 — so you sell. But then the Dow moves to 1100, and it still says sell, and then 1200, and then 1300. What is your recourse? Nothing, except bankruptcy. You would lose money and lose money and lose money. The Wave Principle, if you're rigorous, won't allow you to ride a losing position like that. Of course, you can fight or rationalize the message of the market. I've done it. But that's a personal problem, not an Elliott problem. As Elliott once said in a letter to Collins, "The application of rules requires considerable practice and a tranquil mind."

Do you use stops?

Only when the wave structure demands it. Those that have been triggered have been worthwhile, because they meant I was dead wrong, and they usually stopped us out very close to where the market recommendation was made. There's rarely been any loss as a result. And that's a big plus, because if you can make a lot of money when you're right and keep yourself from losing a bunch when you're wrong, you've got a good system.

I have also gone for long periods without a stop because I was so certain. That has worked every time but one, when I shorted stocks and they kept going up. Live and learn. But I think even *that* position will pay off eventually, by a big margin.

When you were in the trading championship, what kind of a percentage did you establish as the limit for how much you were going to allow yourself to lose?

I didn't. You can't successfully use a fixed percentage to take a loss. All stop-loss decisions must be objective, that is, based on a reason to say "I'm wrong." Let's suppose I'm bearish on the market, and we get an up day, and I buy a put, and then the next day is up. That means one of two things. It either means I'm wrong, or it's an opportunity to buy another put cheaper. If all the evidence still says I'm right, I'll buy another put. That way, I'm using the Wave Principle properly. The decision is not arbitrary. Let's suppose the market continues in the direction I did not expect. It may still be well within the bounds of a corrective process, in which case I would use the opportunity to buy another put. But if something happens in the wave structure to say I'm wrong, that's when I get out, right then and there. So I use the market itself to tell me when I'm wrong. That's my stop. Any other type of stop is arbitrary.

What's wrong with saying before you get in, if this loses 10%, I'm out of there?

You will take a lot of losses that are unnecessary. What happens after you take the loss and the market goes the way your method said? Do you then re-enter the trade at a worse price? With another arbitrary stop that can be hit again? That is a formula for disaster. A 10% stop is arbitrary. You cannot base a system on the arbitrary.

Arbitrary if you say, "I'm not going to lose more than 10%, that's it?"

Why not 9%? Why not 11%?

You have the choice...

To decide on what grounds? Look, your intellectual goal is to be right on your analysis. Your practical goal is to trade according to it. Ideally you should know before taking the trade at what point in your market analysis you will come to the conclusion that your prior conclusion was incorrect. It may or may not have anything to do with how far the market moves.

Is trading with options the same in that regard?

Well, you can't put stops on an options trade; you have to pick up the phone to close out a position. Options are so volatile that stops would kill your account. So you have to approach options from a little different frame of mind than you would a futures contract. If your option is down 50%, by the time your phone call hits the floor, it might be down 80%, in which case you're probably selling the low. In fact, at that point, it may be a screaming buy. You might want to add to your position so that a bounce back to 50% of the original price will get you even. The whole point is, what does the wave structure say? If it says you're still right — the trend is going to turn in this particular direction — then the more the market goes against you, the more you may want to add to your position.

You're saying that trading long term trends makes the most economic sense, but you made a fantastic return trading 200 times in three months.

I paid my broker as much as I made in profits. I spent as much on trades as I profited. You have to be really right to do that.

Much of what you've said so far speaks to traders and investors alike, but it seems like your overall investing philosophy is more like that of a trader. For those that don't want to speculate, are all the guidelines the same?

The time frame is irrelevant. *All* investment is speculation, and there is no speculation more dangerous than one that is confidently viewed by the majority as an investment. Take long term bonds in 1946, for instance. Or gold in 1980. Or stocks in the late 1990s.

Let's say you're in charge of writing the regs for money managers. You're now at the head of the new national agency involved in making certain retirement funds are properly managed. What would be your first step?

First of all, I think the whole concept is immoral. I don't think any government agency should tell people how to invest or whom to invest with. Second, the average regulator is a fundamentalist. He thinks that in order to buy the stock of a company that sells textbooks, you have to go out and make a case that the schools will have a greater need for textbooks next year. That just isn't the case. So, you really can't set rules. The only way to judge the efficacy of a method in the long run is by whether the guy makes money consistently or not.

You've stated that the waves are there to the smallest possible degree. Can a short term trader use Elliott to ride the micro-waves?

One of the great things about the Wave Principle is that you can choose which of the trends you want to trade with. If you bought stocks in 1982 and said "I'm just going to hold these until this giant cycle is over," I'd say that's a perfectly good investment strategy. It is also perfectly all right to have attempted to exit for the intermediate corrections. Some people are day traders, and the Wave Principle is applicable to that, too. R.N. Elliott discovered the basic pattern of market movements, and he found this pattern over and over, even on the smallest degree charts. If you chart tick by tick, you can see it recurring, and I know some super short term floor traders who trade off of that. Of course, they don't pay commissions.

This ability to reflect both microscopic *and* telescopic price trends is one of the things that makes the Wave Principle a unique instrument of stock market observation. But what about when the microscope is telling you one thing, and the telescope is telling you the other, do you play favorites?

My philosophy is to use the underlying trend to the best advantage. It's very difficult, for instance, to make money on the long side in bear market rallies. If you've seen the start of a bull market, you know the difference. Then people are eager to sell because the profits have come so easily they can't believe their luck. So when I perceive that the major trend is up, I will suggest buying, selling and re-buying. When the major trend appears to be down, I will suggest shorting, covering and re-shorting. This way errors in timing will have a better chance of being redeemed by the overall trend. When you assess the underlying trend incorrectly, you lose money, of course, but even then, because you are trading the moves at one smaller degree, you don't get hurt too badly. Unless you're wrong on both, which has happened. But the odds of that occurring are low enough to survive it happening from time to time.

How would you differentiate between an investor and a trader?

To most people, the difference between investing and trading is simply a matter of the degree of trend. Speculating on the minor trends is called "trading," while speculating on the major trends is called "investing." It's a silly division, because it's quantitative and you can't say where the line is. That's why I use the words interchangeably when I discuss strategies. Everyone must have a market opinion at some degree of trend, even if he denies that he does. A buy-and-holder is bullish because of recent history, so he is bullish at Primary, Cycle or perhaps Supercycle degree. Or all three. If he sells later because he's worried, he's made a market timing decision. If he doesn't sell, he has retained his opinion. But he still has one. Investors' actions require a timing of entry, whether the timing is approached emotionally or rationally. Sometimes people's timing is unrelated to a market-timing decision. For instance, someone might sell a stock because there is a family medical emergency. But it is preferable to have good analytical reasoning behind your timing decisions.

Diversification and Other Myths

In recent years, mainstream experts have made the ideas of "buy and hold" and diversification almost synonymous with investing. We just discussed buy and hold. What about diversification? Now it is nearly universally held that risk is reduced through acquisition of a broad based portfolio of any imaginable investment category. Where do you stand on this idea?

Diversification for its own sake means you don't know what you're doing. If that is true, you might as well hold Treasury bills or a savings account. My opinion on this question is black and white, because the whole purpose of being a market speculator is to identify trends and make money with them. The proper approach is to take everything you can out of anticipated trends, using indicators that help you do that. Those times you make a mistake will be made up many times over by the successful investments you make. Some people say that is the purpose of diversification, that the winners will overcome the losers. But that stance requires the opinion that most investment vehicles ultimately go up from any entry point. That is not true, and is an opinion typically held late in a period when it *has been* true. So ironically, poor timing is often the thing that kills people who claim to ignore timing.

Sometimes the correct approach will lead to a diversified portfolio. There are times I have been long U.S. stocks, short bonds, short the Nikkei, and long something else. Other times, I've kept a very concentrated market position. My advice from mid-1984 to October 2, 1987, for instance, was to remain 100% invested in the U.S. stock market. During the bull market, I raised the stop-loss at each point along the wave structure where I could identify definite points of support. If I was wrong, investors would have been out of their positions. The potential was five times greater on the upside than the risk was on the downside, and five times greater in the stock market than any other area. Twice recently, in 1993 and 1995, I have had big positions in precious metals mining stocks when they appeared to me to be the only game in town. In 1993, it worked great, and they gained 100% in ten months. Diversification would have eliminated the profit. And every so often, an across-the-board deflation smashes *all* investments at once, and the person who has all his eggs in one basket, in this case *cash*, stays whole while everyone else gets killed.

* * * * * * * * * * * * * *

The Elliott Wave Theorist
April 29, 1994

It is repeated daily that "global diversification" is self evidently an intelligent approach to investing. In brief, goes the line, an investor should not restrict himself to domestic stocks and bonds but also buy stocks and bonds of as many other countries as possible to "spread the risk" and ensure *safety*. Diversification is a tactic always touted at the end of global bull markets. Without years of a bull market to provide psychological comfort, this apparently self evident truth would not even be considered. No one was making this case at the 1974 low. During the craze for collectible coins, were you helped in owning rare coins of England, Spain, Japan and Malaysia? Or were you that much more hopelessly stuck when the bear market hit?

EWT's position has been that successful investing requires one thing: anticipating successful investments, which requires that one must have a method of choosing them. Sometimes that means holding many investments, sometimes few. Recommending diversification so that novices can reduce risk is like recommending that novice skydivers strap a pillow to their backsides to "reduce risk." Wouldn't it be more helpful to advise them to avoid skydiving until they have learned all about it? Novices should not be investing; they should be saving, which means acting to protect their principal, not to generate a return when they don't know how. For the knowledgeable investor, diversification for its own sake merely *reduces profits*. Therefore, anyone championing investment diversification for the sake of safety and no other reason has no method for choosing investments, no method of forming a market opinion, and should not be in the money management business. Ironically yet necessarily given today's conviction about diversification, the deflationary trend that will soon become monolithic will devastate nearly all financial assets except cash. If you want to diversify, buy some 6-month Treasury bills along with your 3-month ones.

* * * * * * * * * * * * * *

Do you have to forecast the trends with a lot of specificity to make money?

Forecasting the stock market in detail is infinitely more difficult than merely *deciding* whether to be long or short. The decision to be long or short gives the analyst a 50/50 chance of being right over any chosen time period, and even if he's wrong, in some circumstances he can wait for the trend he expected to emerge. Forecasting the shape, extent and time element of the market, however, is an exercise that must always produce some degree of failure, since no forecast could ever be perfect. The market has an infinite number of paths it can take in making either the "longs" or the "shorts" profitable. So forecasting, which is what I try to do in *The Elliott Wave Theorist*, is much harder.

If forecasting is harder than timing, why aren't good market forecasters good traders?

Forecasting and trading are two different skills. Forecasting may come after some study, whereas if you add the serious and heavy emotional trauma of trading real money, an individual may not be able to think so clearly. It is a different skill. Conquering your emotions and being able to act with discipline are two things that successful traders can do that the successful forecaster doesn't necessarily need to perform successfully. Good forecasting is required for good trading, but it alone cannot guarantee profits. If you are wrong on market direction only two times in five, you have an amazing forecasting record. But if one of the wrong times wipes you out, you are a lousy trader.

Do you invest in the markets you tell other people to invest in?

I always follow my own advice. Whom else's would I follow?

Do you trade the way you did in the contest much?

Not any more. I'm lousy at it when I'm only paying part-time attention. I just can't write my newsletter, run a business, and be a professional short term options trader at the same time. But I do invest in the long term trends according to the Elliott wave outlook.

Do you believe predicting the market can be learned?

Yes. Competent market forecasting is not based upon revelation, instinct or gut feel, but upon knowledge. The field is not embodied in a single course or textbook, so the information is more difficult to attain than that for many fields. Nevertheless, as in other fields, some people are just not cut out for it.

How can I become an expert forecaster?

The first key is knowing what doesn't matter. Only then are you ready to learn what does. But in the meantime, here are two axioms to live by: (1) Put 100% of your professional effort into dealing with the markets, but don't expect to get 100% of your fulfillment from it. Make sure other parts of your life matter to you. (2) Don't get married in October. You'll find out that during half your anniversaries, the market is collapsing.

Over the years, one of the striking aspects of your letter is the way it has pieced together the big picture in the financial markets, one wave count at a time. Most other services take the opposite approach. They deduce the direction of the markets by extrapolating down from an elaborate world view or one key market that is said to sway all the others. The influence of the bond markets and interest rates is probably the best example. Everything boils down to the Fed or whatever. By doing just the opposite, you have consistently confounded your colleagues and anticipated sweeping global trends, like the shift away from inflation in 1980. In your own mind, however, do you have any way of reconciling all your forecasts with each other?

I learned my lesson early to treat each market separately, to analyze stocks, bonds and gold on the basis of their own wave structures, without regard to whether they "fit" the other markets. The reason is that markets very often don't fit together according to conventional concepts. By the time the consensus recognizes the obvious "fact" that when market A moves, market B moves in apparent response, the markets cease coinciding. When I did try to "make the markets fit," I found that I made more mistakes. And six months after the fact, there was always a fundamentalist around to explain how the forces of x-flation had caused the changed relationship.

If my forecast for stocks or bonds or gold is incorrect, so be it. It's happened before, at which time I just have to adjust for my error in one market. When I insist that they fit together based upon some presumed relationship, I often find myself wrong on more markets.

But we've seen bonds and stocks rise together for more than a decade. Before that they were both in bear markets. Don't you feel like it would be risky to predict that one would rise and the other fall?

Let's answer that with something that R.N. Elliott was big on: historical observation, i.e., empirical research, not ivory-tower theory. Let's look at one forty-two year period. In 1942, interest rates were less than 3% and the Dow stood at 95. By 1984, after a steady and nearly unrelenting climb in nominal interest rates to the 10-12% area, with real interest rates near their highest level in United States history, the Dow was not at

20, it was at 1200, up over 1163%. Does that fit the theory? Now let's look at a shorter period. In 1976, with the Dow at 1000, short term interest rates were 4%; by 1984, with short term rates at 10%, the Dow was not at 300, but at 1200, and the Dow was the worst performing stock index! Had you shorted stocks in 1976 based on a certain knowledge of where interest rates would be eight years later, you would not only not have become incredibly rich, you would have lost money. Doesn't it strike you as odd that no one was running around that year screaming that "rising rates are bullish for stock prices?"

* * * * * * * * * * * * * * *

The Elliott Wave Theorist

June 2, 1986

Wait a minute. Stocks hit a new high on Friday, and bonds hit a new correction low on the same day? Isn't that supposed to be impossible? Aren't bonds and stocks always in "lock step?" Yep, like gold and silver and platinum and oil and the Tierra del Fuegan army.

* * * * * * * * * * * * * * *

What about over short term periods?

Well, in 1976, when rates were 4%, the Dow stood at 1000; in February 1980, after short term interest rates quadrupled to a record high above 16%, the Dow stood at 870, only 13% lower. In the final collapsing wave of bond prices during that period, from December 1979 through February 1980, the Dow actually rose a net 50 points. The ensuing 130-point drop in the Dow accompanied a sharp *drop* in rates. So percentage-wise, the Dow lost more when rates finally fell than when they quadrupled. Notice I'm not using a minor example. This was a time of the most dramatic moves in interest rates ever. The theory that substantially rising interest rates "kill" stocks would have had the DJIA at 100.

Let's take some even shorter periods. In 1980-1981, bond prices dropped from 87 to 55, a whopping 32 points. The net drop in the Dow during that period of interest rate agony was a mere 52 points. A decline, yes, but hardly a disaster. A bit later, cash T-bonds registered an intermediate term top on November 4, 1982, and declined until May 30, 1984. The net decline in the Dow?...Whoops! It was a net advance of 50 points!

What about short term rates during that period?

Yields on 3-month cash T-bills bottomed on August 13, 1982 at just below 7.5%. Not only was that not bearish for stocks, but the Dow ended its great bear market on August 12th, almost the very same day! As short rates doubled to above 11% by August 28, 1984, the Dow rose 444 points, a full 56%.

Move ahead ten years and take a look at 1994. The bond market had its biggest 13-month decline in U.S. history, and stocks were unchanged.

O.K., maybe rising rates aren't always bearish. But we know from the experience of the last 15 years that *falling* rates are *bullish* long term.

If you had lived in the 1930s, you might conclude, as the consensus did, that falling interest rates are *bearish* for stock prices. As stock market historians know, much of the biggest crash in our history, 1929-1932, was accompanied by falling short term interest rates. The recovery was accompanied by rising rates. At the time, the theory was that stocks and bonds compete for investment capital. So as bond prices rise, money is being pulled out of stocks; as bond prices fall, more money is shifting to stocks. Sounds perfectly sensible, doesn't it?

Yes. In fact, I can't refute it. On the other hand, I don't see anything wrong with the idea that high interest rates, which means *falling* bond prices, compete with stocks. You hear it every time bond prices fall with stocks, people must be putting more money into short term bills, so there is less money for stocks. It makes perfect sense, but it is the opposite point.

Whatever. You should know that even if the evidence had revealed a strong correlation between the stock and bond markets, I wouldn't have changed my mind on the idea of keeping the analysis of each market separate. Market relationships change, as we've seen many times in recent years, and wave analysis is the most reliable forecasting tool available. So use your tools for the job they were designed for.

More important, don't believe everything the so-called experts tell you. Check the charts yourself; you'll be light-years closer to an intelligent decision. There's nothing like a few facts to confound a myth.

But there are times when interest rates at least seem to affect stock prices.

That's true. And it's also the basis of the trap. If a correlation works *sometimes*, how do you know when it will change? And what do you do about it? Let's consider a real-world example, the 1986-1988 period. Bonds made a multi-year high in April 1986. The Dow rose 40% during the next sixteen months as interest rates rose. Perhaps they rose so far that stocks finally succumbed in the 1987 crash. But that's easy to say only in retrospect. Besides, the stock market indicators gave a "sell" near the high of the stock move. If they hadn't, and bonds had stopped falling earlier, then the market presumably would never have succumbed. If there is a lagging relationship at times, which many people claim, then one must discern the lag with some method. Market analysis remains the best method. At most, I keep an eye on other markets as an indication of the economic background for the market I'm following. They can help direct your gaze at the right indicators sometimes, but they are not a substitute for market analysis.

What about the trend of the dollar? Doesn't that affect the bond market, which sometimes affects the stock market?

The Wall Street Journal recently repeated the conventional wisdom that a weak dollar is bearish for stocks. And here the dollar has fallen relentlessly from 1985 to 1995, during which time the DJIA has more than tripled. The desire to cling to a false causality is stronger than reason in the investment marketplace. It will ever be thus. But *you* can be diligent. Study the trends side by side. If you find a useful correlation, I'd love to see it.

Well, maybe rising stocks are just adjusting for the weak dollar. I mean, if a currency is devaluing, then maybe stocks can rise to reflect that fact.

You should write for *The Wall Street Journal.* Question: Then why didn't stocks collapse in 1984-1985, when the dollar soared? And why is everyone desperately hoping for a rising dollar now to make stocks go up? And why is it one way one time and another way another time? These are either difficult questions or impossible ones to answer if there is no consistent correlation. So considering them either complicates your work or ruins it. Take your choice.

I've always heard that interest rates and gold trend together, as both reflect the pressure of inflation. Is that wrong, too?

Very wrong. Sometimes when deflation reigns, rates soar and precious metals collapse. Just look at 1980-1982.

Well, what about gold and other commodities?

Aargh!

* * * * * * * * * * * * * *

Investment Vision

July/August 1990

Before he became editor of *The Elliott Wave Theorist*, Prechter began investing in the early 1970s by buying South African gold stocks. He believed that gold was about to experience a major price rise, and he guessed right. The price quadrupled, and his stocks fared even better.

In 1974, after gold had dropped back to $130 an ounce, Prechter foresaw another big price rise, and bought another round of gold stocks. Here, too, he was right: gold rose to $200. But this time, to his surprise, his stocks languished. The metal moved up, but the companies that mined it did not.

In early 1975, Prechter had a similar experience, when he was convinced that the Dow was about to soar. To prepare for the upsurge, he bought half a dozen low-priced stocks. He was right about the Dow, which swelled by an astounding 25%. But the stocks lagged far behind, rising only 5% — just about enough to cover commissions.

From these two experiences, Prechter learned that even markets that appear to be intimately related don't always move in tandem. Gold stocks generally follow price changes in gold, but not always. And if you're betting on a rise in the Dow, don't assume that smaller stocks will necessarily follow.

* * * * * * * * * * * * * *

O.K., so the relationships among markets, if any, can change. Can market behavior itself change?

Almost every time I meet a group of people at a seminar, I hear a passionately argued case that the market is acting completely differently today from the way it did in years gone by. Some argue that options have increased volatility by encouraging stock manipulation; others argue that options have decreased volatility because of the ability to hedge. Some argue that technology has speeded up the markets because of instant access to information. Others argue that technology has dampened the markets because it makes them more efficient. Some say that futures serve to decrease the volume on the NYSE because they have attracted trading money. Others say that futures have caused an increase in volume on the NYSE because they allow market makers to accept huge blocks of stock, covered with options, which they then redistribute. Last but not least is the old favorite: the market "doesn't make sense any more" — as if it was crystal clear in real time in the past.

As I see it, markets are people, and people never change. The specific tools of the trade are irrelevant to the dynamics of the process. This isn't just a theory. You can prove it to yourself by studying the price action of past markets. It is unlikely that there is a soul on Wall Street who could recognize a difference in either price or volume behavior between a chart of today's stock market and one of a comparable period 40 years ago. And from my standpoint, the wave patterns are still there. The ebb and flow of volume is the same. Prices still channel, and they still meet standard mathematical targets.

You mentioned that forecasting is harder than choosing to be long or short. Why do you bother to forecast — to guess in detail about what's going to happen — when it would be so much easier to just tell people to get in or out?

For one thing, the advice would have to be different depending upon what class of investors an analyst is addressing. If he expects the market to be "up" next week, he might say "buy," with option traders in mind. However, if that rise is to be the final "up" week in an eight-month advance, the better advice for institutional portfolios might be "sell aggressively." If he has no expectations regarding the future, to many investors his advice is useless. In other words, investment conclusions imply a forecast anyway. So you should give your followers your entire perspective, which is the most valuable service you can provide to them. It allows each individual to tailor his own actions to his own situation.

Another aspect is that forecasting gives you a framework for decision making. You still have to be right on the 50/50 question often enough to be net profitable. So you need a method to do that, and projecting trends is part of my method. If the market doesn't follow my forecast, I need to rethink my position.

In general, is there any way for a person to tell a good forecast from a bad one?

There is a subtle way to tell a potentially useful forecast from a useless one. Most published forecasts are at best descriptions of what already has happened. I never give any forecast a second thought unless it addresses the question of the point at which a change in trend may occur. As an example outside the markets, a sportswriter for the *Atlanta Journal* published his ratings (scale 1-5) for each of the players on the Braves baseball team as a forecast of how they would perform in 1984. At the start of the season, he rated 1983's Most Valuable Player a "5," Atlanta's slugger a "4," and the right fielder a lowly "2" due to bad performance in 1983 following two excellent years. Later in 1984, the MVP was batting only .215, and the slugger was batting a dismal .179, while the lowest-rated player, the right fielder, had hit 8 home runs and led the team in batting average and RBIs. The point is not that the sportswriter was wrong in his predictions. The point is that *he didn't make any predictions*, even though he thought he did and said he did. He was merely rating the 1983 Braves in retrospect. He ignored possible bases upon which to *forecast* the 1984 season, things like motivation, new developments or events in a player's life, cyclic changes in playing success, etc. As with most forecasts, these things weren't even considered. Read forecasts carefully. If they are mild-mannered extrapolations of a recent trend, it's probably the best policy to toss them aside and go search for something potentially useful.

Obviously the same holds true in finance.

All the time. When economists say, as they so often do, that they see "no reason to expect anything different" from the recent past, they mean it from the bottom of their knowledge. The linear projections they typically employ result in logic such as that expressed by an economist in a national newspaper, who said, "This rising consumer confidence is good news for the economy. Rising confidence spurs the economy, and the pickup in the economy then serves to heighten confidence." By this line of reasoning, no change of direction could ever occur. That's why absent other knowledge, the only forecasts even worth your time considering are those that predict a *change*. Not because the forecaster is certain to be right, but because it shows that he is thinking and perhaps employing a tool that can anticipate trends.

* * * * * * * * * * * * * *

The Elliott Wave Theorist
May 11, 1981

By early February, it was common to hear that "the market will generally be heading lower, probably testing the 900 level, or even 850." By late February, forecasts were for the Dow to "remain in a narrow range between 930 and 960." By early April, predictions of "a slowly rising market will probably attain 1050 by summer; stock groups will rotate." By late April, the general forecast was for the Dow to "remain in a narrow range between 980 and 1015-1020, tracing out no clear-cut course." Now the talk is that "a declining market will probably persist into the summer, with the Dow testing the 900 area." If you read over those "forecasts," you'll see that every one of them is merely a description of what had already been happening.

* * * * * * * * * * * * * *

So the word "prediction" doesn't necessarily apply to the future!

Right. And it's those predictions about the future that are the tough ones. That's why economists stick to predicting the past, which is a crafty solution. It leads to misery among the people who follow them, but it doesn't seem to affect economists' jobs, so it certainly keeps *them* happy!

Do you think that predicting the economy is possible?

It is not only possible, it is downright easy compared to predicting the stock market. One economist has gotten a lot of chuckles by saying that the stock market has predicted something like 19 of the last 13 recessions. However, that is only a reasonable statement if you believe that a certain rigid definition of a recession is the only one that is viable. In fact, if you look at the ebb and flow of economic activity and generally realize that it lags stock market activity of between zero and twelve months, you will find that there is no better single indicator of what the economy is going to do than the stock market. Not only that, but even 19 out of 13 is infinitely better than any economist has ever done.

* * * * * * * * * * * * * * *

The Elliott Wave Theorist
September 28, 1990

THE ECONOMY

The latest report from Blue Chip Economic Indicators made headlines on September 11 by revealing that "half of economists surveyed say the economy is in *recession or will be by the end of the year.*" For the record, this formulation means *that the majority of economists still do not believe that the U.S. is in a recession,* although, as the article in *USA Today* put it, "business executives and other people have been saying for some time that a recession is already underway." Despite the fact that national magazines know there's trouble, the Administration (like the average economist) still sees no serious problem. Here's the latest, from the September 26, *Wall Street Journal*:

Economic growth slowed to a meager 0.4% in the second quarter, revised data show, well below the 1.2% the government estimated earlier. The White House continued to insist that the economy isn't in a recession, even though the revised figures don't reflect recent soaring oil prices.

What's wrong with such pronouncements from economists and government is that they *hurt* people in the real world. Just ask the homeowners in L.A., where real estate prices were "never going to fall:"

"It's gotten to the point where we can't even sleep at night," said Darryl Jackson, who has been trying to sell his house for nearly six months.

Jackson and his wife, Debbie, are suffering from what some realtors have dubbed the "home sellers' blues" – a sad litany of frustration, anxiety, desperation and even anger.

It's a tune that's being sung by hapless would-be sellers in many parts of Southern California, with backup vocals provided by millions of home-owners in depressed housing markets across the nation.

Sleeplessness. Headaches. Upset stomachs and – as one would-be seller puts it – "a general state of disorientation. I think about it when I'm at work. I think about it when I'm cooking dinner. I think about it when I go to sleep at night.

"It's all just sort of hovering there. I feel like I'm in the twilight zone."

"Frustrated sellers are angry at the world, and they want to place blame on somebody for their problems," said Irene Goldenberg, a family psychologist and professor at UCLA.

As you may see by the last paragraph, denials of financial danger at a peak ultimately lead to serious and dangerous social problems.

When the preceding entry appeared in The Elliott Wave Theorist, *the economy was in the middle of a recession that the economics profession did not officially acknowledge until the spring of 1991. The November 1990 issue of The Theorist added that "a broad poll of 'economic forecasters' by* The Economist *magazine in October showed a clear consensus among international economists that "there is no recession in sight anywhere." All the economies of Europe and Japan were soon experiencing what was by many measures the worst recession since the Great Depression. The Bureau of Economic Research, the profession's official recession sanctioning body, reported in April 1991, that the economy did in fact go into a recession in September 1990. In December 1992, the bureau reported that the recession ended in March 1991. In other words, economists were not able to officially state that the seminal business downturn of the 1990s was on until one month after it had ended.*

* * * * * * * * * * * * * * *

Do *Elliott Wave Theorist* subscribers make money?

Lots of them do. My favorite letter ever was from a couple who made a million dollars in the 1980s following EWT. They moved to Hawaii, bought their dream house, and left the market behind. It has also been a joy to see what a large percentage of the winners in the U.S. Trading Championship have been *Elliott Wave Theorist* subscribers and consultation clients. Obviously, the winners have benefited from knowing the Wave Principle.

Of course, just finding someone who can forecast successfully doesn't remove us from our own clutches. You've said that many of your subscribers have not benefited fully from your predictions. How does this happen?

As a class, my subscribers are by far a higher caliber than most. It takes some market experience to understand what I'm saying, as I do assume a certain base of knowledge. But I do think it is kind of a sad thing that people — because they are people — are more likely to lose money than to make it. Many subscribe to six market letters, and they want all of them to agree at the same time. Whenever it happens, their collective advice is probably the wrong thing to do. Mathematically, each one of them could be successful, i.e., right, 65% of the time, yet there could be unrelenting disagreement!

There are always reasons for people either to refrain from following my good recommendations or to follow only those recommendations that they're comfortable with, which are often the bad ones. Or they wait until I've been right five times and then go with the sixth one. Or they bet each time and bet more the more often I'm right. Once I'm wrong, they'll be the most heavily invested, and then they'll get shy again. There are an untold number of ways for a subscriber to follow a very successful forecaster and still end up at the end of the year without any money.

What's the best way to follow a forecaster successfully?

The only way is to do absolutely everything that the forecaster suggests and do it with an equal amount of capital every time. If the forecaster has a winning record at the end of the year, so will you. But most people try to bring their own judgment in. When they're the least comfortable, they'll read something in the newspaper or another newsletter which changes their mind at the wrong moment, and they'll get out of the position because they never made the disciplined commitment to follow the newsletter in the first place.

You've been up-front about the mistakes you've made over the years. Do they ever make you want to chuck the whole theory?

Suppose you asked a baseball player if he had to change his entire philosophy of hitting because he struck out three times in last night's game. Would it not be legitimate for him to answer, "No, my batting average is still .300, and that's about the best that can be done?"

To provide at least some kind of perspective, I've always said that a correct application of the Wave Principle should generally produce correct calls two out of three times. In many environments, it does better, and in some it does worse. The only thing that application of the Wave Principle has ever promised is that you will have a hell of an edge over other approaches, which will make you right more than almost anyone else. And that's quite a lot.

Still, you will not find the next 20 years of stock market prices plotted before your eyes. Don't forget that A.J. Frost and I were Cycle degree bullish during most of 1975 through 1982. Low priced stocks rose almost nonstop throughout the period, but there were times when the Dow fell for as long as 12 months. Was that a failure of the theory? If you think it was, then don't use it. If overall you believe it provided a perspective that no other approach could or did, then retain it as something of value. I think the current period is analogous, because a top of Grand Supercycle degree is forming, and the aftermath will make abundantly clear what I've been talking about.

* * * * * * * * * * * * * *

The Elliott Wave Theorist

(from the publisher's note, included in every issue)

Be advised that the market timer that never makes mistakes does not exist. Long term success in the market demands a recognition of this fact.

* * * * * * * * * * * * * *

During the 1990s, you repeatedly expected the market to top out and turn down, but it continued to new highs. Has it been a difficult time emotionally?

Being wrong on a market is an excruciating experience personally because I work so hard to be right. It happened once before in bonds for six months and another time in gold for about a year. No one who hasn't had his every word scrutinized on an international stage can possibly understand the experience. But as another prominent analyst likes to say, "It comes with the territory." Each of those earlier times, the market ultimately moved in the way I was expecting it to and resolved its technical conflicts. I expect the stock market to do the same. The problem this time is that the degree of trend change is so large that to most people's perception, I have been wrong for a very long time. But it's only Act Three, and the climax has yet to occur.

When people fail to become "professional" in their approach to the markets, they frequently exit the way frustrated gamblers leave Las Vegas: absolutely convinced that the deck is stacked in favor of the house. Usually, there is a feeling that the game used to be fair, but it somehow became rigged against them. Is this accurate?

Yes and no. The game is not rigged, but it is *stacked* against them, because their opponent is their own unconscious emotional mind. Can *your* cerebral cortex beat your very determined unconscious mind?

But you have to have some sympathy. Looking back on paper, October 1987 is just a line on a chart, but as they lived through the crash, many found it very hard to understand how values could legitimately go from where they were on August 25, 1987 to where they were on the morning of October 20.

Well, of course I sympathize, both with the pain and the lack of understanding. All I am saying is that the latter must be fixed before you'll have a chance of avoiding the former.

How?

Most investors believe that they are dealing with a law of cause and effect with the market's action on the "effect" side of the equation. The market does operate in a cause and effect world, but is a reading of what is on the "cause" side. The market's behavior itself just IS. It is a manifestation of naturally rhythmic mass mood change. Any student of the market, as opposed to a theorizing model-builder, will have to come to that conclusion. George Lindsay, in his very last market letter, published in February 1985, said this: "Is it a 'crazy' market? Most professional market men call this a 'crazy,' 'outlandish,' or 'weird' market. I can see nothing about it that differs materially from other strong advances...." That is from a man who wrote market commentary for 34 years and saw all types of markets. A fox only appears to be crazy if you expect it to behave like a chicken. Similarly, the market only appears "crazy" if you expect it to behave according to the laws of physics rather than those of sociology, upon which it is actually built.

* * * * * * * * * * * * * * *

The Elliott Wave Theorist
September 30, 1985

THOSE EVIL INSTITUTIONS!

Lately a number of dire warnings have been issued regarding some institutions buying index futures and selling stock when they believe that futures premiums are too low. Some have gone as far as to say that this simple arbitrage game "threatens the integrity and stability of America's stock markets." Every imaginable new structural event in the history of stock trading has produced such pronouncements. They usually appear during downtrends when people are losing money. In the 1910s, "the big money boys" were supposedly "rigging" the markets. In 1929, the "shorts" had "engineered" the crash. In the later 1930s, the Dow Theory's popularity was blamed for the occurrence of several "confirmed" tops and bottoms in the market. In the late 1970s, options were supposed to be the tail that "wagged the dog." Now it's futures contracts! The danger in believing these theories is that market losers will place the blame for their losses on someone else and thus fail to learn anything about trading. (I hate making mistakes, but I don't blame someone else for them.) Such an "out" is almost irresistible, like a conspiracy theory. Here are some observations on the latest concern:

1) The wave structures on the hourly chart look no different from those of the past, so no effect of this nefarious practice is evident. The times when these structural selloffs and rallies are supposed to be occurring just happen to fit right into the "third wave" position of the smaller waves, a natural place to expect volatility.

2) I was told at a meeting of the San Francisco Society of Technical Analysts that computer studies of volatility showed no support for the widely held belief that the market is more volatile today than at all other times in the past.

3) I haven't yet spoken to an institution that has gleefully explained its wildly profitable "program selling" schemes. Could the extent of this practice be a fantasy? Suppose the occurrence of low premiums is largely a natural event when tuned-in floor traders determine that there are large blocks of stock for imminent sale? Then the low premiums would reflect what the value of the market is to those closest to it. After the selling occurs, the premium returns. Ultimately, the extent of this practice will be revealed in the extent to which the institutions outdo their prior-year performances relative to the market and to the public, which can't afford to conduct program selling.

4) The idea that arbitrage tactics will "snowball" the market into a bottomless pit or unstoppable rally is ridiculous. It's the same case we hear every time the market makes a major bottom. Remember? It goes like this: "The margin accounts' equity is so low that it will force more liquidation, which will force the market lower, which will force more liquidation," etc. There's always an article to that effect on the week of a bottom.

5) At some point, the arbitrage game becomes only marginally profitable. When a large enough number of institutions catches on to the profits available, they will act to keep a very tight rein on futures premiums. The arbitrage will then be just another service, like shoe-shining, and will be paid accordingly.

6) Arbitrage is actually a good thing. It provides, without intention, a service for less accomplished traders, particularly the public. If futures premiums were not arbitraged, their values relative to the cash markets would fluctuate even more wildly than they do now, precisely as they did on Value Line futures in 1981, before arbitrage. Then it would be even harder for the "average investor" to profit. The professional traders, who can smell panic and greed, would do even better. If I were a professional trader, I would be all in favor of outlawing the practice of futures premium arbitrage.

I recently received a letter from a subscriber who quit investing in the market, saying, "the odds of figuring out the direction of the market have changed drastically since these institutional programs have begun to dominate the market. The *Business Week* issue of September 16 finally convinced me I have no chance." I think *that's* the poor guy who was done a disservice, by those who blame their difficulties on manipulation and conspiracies. Once the market turns up again, you probably won't hear any more about it.

* * * * * * * * * * * * * * *

Will you at least admit that professional traders have an unfair advantage because they have instantaneous access to resources that part timers and amateurs do not?

Think a minute. Isn't that the case with every business? Why would anyone expect a professional commodity trader to trade as poorly as does the general public? So they have an advantage, but it is not an "unfair" advantage.

Even then, there are several points to make. First, if anyone would like to become a professional, he can choose to give up his life and crawl into the pits with the professional traders, thereby gaining all the latest "information." Secondly, the "information" he gets is, nine times out of ten, erroneous or misleading or irrelevant to the trend of the market. Finally, even a cursory examination of commodity charts shows a remarkable propensity to trend, and split-second timing is really unnecessary. If you call the trend right, you'll make money. If you make a lot of casual assumptions about hot, up-to-the-minute "information" without studying the way markets act, you'll deserve to lose every penny you put at risk. In fact, it's long been shown that the in-and-out trader who relies on the latest news flash has the worst results. Many so-called "insiders" blow themselves out in just that way.

What about the manipulation of computer programs? We've seen the markets do some pretty crazy things when program trading was in force. Traders on the floor know those programs are there, too. Is it not logical to assume that there are times when insiders know the trend is artificial and short-lived, but the computers don't? At such times, can't we conclude that they are going to push prices to a certain point and create an exaggerated response?

I'd like to meet these insiders who *know* that a trend will be short-lived or long-lived! Even the idea that traders can "muscle"

prices into triggering computer trading systems is probably un-
true. In the first place, they can only buy or sell enough to do it
if the other side of the market allows them to, in which case
prices would probably have gotten there anyway. If someone
could actually conspire to "trip" a rush of computer-generated
buy or sell signals, then there is a problem in the computers'
trading systems. Anyone who designs a trading system that
purposely buys strength and sells weakness is going to be whip-
sawed. There is just no wishing away that fact, and griping about
conspiracy is the way most program designers and salesmen
cover up for an ill-conceived system. And if such activity is part
of the trading game, then the computers had better factor that
into their programs, right? Is it really a legitimate gripe that a
simple-minded trend following system, which most technicians
can construct after their first week of training, won't make you
rich beyond your wildest dreams?

So conspiracy theories are an easy scapegoat.

Conspiracy theories have an appeal, not only because the
money loser can rationalize his failures, but also because it keeps
him from having to admit he's too lazy to do the exhaustive
work required to figure out how to make money at trading. They
are a substitute for taking responsibility.

**You've said that such theories do have one merit. When an analyst
finds that one such theory is believed by most people, he or she can be
sure that they are close to a market turn, usually a bottom. What are
some other characteristics of a major market bottom?**

General despair. Investors completely give up. Sometimes
you even begin to hear arguments as to why that market really
has no reason to exist. For instance, in 1932, people said capitalism was dead, stocks were dead, and they'd never go up again.
We had that situation in gold in 1971, when the government
decontrolled it. Several economists came out and said that as
soon as they took off the price controls at $35 an ounce, gold
would drop to $6 an ounce because it had no industrial utility.

**The market is an amazing beast. It even manages to do damage on the
way up. Richard Russell has said that the "diabolical objective of bull
markets is to advance as far as possible without any people getting
in." The opposite is apparently true in bear markets.**

Exactly. It's the old story. Bull markets climb a Wall of Worry. I made up a parallel maxim: bear markets slide down a Slope of Hope.

You anticipated this idea in the great bull market when it was just getting underway. You said, "Somehow the Dow has to get to 3600+ with almost nobody aboard."

All I really meant was that for the mechanism of the market to be satisfied, there must be reasons for people to disregard really important advice at the time it is most important that they actually take it. The psychology of 1984-1985 was exquisitely instructive in this regard. Advisors, newspapers and brokers *hated* the market. They were amazingly bearish. So the market went up with the fewest possible people participating. In fact, they were shorting and losing money as it rose. The history of markets shows that over 90% of investors cannot make money in the market. The few successful ones you occasionally hear about usually took the approach of long term buy-and-hold, without regard to trend, and they were lucky enough to be in a multi-year bull market.

But so-called typical investors just don't make money for long. They get interested in the markets at the top of every bull trend, and they get scared out at bottoms. The short term traders lose even faster. They're sending 2% or 3% of their accounts to the brokerage industry in commissions every week or so. How long can you survive that without a good rate of market success? Since people's hopes and fears are the engine of the market — their hopes make it go up and their fears make it go down — the result is that most people must lose money. It is their fears that make them sell near bottoms and their hopes that make them buy near tops.

Let's say you could dissect the average investor's stock portfolio over the course of a full cycle. What would it reveal?

More than 75 years ago, Don Guyon, the pseudonymous author of *One Way Pockets*, wanted to discover why his clients always lost money in a complete bull-bear cycle. It might be argued, he reasoned, that at worst, they should have broken even, since at the end, prices were back to where they were at the start. He found that the answer lay in the clients' temporal orientation to the market's future. At the beginning of a bull market, he found all his clients were traders. At the top, they were all "investors." This is not only precisely the opposite of the correct orientation for making money, but also entirely natural for human beings and a key reason why the market repeatedly behaves as it does.

* * * * * * * * * * * * * * *

Don Guyon

One Way Pockets

When the bull market was in its infancy, each of the accounts showed purchases of industrial stocks at prices which a few months later appeared ridiculously cheap, yet advances of from one to three points brought these stocks back to the market. When Steel was in the 60s and Baldwin was nearly 100 points below the figure it finally reached, the accounts showed scores of completed transactions yielding profits of less than two points, liberally interspersed with losses. Then as a gradually higher level was established, these stocks were repurchased, usually at prices considerably higher than those at which they had previously been sold. At this stage, larger profits were the rule; three, five, seven and even 10 points were taken. [Later,] as one after another soared to unheard of heights, stocks were bought freely, and they were not for sale even when the purchaser had ten or fifteen points profit. What was fifteen points? Hadn't Bethlehem advanced over 500? The customer who three months ago had been eager to take a point profit on 100 shares of stock would not take ten points on 1000 shares of the same stock now that it had doubled in price. Just why the public should almost invariably do the wrong thing on Wall Street can be explained only on psychological grounds.

* * * * * * * * * * * * * * *

Your contention is that we're experiencing a long term top of historic proportion. Is there evidence that the long term orientation is the predominant orientation today?

The Elliott Wave Theorist has gone to great lengths to show that the entrenched "focus on the long term" buzzphrase of recent years is of paramount importance in judging the psychological condition of today's market. Such exhortations are always made at market tops. "Buy and hold stocks regardless of anything you see, hear or read," the wisdom now goes.

"Focus on the long term and hold your stocks" is what people said right after major peaks in 1930, 1946, 1969 and 1973, too. If a long term bull market ever "rings a bell" as it forms its top, this is it. Back in 1974, 1978, 1979 and 1982, you almost never heard that kind of commentary. The public certainly had no truck with it. Today, it's everywhere. People are writing books about how if you just buy stocks and hold them, you'll get rich. I think that's an excellent description of the past, but I don't think it's going to describe the next 10 years *at all*.

Do you feel the same way about equities today that you felt about gold in 1980 — that they both exhibit the same level of overvaluation?

No, this market is far crazier. Gold was reasonably priced at $850 compared to the Dow and NASDAQ today.

When will we know for certain that we have seen a market top?

For *certain*? When it's too late to act!

If you don't know until it's too late, should traders try to pick tops?

By all means, yes. Waiting for certainty means waiting long enough to miss it.

At what point in the Dow would a crash scenario become a possibility?

Any time it's open.

You know, if the most popular investment gurus of the day, Peter Lynch and Warren Buffett could hear our discussion, they would say, "It's nice to talk about declines, but nailing down when they are going to occur is almost impossible. So, individual investors should just buy the best stocks they can. If they diversify internationally, they can't get killed because they will have to spread the risk out all over the world. Forget about trying to forecast everything." What would your response be to that?

I have a lot of respect for those people because they have risen to the top of their field. However, their field is stock picking. They have been professionals during one of the most rewarding periods in history to be a stock picker. The trend, for the most part, during the past 40 or 50 years has been up. When that situation changes, so will the fortunes of the stock pickers.

But they have a point. Buying and holding works.

It *has* worked. That's different from saying it works or will work. It is also easy to say now. It was not easy to say in 1949, when almost no one followed that advice. So this supposed intellectual point is simply a description of the past. Has it "worked" for bonds since the mid-1940s? Has it "worked" for gold for the past twenty years? Buying always pays off as long as the relevant trend degree is up. When the trend is down, you could just as easily say that one should *sell short and hold.* If buy and hold is in, then market timing should be out, which it is today. It's more or less routine to hear about some new study that shows all the gains over the last 100 years came in less than 100 specific days, and investors should therefore be in the market every single day. In the second half of the 1970s, after the market had cycled for a decade, market timing was all the rage.

We certainly touched the opposite extreme in the recent mania as more than 92% of the respondents to the separate surveys said they were "in for the long haul." Even if stocks plunged, 75% said they would not sell. That conviction is the reason many analysts say the average investor is a "stabilizing force." They say it shows investors are far more market savvy than ever.

Today, to be "market savvy" means to be clueless about market fluctuations, valuation and history, and to buy and hold stocks without a second thought. The *truly* savvy people took such action in 1974, 1979 and 1982 — when *The Elliott Wave Theorist* said to "buy and hold" for the long term — *not* in 2000. In truth, these findings are a devastatingly bearish technical indicator. Taking these statistics at face value, however, analysts are concluding from the public's conviction that investors will continue to buy stocks no matter what and thus keep the market from falling. The only problem with this assessment is that people have minds, which they are inclined to change from time to time when dealing with investments.

Does this buy and hold attitude, in and of itself, mean that the top of the stock bull market is in?

These studies do not pinpoint the day of the top. However, they do provide critically, if not decisively, important information about the market's psychological state. The evidence EWT has been presenting is not merely of anecdotal interest. It is crucial to understanding that the state of the market is typical of the distributive phase that unfolds at the end of a long bull market. When investors are standing stock still (pun intended) mentally, they are in for trouble.

You've said technical analysis is up against "something of a brick wall" when it comes to gaining acceptance among fundamentalists but added that technical analysis has had its moments such as the 1970s and the 1930s-1940s, when it was widely in vogue. Did the bull market of the 1980s and 1990s help or hurt the cause?

In long term bull markets, no one really needs market timing because the market is always going up. This was true during the 1950s and 1960s, a period of market strength. And it has been mostly true since 1982. From 1966 to 1982, though, the market was very cyclic, so investors couldn't sleep like babies with a buy-and-hold blanket like they do today.

But timing is still the most important thing?

R.N. Elliott said quite properly in 1946, "In the matter of investment, timing is the most essential element. *What* to buy is important...but *when* to buy is more important." Regardless of today's bull market rhetoric, that is still true. Once you are satisfied that the trend is safe, you can then concentrate on stock selection. In fact, just to demonstrate that this is not a new viewpoint for *The Elliott Wave Theorist*, I will read this quote from over 12 years ago, in April 1983: "Large institutions will probably do best by avoiding a market timing strategy and concentrating on stock selection, remaining heavily invested until a full five Primary degree waves can be counted." That statement was possible only because of the luxury of having a perspective on the market from a timing standpoint. The gist was, "Now you can forget about timing for awhile." Now that timing is wholly forgotten, it is again absolutely crucial to success. The persistent rise, particularly over the past decade, has brought back into fashion the recurring belief that market timing is passé and useless, if not counterproductive: "All one needs is good stock selection. Just stay in good stocks, and you will make money and be safe." Well, we'll see.

So, who's right? Or is it just another timing play — a relative thing in which technicians are right at tops and fundamental buy and hold strategies are right at bottoms?

Technical analysis is the correct way to approach markets because it accommodates both bullish and bearish positions. "Buy and hold" is not ever right philosophically. It only appears so when the trend is up. The top technicians were bullish at the 1982 low. There are magazine articles to prove it. A very small handful of technicians are the only people bearish here at the top. The craft will only expand in influence as the years go by.

Technical vs. Conventional Approaches

So the timer and the buy-and-holder are both in favor at exactly the wrong time.

When thinking technically, one continually notices this kind of irony. It is precisely the position of the market in its overall trend that induces people to say that the position of the market in its overall trend is either irrelevant or crucial. But to your question: Which approach is *in favor* at a particular time is irrelevant to the essential validity of the approach. Popularity simply means that it is embraced by more novices. The only useful message results from the fact that an approach — and its message — are popular at a given point, which is a technical fact about the market environment.

Psychology is key, but can a big enough event change psychology?

I become a little more radical every year with my opinions on that. I believe that *all* external social events *follow* changes in the market. They are not events that affect the market. Changes in mood show up immediately in financial markets and later as fundamentals. If people become more optimistic after a period of extreme pessimism, it is only natural that a few months later the economy picks up, because those changes toward optimism result in decisions that expand economic activity, and that change shows up in the economic indicators a few months later.

What about trade agreements? Aren't they almost certainly going to have a positive effect on business?

This may be difficult to accept if you have been steeped in financial "analysis" from newspapers, magazines and TV, but the passage or non-passage of a trade agreement or any other political resolution has no causal forecasting value whatsoever for financial markets. A trade agreement or a peace treaty or whatever might *coincide* with a market turn but not because the decision per se went pro or con. Even if the future of that treaty were known to you before it went into effect, you wouldn't know what to do in the markets. It's mind boggling to see how much energy goes into discussing such supposed indicators of market behavior. Yet no one has done one bit of study to see if there really is a correlation between trade treaties and markets. They just barrel ahead confidently on unencumbered assumption.

Markets reflect social mood, and mood trends eventually produce social events. Since mood precedes events, you cannot forecast mood using events. The only forecasting value that some events possess is that certain events can occasionally imply an *extreme* in mood, further implying that that mood is more likely to reverse soon than to continue. However, this is not to say that the event itself is causal. Analysis based on events is a complex task that requires a good deal of sophistication about the correct relationship among mood, markets and social events.

Why do you say "supposed" in referring to the indicators used by conventional analysts?

They are truly not indicators at all. They are utilized because of a simple *presumption* that they are valid, not because of any rigorous back-testing. Conventional analysts do not bother to study history. They merely assure us, for instance, that the passage of a trade agreement will guarantee another decade of rise in stock prices because it *seems* as if it should. Wouldn't it be a delicious shock if a light bulb suddenly lit up in some reporter's head and he or she asked, "Pardon me, but have you by any chance *checked the historical record* to see if trade agreements in fact are typically followed by stock market rallies?" Don't hold your breath. The reason conventional analysts get away with their suppositions is that they sound utterly reasonable to the average man on the street, who is unsophisticated in the ways of markets. Technicians, on the other hand, *do* study history. That's what a chart *is*.

So, ultimately the technical evidence will manifest itself in some fundamental form. Does that mean you can forecast what most people call fundamentals?

Absolutely. When gold was $850, we had the knowledge that it was likely to drop to more than half its value, and when stocks were at 900, we had the knowledge that the averages were likely to quintuple. Armed with that information about the coming change toward positive social mood, *The Elliott Wave Theorist* was able to make a lot of forecasts regarding what the "fundamental" environment would be like in ensuing years. I said that disinflation was likely, that there will be an improving economy, that the president in power would get re-elected, these kinds of things. I think you can apply the same idea right now. As long as you are pretty well on top of your forecasting, you get a tremendous advantage over most methods of reading the market because you have something very few people have: perspective. Then you can forecast a lot of fundamental events. Elliott and the markets have always been a greater value in forecasting fundamental events than vice versa.

You look first to the market. And that's as far as you really have to go, because in the market itself, you have everything you need to make money. But as a secondary exercise, you're saying you can actually extrapolate the kinds of fundamentals that normally accompany the style of market you're predicting. Then how come anyone who reads the papers or listens to the news or knows the first thing about supply and demand from Economics 101 knows that the game on Wall Street is played by scores of analysts and economists who get paid big money to chase down the factors behind every little squiggle in interest rates and stock prices? They all start with the fundamentals, which is the opposite point of view.

Quite so. One of the great paradoxes of forecasting is that so-called "fundamentals" (i.e., current events and conditions) have no value in prediction, and yet that's where people focus their attention when attempting a peek into the future. On the other hand, forecasting based upon the tenets of social pattern allows one to predict "fundamentals" to some degree. In other words, when an analyst understands some of the truly meaningful indicators of coming social trend change, he can then describe some of the types of events and conditions likely to follow. The markets are the best forecasters of economic and social conditions. I think that economists should use markets mainly for that purpose, but of course, they don't.

Another example of this paradox in action was the barrels of ink that were used by the financial media to discuss what effect the "Crisis in the Gulf" in late 1990 would have on the stock market. There is no way whatsoever to guess at such a thing, since its extent could not be predicted at any point using only the knowledge of its current state. On the other hand, not a drop of ink was used in discussing the fact that cycles of market prices, and thus social mood change, are valuable in predicting things such as international conflicts and their extents. The fact that the stock market was at a four-year cycle bottom, and that by one count, it was ending Primary wave ④, increased the probability of armed conflict. *At the Crest of the Tidal Wave* predicts an increase in warring on the heels of the coming great bear market. Thus, understanding how wars have fit into such patterns in the past is valuable in predicting a dramatic increase in the likelihood of war, whereas the outbreak of war has no value for predicting the course of stock prices except to indicate that collective emotions are negative.

Could you use a strong trend in stock prices to predict that a seemingly important crisis would have no importance to the trend in prices?

Oh, yes. If the stock market is in a large impulse wave, no crisis will derail it. Here's a chart of nine years of stock market action. A complete surprise to the entire country was the assassination of President Kennedy. Can you point it out? Here's another chart of recent weeks. Can you identify when the U.S. government was forced to shut down in a budget crisis?

* * * * * * * * * * * * * *

Examine Figure 2-1 on the next page. Try to guess which bar represents November 1963, the month of the Kennedy assassination. Then examine Figure 2-2 and try to guess what week the U.S. government shut down amidst an unprecedented budget confrontation between the president and Congress. Then check your guesses against the actual dates, shown in Figures 2-3 and 2-4 on the following page.

* * * * * * * * * * * * * *

You might ask, what about peace treaties? Or the San Francisco earthquake? Or the assassination of President Lincoln? What about the hurricane that devastated the coast of Florida and South Carolina or the floods that damaged so much of the Midwest? Are there corresponding market moves? No. The patterns of the market go around and through events of that type. It is moving in its own cycles of optimism and pessimism and is not buffeted by such events. If you go back far enough in history, you will find that almost any recurring type of fundamental event will appear to coincide with a rising market in some periods of time and with a falling market in other periods of time. A severe change in mass psychological mood always results in major events, but such major events do not cause trends.

Dow Jones Industrial Average from ? to ? Find the bar that is November 1963, the month of the Kennedy assassination

© 1995 Elliott Wave International

Figure 2-1

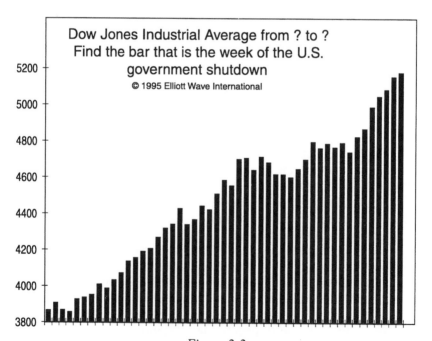

Dow Jones Industrial Average from ? to ? Find the bar that is the week of the U.S. government shutdown

© 1995 Elliott Wave International

Figure 2-2

Are you saying that if you were in the stock market for technical reasons and you somehow obtained secret information five minutes ahead of time that the president would be assassinated, you wouldn't lighten up on your position?

I would buy some puts and sell them five minutes after the announcement. Otherwise, I would not change my position.

But if you knew ahead of time what the major events were going to be, how can you say that even that would not help you to know what the markets would to do?

If the devil had come to you in early 1986 and said, "I've got some inside information. The Democrats will take over the Senate by a wider margin than even they expected. We'll have the biggest financial scandal on Wall Street in 60 years – the Milken/ Boesky insider trading debacle – and Ronald Reagan, the most beloved president in history, will be caught in the midst of a national scandal regarding Iran." What would have happened if you assumed the news would have an effect on future trends and you shorted a bunch of stock? You would have lost money. Suppose you knew in 1992 after 12 years of Republican reign that a Democrat would get elected, enact the largest tax increase in U.S. history and attempt to socialize the entire medical industry of the U.S. Would you have sold? For market analysis, these so-called "fundamentals" don't work.

Ultimately, however, isn't it reasonable to say that the driving force behind long term appreciation is always the same fundamental force: earnings? No matter what 20th century success story you're talking about, Coca Cola or IBM or Microsoft, the common element was an ability to deliver on the bottom line. So if you can forecast profits, can't you be expected to forecast rising stock prices?

How many people forecasting profits predicted the stock market one year ahead in mid-1929, mid-1930, mid-1931, mid-1932 and mid-1933? Or 1984, 1985 and 1986, when economists were bearish? The stock price is the best forecaster of earnings and profits, not vice versa. Now, once you have established that a bull market is in force, which is a task requiring technical analysis, then you can perform one type of useful fundamental analysis: you can set out to learn more about a company than the otherwise best-informed people in the marketplace. A really dedicated fundamental analyst who gets inside a new company

Figure 2-3

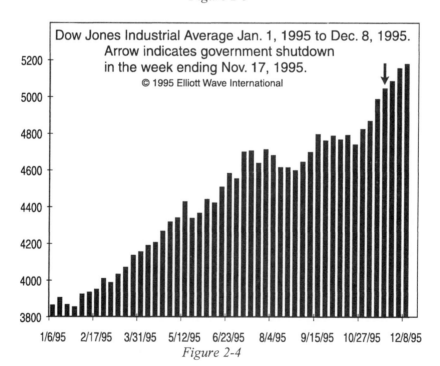

Figure 2-4

and believes it has a huge advantage over the competition and believes that its stock price does not reflect that potential can make an intelligent choice. He is, in effect, predicting profits and therefore the relative price of one stock.

In the area of individual stocks, can fundamental approaches be effective in ways that even the Wave Principle is not?

Sure. In fact, I think stock selection is the only place fundamental analysis is valid. A guy doing fundamental analysis has to do his homework, he has to be on top of the company, he's got to know the key people, and he has got to really know what is going on. He has to have a good feel for the future and the competition in that area. So I think it's a valid approach in picking undervalued and/or emerging companies. This approach takes immense work. You're not just talking about investigating Microsoft. You're talking about investigating 100 or more companies just to *find* the next Microsoft. This approach only works on the micro level, and *only after* the macro level is judged to be acceptable for the exercise. Otherwise, a bear market will kill the stock price of your presumed new Microsoft.

Is there any point in a market cycle at which Elliotticians and fundamentalists will agree?

There is a stretch in the fifth wave of a bull market when Elliotticians and fundamentalists are on the same side. But Elliotticians know it's late in the trend, and fundamentalists think it's early.

Mark Hulbert of the *Hulbert Financial Digest*, a newsletter rating service, has compared the performance of two groups and said that fundamentalists had "about an equal showing" with technicians.

This equal showing has been achieved during a period of consistently rising prices. It would be dangerous for someone to assume that these two camps would also perform equally if the market entered a bear market. It has been rather widely recognized that fundamental analysts get killed in bear markets because they are almost always "long." Undoubtedly, many technicians will be wrong as well, but the top performers will be technicians. To make assumptions using only data from bull market years will prove to be a dangerous thing when market behavior changes. The mere possibility that technical analysis can serve to help an investor avoid a bear market of historic proportion or duration gives it an edge.

James Cloonan, president of the American Association of Individual Investors, has reported that the likelihood of loss in buying and holding a diversified stock portfolio falls to 4.3% once the holding period reaches five years. That's with stock portfolios begun in each of the past 50 years. The odds are even better when considering a diversified portfolio of small stocks.

The fact that most of the past 50 years has seen rising markets says little about the future. To rely on that record in justifying a fully invested position is no different from relying on a mechanical technical trading program fitted to back data.

* * * * * * * * * * * * * *

The Elliott Wave Theorist
July 6, 1979

Those of you who have heard A.J. Frost speak have heard him refer to technicians as *falcons*. Falcons, you may have heard, fly in a widening spiral to confuse their prey, and then begin descending in a contracting spiral until they zero in on their prey and strike at speeds of up to 200 miles per hour. You might ponder the following headline from a *Wall Street Journal* front page article: "Rare Falcons Adapt to a New Habitat Teeming With Prey — Stately Birds Soar and Hunt Amid Heights and Canyons of a Modern Wilderness." Are the daily, weekly and hourly charts of the Dow Jones Industrial Average the "Heights and Canyons of a Modern Wilderness?"

* * * * * * * * * * * * * *

What about the academics? Whose side are they on?

The most widely accepted model of stock market behavior among academics is built upon the premise that all investment is based on rational decision-making processes in an environment of random price movement. Does that make sense to you?

When you put it that way....

No, *they* put it that way. And in fact, each idea on its own is as patently false as putting them together is illogical. Most investments are made for emotional reasons and because everyone else is doing it. Such are not rational decisions. And as far as randomness is concerned, the Wave Principle disputes that. Study the charts. The major events do not show up, as we discussed earlier, but the wave patterns do. In fact, we're making headway in *proving* that the market is not random. More on that in a coming publication.

But most "ivory tower" types still argue that neither technical nor fundamental systems are any better than a thrown dart.

Right. This comes from the "randomness" idea, which comes from EMH — the Efficient Market Hypothesis — which has held academia captive for decades. I think researchers knew (accurately, to be sure) that they were smarter than most other people, but then they discovered that *they* couldn't make money in the market. So they were ripe to conclude that therefore it must be a random walk, because otherwise, they could figure it out.

When people demonstrate that they can do better than chance with a method over a long period of time in a speculative market, they have essentially refuted the random walk hypothesis. I know traders who make a six- or seven-figure income every year trading stock index futures, using the market's emotional patterns to guide them. The Wave Principle can even make a precise forecast every so often, and the total record is way better than chance. Examples of some predictions using the Wave Principle are Charles Collins' prediction in 1957 that the top of Primary Wave ⑤ would be 1000 and Hamilton Bolton's prediction in 1960 of the top at 999. On February 9, 1966, the 3 p.m. hourly reading reached a high of 995.82, less than ⅓ of 1% error. A.J. Frost in 1970 forecasted a bear market low of 572. In December 1974, the DJIA hourly reading low was 572.20. In the summer of 1976, I predicted the expected low for the fourth wave expanding triangle in progress would be Dow 922. The low occurred at 11 a.m. on November 11th at Dow 920.63. In 1980, I forecasted a drop in gold to $477. It fell to $474. Then I forecasted a rally to $710. It topped at $720 in September. While we cannot do such precise forecasting all the time, we can do it *sometimes*, and that means the market is not random.

From 1995 through 2000, many academics have been advocating a "buy-and-hold" approach to stocks, saying that while fluctuations in

stocks were random, the long term uptrend was reliable. So they said, "buy stocks for the long term."

Yeah. They weren't saying that twenty years ago. *Now* they tell us. What's really going on is that they are predicting the past. I can do that, too. So can you. But these irresponsible people have taken the step of advising average people that because stocks have gone up so persistently for years, they should buy *now* and hold for the long term. They say *you* should buy stocks now because *they* can't time the market. I guess we'll see how *that* advice, and that's what it is — advice — works out.

But you seem to be an advocate of long-term orientation.

Most definitely! But a *proper* long term orientation. *Elliott Wave Principle* presented one in 1978, and I'm presenting another one now.

To give them their due, in recent years, some academicians have uncovered cracks in the efficient market and random-walk theories. How does this make you feel?

It is very heartening. Not only is the technical analysis profession roaring toward the realm of science, but science itself is roaring toward technical analysis. In fact, it will change our profession over the next decade in a most shocking way. The latest scientific frontier, that of complex systems, will eventually make conventional analysis, involving the idea of causality from events to markets, obsolete, just as those same studies are swiftly making obsolete the idea of random walk. Complexity theorists recognize nature's processes of self-organization. Now that that principle is understood, it is only a short step to realize, as some have already done, that society operates the same way. That's why free societies are more successful and productive than controlled ones. They self-organize far more efficiently than any human directors could make them do. Nature's processes of self-organization, furthermore, are patterned. This applies to human self-organization as well, which is exactly what R.N. Elliott said and exactly the phenomenon that technical analysis studies. The market has the same paradoxical order in its wildness that nature does. Its order comes from its wildness, i.e., its interactive organizational mechanisms, not from imposition, such as one finds in a garden.

So the ivory tower is coming up to speed?

Well, sort of. The studies I've seen are based on physics, which ultimately won't work, or they admit to a slight psychological component to stock price activity by investigating whether the stock market occasionally "overreacts," when in fact it does not "react" in the first place; its patterns are endogenous. I have maintained that academic study should be focused upon the patterns of human behavior in the area of self-organization, and increasingly, if haltingly, that is exactly where it is being focused.

Basically, the long-held academic point of view is that market predictions are impossible. Your view has always been that they are difficult, which philosophically is a world of difference.

True, and mine is a lot more fun.

Society and
the Grand Supercycle

Now that we've covered the money-making aspects of the Wave Principle, we can move on to the some of its larger implications. Over the years, you've extended your stock market studies to the economy, popular culture and social trends. This extension has pushed the debate into its largest possible context. On Wall Street, it is common for observers to consider the market's performance a by-product of politics in Washington or the latest global crisis, with such phenomena cited as causal explanations for market behavior. According to you, the correct temporal relationship is the other way around. The market precedes social change because the market is a "coincident register of mass emotion." Thanks to its long history and the diligent record-keeping of market pioneers, it is clear that the market is a precise recording of mass mood in finance. In your 1985 report, *Popular Culture and the Stock Market*, your most recent book, *The Wave Principle of Human Social Behavior* (1999) and issues of *The Elliott Wave Theorist* beginning in 1979, you've focused on the connection between the market and everything from the popularity of exercise to the cancellation of TV shows. The first question is: Is there really a foundation for making such sweeping observations?

Yes. Exactly. Almost everyone believes that *social actions cause changes in social psychology.* If that is true, then events must be so perfectly determined that they create the Elliott wave patterns we see in the markets. For people to claim that the latest idea from the White House or the latest law passed by Congress or the latest statistic on the trade deficit or earnings or war or natural disaster has any *effect* on the market's pattern, that such things are *determinants* of stock prices in any way, is suggesting a far more radical view of the harmony of the universe than I am. In other words, to argue that events cause the state of social psychology is to argue that *events* are patterned, which is determinism. In that case, free will is invalid, in which case no one could make money from the Wave Principle, which we have shown can be done.

On the other hand, if *social psychology guides the tenor of social actions*, then it is only mass psychology, which is apparently a process governed by the unconscious mind, that need be patterned to produce structure in markets. Its patterns underlie social behavior, and behavior ultimately produces results in the form of social action that are viewed as important events.

So given moods, or wave counts as you call them, always produce the same events at similar junctures in the count?

No. Social events are manifestations of a patterned social mood, but the moods may be manifest in countless ways. Social actions are an outlet for the patterns of mass psychology, expressing it in diverse ways that give rise to the myriad events of human history.

You don't consider fundamentals?

On the contrary, socionomists, as I call us, are the only ones who do so properly. The patterns of social psychology that occur naturally *are* the fundamentals of the market. They are what cause what most people *think* are the fundamentals.

On Wall Street, analysts contemplate the ramifications of events in Washington, Tokyo and all points in between as much as the people who make their livings there. Then they proceed to build a market opinion from an initial observation about a political or social event that they see happening. They say, "The Democrats are going to win, and the president is going to do such-and-such, and that's going to cause stock prices to..."

Right. And they have about as much success predicting markets as economists have predicting the economy.

Isn't it possible that there is no pattern — that the five wave subdivisions in the market since 1932 are an accident?

That's the typical response from Wall Street observers: "Another coincidence." When patterns of this tremendous size continue to work out time after time, it becomes a matter of faith to continue to believe that the Wave Principle is *not* reflective of stock market behavior.

It's an elegant idea, but in the workaday world of Wall Street, the average broker or economist or reporter is going to say, "Ellio-huh? The Fed just raised interest rates."

And what do they say when the market goes up despite a rise in rates?

They don't talk about it.

Right. They find a different event they perceive as positive and say the market went up today because of that. It's easier than saying it's because a given wave pattern may or may not be in effect. A rise in rates is a matter of fact. That's something a broker can sell, an economist can speculate upon, a reporter can write about and an investor can grasp, all without doing any research.

If everyone believes in the significance of an event, isn't such an event significant?

Many people believe in ghosts, but that does not make them real. Nor have they escaped the question of "maybe it's meaningful and maybe it's not." If it's something to "speculate upon," historically speaking, there is far more uncertainty as to implication as there is with a wave count.

A belief in the power of the Fed or earnings equals a belief in ghosts. Maybe you don't realize how heretical this sounds.

I actually took my position for granted for a dozen years. Then I began to discuss it with people and realized that they had never thought of the idea and never considered it. But after they hear it, most people *do* see the internal logic of it fairly quickly and right away become quietly thoughtful.

The logic may be compelling but the implications that flow from this idea demand an enormous reordering of one's mindset.

Yes, and accepting it as depicting reality is a bigger step. I am confident that people will take this step, though. I may present a radical theory of social causality, but it is the only one that makes sense.

The Wave Principle presents a profound truth: sometimes the dynamics of social psychology are impelling the mass mood toward optimism, and sometimes toward pessimism, regardless of all news. Events do not shape the market; it's the forces behind the market that shape events. Events are *results*, and when you know what they result *from*, i.e., social mood trends, you can often predict the general tenor of such behaviors. If one knows the species of a tree, he can predict what kind of fruit it will bear. Events are the fruits of a bull or bear market in social mood.

Yes, but you have to predict the tree, too, if you're after investment profits.

Yes, you have to recognize extremes in psychology, which requires knowing the patterns. The natural path of psychological development is described by the Wave Principle. When wave five ends, it's time for a reversal, regardless of all other possible considerations.

This idea elevates the status of technical analysis, certainly to a level well above the more accepted methods on Wall Street. But it also suggests that technicians who grasp the psychological components of the market can do things even they don't routinely attempt: anticipating some of what's in store for society at large.

Right. With this background, we can appreciate the wider applications of market analysis and realize that it is the only basis upon which to do what man has forever wanted to do: predict the future, at least in some areas and to a limited degree.

If that's all true, market technicians should be successfully predicting all kinds of changes in our social experience.

Yes, and I am not alone in this realization. Bob Farrell of Merrill Lynch observed that he is often able to make forecasts about upcoming changes in the market's backdrop based upon the implications of his market analysis. I argue further that such is the *only* logical direction of forecasting between the two sets of data. If we are dealing with a mass psychological condition that pervades our collective life and expresses the direction in everything that we do as a group or society, the predictive possibilities can't stop at stocks.

So people following news for clues to market direction are wasting their time?

Of course, and I am not the first to say that. But I am the first to recognize the depth of the irony and paradox behind the exercise.

Explain.

It is not precisely correct to say that news and other extramarket events and conditions are irrelevant. For one thing, they can provide a basis for the *rationalization* of a market opinion formed simply by one's emotional state, the pervasiveness of which is precisely *why* markets are patterned. It is rationalization that allows people to avoid exercising reason and therefore to act on the basis of their emotional states. So the pervasiveness of people's pretending to follow news is why markets are patterned and why following news cannot work.

Is that all news is good for?

No. When you understand the cause of news, you can occasionally use the news to help understand the psychological climate. When news is extreme, it can help confirm the passage of an extremity in mood.

But we've all seen the stock and bond market bounce or dive on the release of money supply or Consumer Price Index figures.

Sure, for a few minutes. And sometimes it *doesn't* react, does it? It need not do so because after all, what created the money supply figure and the CPI figure in the first place but people acting in concert *before* the number was announced? Their actions are in the fabric of our experience well before the number comes out, and the motivations that produced it come even before that. The release of such figures never changes the market's larger trend. On all time horizons longer than two minutes, news *lags* the market.

Although fundamentalists seem to be completely in the dark about the temporal relationship between the market and news on the larger scale, technically-minded analysts have recognized it for decades. They say the market "discounts," or correctly guesses, the outcome of a vote or a war.

This theory is initially enticing because in preceding social and political events, the market may appear to sense changes before they occur. However, the idea that investors are clairvoyant regarding social conundrums is somewhat fanciful. Did investors panic in 1929 because they suddenly realized that the worst depression in history was coming and that ten years afterward, Germany and Japan would be bombing their neighbors? The very idea is revealed as absurd if you take the time to contemplate it. Not to mention the fact that by early 1930, they were complacent again.

So what *is* happening?

The market doesn't "see into the future," as the discounting concept suggests; it records, like a barometer, the causes of the future. Increasingly optimistic people expand business; increasingly depressed people contract their businesses. The results show up later as a "discounted" future.

If all the conventional news-mongering is just empty talk, isn't it therefore just a harmless activity?

Sure, if you have no stake in the market, social events or your own time. But truly, this false premise of market compulsion by news leads to a fog of uncertainty in every conceivable area of anticipating the social future, from market forecasting to anticipating cultural trends to predicting elections to planning for the comfort and well-being of your family or the safety of your nation.

The Economy

Is the economy as strong as everyone says it is?

No. I've examined dozens of charts of economic activity. Despite the fact that the Dow is at new all-time highs by a huge margin, the recent peaks in the rates of change of economic activity are *lower* than those of the 1960s and 1970s. That difference reflects a fundamental change in the health of the economy and says that what we are experiencing is not just the end of the expansion in force for the past few years. This loss of expansionary momentum reflects a top of much larger degree.

Can the Wave Principle account for this relative weakness?

A fifth wave in the stock market always diverges against the third by technical measures. In other words, even though prices are at a new high, the rate of change is less, the overbought condition is less, the breadth isn't as strong. The same thing is true in terms of the economic results, which are likewise weaker. For instance, the economy during Cycle wave V has been productive, but there is a much wider disparity between the stock market's valuation and economic performance today than there was in the early and mid-1960s.

Does this underperformance in capital intensive endeavors in the 1980s and 1990s fit the Elliott wave thesis?

Yes. What occurred in the late 1960s was not the ultimate extreme in psychology, which occurs in the fifth wave, but the extreme in the *ability to render real* the bullish psychology of the time, i.e., to translate ebullience into actual capital production. This is accomplished most effectively in the third wave.

If the 1980s/1990s were to their preceding decades what the 1920s were to their preceding decades, i.e., wave V, then the economy should have painted the same picture back then. Did the economy underperform it in that wave V?

In fact, that's exactly what it did. In *At the Crest*, I show a chart of business activity from 1919 to 1929 that shows the same phenomenon that has occurred from 1972 to the present. The peak in economic activity at the end of wave V in stocks in

1929 was lower than those within the preceding wave IV and undoubtedly the preceding wave III as well. The same thing is true today, and I think the result will also be the same.

But there are valid reasons to expect excess capacity to be consumed this time. Eastern Europe, India and China, for example. Those markets weren't even open to U.S. manufacturers in 1966.

First, it is just such hopes that create the psychological environment for a top. But like all such arguments based on so-called "fundamentals," it has two sides. In your example, those countries are not only consumers but they are also becoming producers. Very cheap producers, too. Won't that be a negative influence on U.S. wage rates and profit margins, at least temporarily? Look, you can spend all day discussing "fundamentals" like this, but the fact is that economic expansions since 1972 have reflected a slowing long term trend. That fact overrides every "yeah, but" you can come up with.

The majority of pundits is saying that positive changes in the worldwide outlook for capitalism and other favorable "fundamentals" are bullish for stocks.

Of course they're saying that. How else could the global stock market make a top? The worldwide outlook for capitalism in 1942 was terrible, so it was a great stock buying opportunity. In the coming bear market, the public's image of capitalism will suffer again.

You say that the coming stock crash will lead to a depression. If so, wasn't the 1987 crash wrong? The economy has gone on to record activity and new highs.

Not all crashes lead to depressions. The 1962 crash, for instance, which was Primary wave ④ of Cycle wave III. The 1987 crash was in almost the same position as that one: Primary wave ④ of Cycle wave V, although because of its large price movement, I didn't realize it at the time. That corrective pattern did lead to a recession, though, in 1990-91. But the coming crash will be different. It will be much larger, part of a Grand Supercycle bear market.

What time period does the current long-term pattern in the markets have the most in common with?

The 1720 peak. That's when the investment manias associated with the South Sea Bubble in England and the Mississippi Scheme in France ended.

Will the bear market be similar to the one that followed that peak?

Similar, yes, but while the bear market of the 1700s produced 64 years of a zigzag pattern, a very simple down-up-down shape, this one is likely to be a sideways pattern, which will manifest as plummeting major declines punctuated by tremendous rallies back to near or slightly past the old highs. If you take a look at the Dow Jones Industrial Average chart from 1966 to 1982, you can get an idea of what I'm expecting. But it will occur on a larger scale.

What about the accompanying economic turmoil? How quickly will depression arrive?

Because the economic changes that are occurring are of such a very large degree, they will occur in a fashion different from the slam-bang progression of typical recessions of the past fifty years. I think the economic expansion in force since 1991 is ending, and we will then have another contraction which is deeper than the last. After it's gone on for awhile and economists actually recognize it, you will undoubtedly hear continual reiterations that it's just a "mild recession." Any recoveries will be met with fanfare and assurances that a new boom is underway. But any bounce will just be a bear market rally against the larger trend. When the bottom is reached, the economic devastation will be front-page news, just as it was in 1933.

When will the depression end?

The bottom of the first depression will occur about a year after the first Supercycle degree decline ends in the stock market.

Can you be more specific?

Cycles suggest that the economy should bottom anywhere from 2004 to 2013, perhaps twice or more in that period, sort of like 1933 and 1938.

We've never had a period like that except the 1930s.

There have been several, actually. The 1930s is one. The 1840s and '50s saw two depressions back to back. There was a pretty bad time in the 1890s. There were several major examples in the 1700s. So that's the magnitude we are talking about, yes.

Do you see the same thing happening globally?

A Grand Supercycle bear market and depression will be worldwide, for sure. That's too big a degree to have only local implications.

Many people would indignantly say, "Today is not like 1929."

They're right. It's worse.

Worse than in 1929. Why?

Because it seems better, of course. People are more optimistic than ever before, at least as far back as our data go. And look at the results. When but at a major top in worldwide social mood would you ever have had the Berlin Wall come down, communism rejected, sanctions lifted on South Africa and the idea of "a new world order?" This type of psychologically induced event on the world stage, including Mideast, IRA-English and Bosnian peace agreements, 20 American free trade agreements in 34 months and, in October 1995, a photograph commemorating the largest gathering of national leaders in world history, has continued right through today with the normalization of trade ties with China.

This is bad news?

It's a huge top. At the bottom, international tensions will be high and include active conflict, as always. That will be bullish ....which means for the *future*.

What will be the prime indication that the great economic contraction is about to start?

The stock market will be the main indication. When the Dow heads down in a big way, we'll be off the cliff.

How far will stocks fall?

The average stock will fall at least 90%. Many will fall to zero.

* * * * * * * * * * * * * * *

From a long term perspective, Prechter's outlook has remained surprisingly static. Here's an excerpt from an interview that was done with Joe Bradley in 1979. On Grand Supercycle issues, it is not materially different from another one with Joe Bradley that was conducted in November 1995.

Investor's Hotline
June 14, 1979

Fasten your seat belts for one of the most dramatic forecasts ever made on *Investor's Hotline*.

A couple of people I spoke to concerning A.J.'s forecast said that he has been calling for these very high stock market figures for two or three years and that a number of these forecasts were actually called incorrectly. Is that true or not?

Well, from one viewpoint it is. I've been doing the same thing. As we approached the low, as matter of fact the first time he and I were interviewed in *Financial World* magazine in October 1977, we said, "We're coming toward a bottom right here. And it's going to be the bottom that's going to lead us up to above 2,000." Well, we got a bottom a few months later. Actually, it was one month later that most stocks bottomed. He and I were both saying, "We've made the bottom that's going to lead the market up to 2,000." But if you'd acted on the advice and expected to be at 2,000 within six months, or even by the next year, you would have been wrong. From that standpoint, we were wrong. [Still,] I think the next important move is going to be up and break the Dow out to new all-time highs. I think if you want to buy stocks cheap, you should buy them here. Right now, I think the safest speculation in the world is that the U.S. stock market is going to go up.

We'll probably have an environment where we'll see stock speculation like we haven't seen since the late 1920s. And actually, if Elliott's right, we're absolutely going to dwarf that particular bull market in terms of speculative frenzy, because we're not just starting a fifth wave of Supercycle degree. We're finishing off a fifth wave of a Grand Supercycle as well.

There's one other minor thing — or maybe it's not so minor. That is that England has just elected a Tory (Margaret Thatcher), the Canadians have just elected a conservative and the trend in the Western world is very obviously away from socialist policies. Now, whether or not that occurs here — we may even end up electing Ted Kennedy; I don't know — but the drift is certainly there. And I would think that merely that perception is something that could stabilize us for a few more years and give that feeling of "Hey, we've got it licked." Whether we do or not.

Once it reaches a bigger high several years down the road, it's going to be set up for an incredibly important crash. You can't name a crash in history that hasn't occurred from a period of euphoria and extremely high expectations. Right now, we are nowhere near that point. But I think we will get there, and at that time, when the gloom and doom seminars only have six or seven people attending instead of 6,000 or 7,000, you will really be set up for a problem crash. [Note: the 1999 New Orleans Conference averaged one-twentieth as many attendees, and the organizers have contemplated dissolving it. Prechter has encouraged them to keep it going because the coming bear market should energize the conference. – Ed.]

* * * * * * * * * * * * * * *

But you've moderated your stance a bit since 1979, I understand.

Yes. We cited 41-381 in *Elliott Wave Principle*. The lower end of that range is not feasible. I see two strongly indicated levels: 161 and around 390. I've been using the phrase "below 400" for my target. So buy the Dow under 400.

What about war?

Bear markets bring wars, but the biggest war of the Grand Supercycle bear market will probably take place mid-century. Not at the first price bottom but near the second.

What would you say to a cynic who finds it odd that your work would coincide with the greatest shift in the course of human progress in 200 years and concludes that the only thing this opinion really demonstrates is the need for market analysts to feel as though they're living at a critical moment in history?

It's a sophisticated point about human nature. I have made the point myself, in other contexts, such as in discussing "end of the world" people. Last year, when people said Y2K would mark the end of civilization, I said to ignore it. Whether it's giant meteors, the hole in the ozone layer or whatever, many people seem to be able to justify believing passionately that the world is about to end a few months from now. But the stock market always falls a long way before social strife erupts, so I was quite sure that Y2K would be a non-event.

The cynic will say that at least Y2K had a definitive end point. Is it possible that your pattern is just a more flexible series of appeals to the "Armageddon" people?

If the cynic doesn't bother to look at the patterns and has no historical context, then his perspective makes mine look psychologically self-serving. However, if he were to read all the Elliott wave material from R.N. Elliott through Charles Collins, Hamilton Bolton, A.J. Frost and myself, he would understand that our reading of the long term wave pattern has been consistent for sixty years, anticipating the juncture that we now face. It has been anything but an "end of the world" stance. We've been mostly bullish, in fact, super-bullish, except for 1966-1974, which was the wave IV correction, and in the 1990s as we awaited the end of wave V. The final answer to the true cynics is, "Watch what happens," because that is the only thing that could convince them.

It seems there has to be some fundamental change in our current monetary stability to produce such an extended decline.

The most widely held belief with regard to the future course of national financial affairs is that inflation will accelerate, or, at minimum, continue. I think the case for an impending deflation is overwhelming. The next monetary trend should be a period of severe deflation, just as occurred in 1835-1842 and the 1930s.

Really? But when economists worry, they worry about inflation.

Now they do, sure, because it's no longer a threat.

You're saying —

I'm saying that economists worry about dangers in the past because they don't use tools based on patterns of change to anticipate the future. The 1970s made them fear inflation. But it's not the '70s. It's more like the late '20s.

In recent years, economists are actually thrilled because inflation is down around 2%, so their worries about inflation have dissipated. And the economy is growing, so they continually refer to it as "the best of all possible worlds."

Yes. I think it's hilarious. The biggest monetary danger signs in three generations, and economists interpret them as positively the best news that could be imagined. They will change their minds.

So some day, people will *want* inflation?

Take for example the real estate crunch of 1990. Some people suffering from that minor deflation were already prescribing "cures." *The Wall Street Journal* ran two guest editorials on the desirability of government policies that would regenerate the multi-decade phenomenon of real estate values rising faster than the CPI. The essential message was, "Bring back the real estate bubble," delivered under the illusion that the bubble period was normal life and should last forever. Well, the incredible thing is, the bubble reflated! Now we're right back where we were in 1989 except that the distortions are even greater. A perpetual credit-fueled bubble is not possible, either mathematically or psychologically, but people will certainly *want* it to continue. The same desire will extend to the stock market as it falls, and the economy.

In the 1970s, when the economy and the stock market sputtered, real estate did reasonably well.

As big as the disaster in stocks is likely to be over the next five to ten years, it will almost certainly be matched by the upcoming disaster in real estate related investments. The 1970s were inflationary; the next period of difficulty should be deflationary.

Are there manifestations of euphoria in real estate?

In the past five years, people have been erecting "McMansions" all over the place — million dollar homes crowded in like condos. It's all financed with credit, and that game is ending. The trap is set.

Credit will contract?

Yes, from long term bonds all the way down to the broader measures of the money supply.

The credit implosion you see leads you to contradict the most deeply held convictions on Wall Street, like the conventional belief that bonds

rise when the economy slows. You have most of them falling in a weak economy.

It's plainly not good for bond values if the issuers of bonds, i.e. the borrowers, suffer financially to the point of not being able to pay interest or principal, is it? In fact, billions of dollars worth of bond defaults in recent years clearly reveal the problem. What economists should say is that (1) in an environment of general growth and inflation, (2) when only a recession occurs, and (3) when the recession brings a reduction in inflation, *then* bonds typically rise in price as interest rates fall. Unfortunately, to most economists, the post-World War II period is the only relevant history, so bond investors don't place their view in the larger context of economic possibilities.

At what point might the economy deteriorate so substantially that its condition and trend are no longer bullish for bonds, but bearish?

When it reaches depression, and a depression is exactly what is on the agenda if the stock market falls to the extent that the Wave Principle suggests. The only way for a bond investor to survive a depression is to hold bonds issued by a strong borrower. Weak borrowers, such as most corporations and municipalities, will default. As investors come to the realization that default is a risk, rates on weak debt will rise as its prices fall.

What happens to the dollar?

During the deflation, the dollar's domestic purchasing value should rise as debt instruments denominated in dollars are defaulted upon. As dollars disappear, the value of the remaining dollars will rise. The same thing has been going on with the Japanese yen in terms of how much you can buy for it in Japan. But how the yen or dollar will perform against other currencies, I couldn't say. We'll have to follow the wave counts.

After the initial deflationary hit, what will turn currency values back down?

It will be the pressure on national governments to create paper money to pay off their debts. Which ones will be destroyed depends upon what course each government chooses when faced with bankruptcy. I am not optimistic that most will take the honest course. Whether or not all paper currencies eventually go to zero, it will be wise to own gold after the deflation.

So in the very long run, the dollar is in trouble?

I think so. Did you know that Roman inflation persisted, in recurring waves, for *over 400 years* before the monetary rot was thorough enough to allow invading armies to successfully sack the city? We've had nearly 70 years of dollar inflation in the U.S. Can you imagine what another 300 years of persistent dollar inflation would do to the political fabric of the United States?

Is there an alternative?

The only way to guarantee that politicians will never again inflate is to introduce private money and ban legal tender laws.

Private money? Do you mean gold coins issued by a private mint?

Not *a* private mint. By anyone who wants to issue it! The marketplace will choose the soundest forms of money, and competition will insure that the science of money is advanced. Compare the old telephone monopoly to cell phones and the Internet, and you'll get an idea of what would happen.

The Cultural Realm

A reader once sent a letter to *Barron's* with a hearty "phooey" to your "Popular Culture" article and accused you of implying that investors should have been reading *Women's Wear Daily* instead of *The Wall Street Journal.*

That's exactly what I was saying.

What's the difference?

There is little difference in what they reveal about the current mood. When *Women's Wear Daily* is showing frisky fashions, *The Wall Street Journal* is in a frisky mood, too. The problem is that the Journal also gives opinions on the markets and the economy, and people take them at face value rather than for what they are: an expression of the prevailing mood. It wasn't always this way. Back in the 1920s, the Journal was run by a technician — a Dow Theorist, to be exact — named Hamilton. Before the market crashed, he warned readers in a famous article called, "A Turn in the Tide," which I adapted for the title of my 1995 book. But when I read the Journal today, I am appalled. The current managers of the editorial page publish the most excessive cheerleading for the bull market imaginable, in the face of historically bearish conditions. If these articles had come out in 1974 or 1984, they would have been useful, but not now, of all times. William Peter Hamilton must be spinning in his grave like a chicken on a rotisserie. So you're much safer with *Women's Wear Daily*.

This alternating current of ebullience and conservatism goes back to the most basic Elliott wave idea: Bull markets give way to bear markets, and vice versa. What are the essential ways in which bear market moods differ from those of bull markets?

In bull markets, people focus on progress and production; in bear markets, they focus on limits and conservation.

OK, I can see that. What else?

Bull markets result in increased *harmony* in every aspect of society, including the moral, religious, racial, national, regional, social, financial, political and otherwise. Bear markets bring *polarization*. With that realization, you can predict increasing cooperation in all those areas in bull markets, and increasing conflict in bear markets.

It's hard to imagine turning bearish when peace is breaking out all over or turning bullish on society in the depths of scary times.

A scary world is perfect for stocks and a perfect world is scary for stocks. When the world appears perfect, most investors have their money in the market, and there is little or no buying power left to fuel the uptrend and nowhere to go but down. When it appears scary, stocks are cheap and hold huge upside potential.

So people get it backwards.

Exactly, people consider these to be the events that *shape* their futures, but they only reflect the *past* trend of social mood.

What is it that people are unprepared for now?

The bear market will bring back nationalism, racial exclusion and perhaps even religious conflict. Thinking *technically* about events, that is, observing what they reveal about social psychology, prepares you for those changes, whereas trying to predict the future from the events themselves leads you to the opposite, and wrong, conclusion. It cannot be stressed enough, because life-or-death decisions can depend upon your assessment. Notice what marks the major bear market lows of just the last 200 years — the Revolutionary War, the Civil War and World War II. Those were buying opportunities.

Can you illustrate how this plays out over the course of a specific wave? Start with the last Supercycle bottom.

At the bottom, the collective mood in Germany was so negative that its expression resulted in the assumption of power by Adolf Hitler. Hitler's popularity actually climaxed in July 1932, the very month all major world stock markets bottomed out. Now, was his popularity bullish, as a conventional analyst would be forced to conclude by the outcome, or was his popularity an expression of the negative social mood?

Clearly, Hitler could not be described as bullish for Germany or the world. But stocks did go up after he came to power. You're disagreeing with economists who say war invigorates the economy.

And I'm happy to do it!

But if Hitler's popularity was an expression of the trough in social mood, why did things get worse instead of better in Europe from that time forward?

"Things" got worse, but mood and stock prices did not. "Things" are the events that result from the mood. In that case, the consequences of the popular action resulting from the deeply negative mood of 1933 took 12 years to play out. The representatives of the negative mood gained great political power at the low.

Why didn't the U.S. see the rise of a similar figure?

Because even though the mood was there, the negative forces never achieved as much political control as they did in Germany. So the events here were less dramatic. China had the same misfortune in 1949. The negative mood brought about a communist takeover that had terrible consequences for 30 years.

The content of popular movies is another cultural trend you've covered. Have there been any similar rumblings recently?

In Primary wave ④, there was some horror. Kathy Bates won best actress for *Misery* in 1990, the year of a stock market correction that in terms of the Value Line index ended a three-year bear market, which included the 1987 crash. *Misery* was a mild horror film, too, and by some definitions, not a horror film. In 1991, when the recession was in force, *Silence of the Lambs* won three Oscars, including Best Picture. That wasn't a horror film in the classical sense, either. When the market falls 90%, we'll have really horrible movies.

Like what?

Well, the previous fourth wave usually gives you a hint. The 1921 low gave us "Nosferatu," which presaged the vampire films of the early 1930s. The 1962 low gave us "Psycho," which presaged the slasher films of the early 1980s. I think it is significant that Hollywood produced "American Psycho," albeit in mild form. I think the new trend in horror movies as the market crashes will be something we have never seen: torture films.

Gross.

Tell me about it.

You were a musician back in the late 1960s and early 1970s. This background has obviously been an asset to you. Actually it helped the whole thesis gel in your mind! What prompted recognition of a connection between the trend in the market and pop music?

Well, The Beatles' *Revolver* album affected me viscerally. Although I have come to appreciate it since, I hated it when it came out. *Sergeant Pepper* was even worse. Besides two or three songs, where were the inventive melodies, harmonies, chord changes and joy that had made them stars? It was in thinking about that change years later that I realized that the melodic, energetic and rather innocent (at least in retrospect) music of 1958 to 1965, which included doo-wop, teen idols, girl groups, and particularly in the final two years, the "British Invasion," stopped dominating the charts precisely at the end of Primary wave ⑤ in 1966. Quite abruptly, it nearly disappeared. Following the second peak in 1968, it was gone.

You connected what you experienced musically to the trend change on the stock chart?

Yes, and that's what eventually triggered the realization that *everything* worked this way, *all the time*. Not just music. Not just in 1966.

Did The Beatles change the public or did the public change The Beatles?

Pop cultural heroes are made by the public, so the public mood determines who's popular. The mood can also affect the creative direction of the heroes as well, so there are two effects.

You have maintained that a song dominated by major keys, harmony, melody and musicality is representative of a bull trend while one dominated by minor keys, starkness and noise characterize a bear market sound.

You can literally hear the difference between a bull and a bear market hit in the composition of the music.

On *The Beatles*, which was known to most people as "the white album" of 1968, for instance, Lennon sang "She's coming down, yes she is," and on his 1980 comeback album, *Double Fantasy*, he declared, "Hard times are over, over for a while." Applied to the stock market, those are two pretty good calls.

Yes, but let's not isolate a few lyrics to make our point. That's a typical approach to cultural analysis, and it's not scientific. Lennon wrote a lot of lyrics. But as a whole, your point is correct. His bull market lyrics stand in immense contrast to his bear market ones. What we need are objective statistics on pop music style and content and to see if the chart matches the stock market. I think it would demonstrate that mood and its expression through myriad outlets is an objective reality. It is difficult to prove because the social sciences are so primitive and data so scarce. Some day, people will start collecting the proper data. We may do it ourselves to prove the point.

But people shouldn't require data to understand what you're talking about if they experienced the changes firsthand. Do you find that they can relate to the message on some basic level?

Sure. Remember U.S. Secretary of the Interior James Watt's embarrassment when he canceled the Beach Boys concert in Washington, D.C. in 1983 to keep out "undesirable elements"? Everyone laughed at him because they knew the Beach Boys don't attract undesirable elements — they're a bull market band. But no one could articulate that point; they just knew it was funny.

* * * * * * * * * * * * * * *

People
May 11, 1987

Most stock market analysts happening upon a song by the Sex Pistols in the late '70s would have simply changed the station. Analyst Robert Prechter, a former rock drummer, heard the punk group and cried, "Buy!" Such dark anthems to angst, Prechter reasoned, must signal a low point in the general public mood, meaning that both an emotional and a market improvement lay ahead.

The screwiest thing is, he was right.

* * * * * * * * * * * * * *

Let's say you were advising the president. The stock market is way down, the music has become atonal, the art is ugly and his or her popularity is sinking to an all-time low. Can't you tell him how to change the trend?

Of course he can't change the trend! The trend is hundreds of millions of people interacting. Ask any president who's tried. The few times that there may have appeared to be a success were simply times that the populace was ready for a leader to escort them in the direction they were going anyway.

So you could not advise a leader on how to avoid war, just that it is probable?

I'm not a political advisor. But isn't it valuable information for a nation to know that the risk of war is heightened? Or for that matter, insignificant?

How have your pop culture studies been received by your colleagues?

Initially, it got a strong reaction from the financial community, either positive or negative. Today, the cultural trends analysis is the most popular section of our publications.

While my method is a complete inversion of the way everyone else approaches the relationship of extramarket events to the market, it is the only valid approach. It is so sensible that all many people need is to be exposed to that viewpoint to become receptive to it.

What about the academic community — has it corroborated your theory to any extent?

I'm working on it. There are some positive initial signs, for instance from physicists. There hasn't been much in the cultural area, although in 1990, Harold Zullow, a researcher at Columbia, got together a research team to study the optimistic vs. pessimistic rumination reflected by popular song lyrics of the past forty years. He concluded that changes in the aggregate sentiment expressed in popular songs precede changes in the economy.

So this study supports the broader case you presented in *Popular Culture and the Stock Market* in 1985?

Yes. I argued that tempo, melody, harmony, dissonance, lyrics and noise are all important in reflecting the social mood. While Zullow's study was very narrowly focused, it was presumably meticulous, and that's what's needed to attract attention to the idea. Further, because stock price change precedes economic change, this study supports my case that stock market and pop musical changes are coincident.

By the way, is your Pop Culture article still available?

It should be soon. I'm going to reprint it in a book I'm compiling called *Pioneering Studies in Socionomics*.

OK, great. Now let's go back to the fitness craze, because that idea really makes sense to me. It began gathering steam in about 1980. Then as the bull market roared through the mid-1980s, the craze matured with Jane Fonda's bestselling workout videos and Jazzercise classes in storefronts across America. In 1988, you predicted its demise. It seems to be happening.

I agree. I think the upside momentum for the fitness craze peaked with the "no pain, no gain" slogan at the third-wave peak in 1987-1989 and began slipping in intensity as the bull market settled into its fifth wave. Over the past few years, a slew of major articles have revealed the existence of an "obesity crisis." Today, we have the opposite of 1980, when the fitness fever was catching on. When the stock market turns down, many health clubs will go under.

If cultural trends ebb and flow like the market, you should be able to make other predictions like this one. How successful have you been at this?

We've had a number of accurate calls. For instance, *The Elliott Wave Theorist* predicted the feel-good pop music of the 1980s, the top of the art bubble in 1989, and a sharp drop in attendance at baseball games. EWT said Michael Jackson was in trouble in March 1991, right after he signed a $1 billion contract with Sony. Soon afterward, the "King of Pop" was accused of child molestation, and his album sales crashed despite massive promotional efforts.

Such forecasts may seem trivial until you realize that you can predict wars, and even their severity, using the same methods. All of the forecasts I just mentioned were strictly technically based, on the premise that mass psychological trends produce social events.

Even with intimate industry knowledge, show biz insiders would be hard-pressed to forecast something like Jackson's decline in popularity — especially when you consider when your forecast was made. We know that insiders were making the opposite bet, by the price Sony agreed upon to sign Jackson. Is it typical for companies to sign big contracts at the peak in an entertainer's popularity?

Now you know why they call it paying "top" dollar. Remember when *The Cosby Show* was sold into syndication for the highest amount ever? It was at the top of his popularity.

* * * * * * * * * * * * * * *

EDGE

January 1995

An analysis of the sentiment that surrounded THE pop music idols of the 1930s, '40s, '50s, '60s and '80s shows that they all came in on creative, energetic bursts of public enthusiasm that resembled panic buying on Wall Street. From Goodman, the King of Swing, through Presley, the King of Rock 'n' Roll, to Jackson, the King of Pop, there is the same meteoric rise. Popular accounts consistently refer to all as episodes in which teenagers were gripped by an unexpected and mysterious delirium. As they swooned and fainted, the rest of the population looked on with a mix of curiosity, bafflement and disapproval. Jackson's white gloves were banned from schools. Goodman's swinging fans were called "deeply disturbed" victims of a harmful nervous disorder. In both cases and each case in between, the artists and their handlers could barely explain, let alone recreate, the feverish emotional high they had triggered.

In 1943, as Frank Sinatra's star was lifting off, his manager George Evans put his finger on it. He told the *Chicago Tribune News Service* that Sinatra's talents provided an "initial impetus." His own planting of "organized and regimented moaning" in Sinatra's crowd accounted for some of the panic. But there was something larger at work.

"Frankie is a product of crowd psychology," Evans finally concluded.

This is, of course, Prechter's point.

* * * * * * * * * * * * * * *

The crowd can be harsh when tearing down a person.

It is not the *person* that matters to the crowd. It's the *persona.*

I thought it was very well said by Richard Gere. He was married to Cindy Crawford, who is considered one of the most beautiful women in the country. The rumor going around was that they're both gay. He said, "You know, some people are really torn up inside. Their lives are all messed up. They think that it's soothing to their own misery if they can tear down somebody else in the process."

I'm glad you quoted that. We've gotten into a topic that seems to be far from our original topic, markets. But it isn't. As that quote reveals, the public perception is not necessarily based upon an action of Richard Gere or Cindy Crawford or Michael Jackson. Their images are in the collective mind of the public. The public can place them in star status, and it can remove the sanction. It is the same essential change in the collective mindset that marks the onset of a turn in the stock market.

During the wave ④ correction, even lower tier "nice guy" heroes were attacked, including kiddy characters Barney the Dinosaur, who was viciously excoriated and beaten up at malls, and Bert & Ernie, whom rightist groups accused of subversive homosexuality. Nothing is sacred.

Not exactly. They were attacked *because* they were sacred.

Who are the most recent heroes? They should be the last bull market heroes for a while. Are they falling into disrepute yet?

The stock market itself provided the biggest heroes. The fame of billionaires Warren Buffett, John Templeton, Bill Gates and George Soros have risen to heights normally reserved for a select group of movie stars and athletes. Alan Greenspan has been called a genius; if we were a monarchy, we'd have knighted him by now. He and Gates were probably the brightest stars. In 1996, *Newsweek* put Gates on its cover and said he might be the king of the future itself. He was the "richest and maybe the smartest man on the planet." His book, *The Road Ahead*, and other books about him were super optimistic about the future. Naturally, they describe the road behind us, not the one ahead. Tomes like these are top signals.

Even when you do get bear market entertainment, it's not total misery. I mean, people must like them or they wouldn't watch. Would they?

Of course they like them. People come out of the theater smiling after seeing *Macbeth* or *Phantom of the Opera*, but they are horror plots. The same thing was true of *All in the Family*, a bear market TV show from the '70s with endless screaming, insults, stupidity, anger and argument. But people liked it. This is not some kind of anomaly; *it's my whole point.* People enjoy such entertainment more in bear markets.

You say we are in a "topping phase," and I can hear it in the bubble gum music that's popular: Back Street Boys, 'N Sync, Britney Spears. What's the next trend?

A bear market. And when that happens, bubble gum will disappear fast.

I just thought of a change that's already happening. Dressing down is a phenomenon that started with the wide-scale corporate adoption of "casual Fridays." Dress-down days gradually came to encompass the entire work week in many sectors of the economy.

Yes. "Popular Culture and the Stock Market" listed "anti-fashion fashions" as characterizing the falling-transition phase of social mood. The last times something like this happened were in the early '90s correction, with the grunge look, and in the late 1960s, with the hippie look.

The cultural shift was usually out in front of the economy. What does that tell you?

It confirms that mood governs actions, not vice versa. The down-scale fashions of 1967-1970 and, once again, in the late 1990s, *preceded* the first recessions in a decade in both cases. The mood behind fashion is father to the outcome. In 1969, people wanted desperately not to look prosperous, and lo and behold, a few years later, they weren't. Fashion signaled a mood change, which had tangible results. The current replay should have a similar outcome.

What about the duration of the movement toward casual fashions? It took almost ten years, several years longer than the last big down swing. Is this significant?

It certainly could be, because after centuries of formal business fashion in Western civilization, this is a relatively rapid change that fits the idea of the end of a Grand Supercycle up-trend in social mood. Here's another interesting item along the same lines: The U.S. government is bringing timberwolves from Canada and releasing them in national parks in Wyoming and Idaho. As a proponent observes, "It is a symbolic act." Civilization eliminated the wolf from the U.S. and tamed the wild a half century ago. The desire deeply embedded in the environmental movement to return to primitive times is not unlike the desire in the hippie movement of the late 1960s to return to a life of simple poverty. When the recession hit, they got what they said they wanted. These ecologists may ultimately get what they claim to want as well, if not what they envision.

You've said nostalgia is big in fifth waves. This would explain all the oldies radio stations.

Yes, and why, in the early 1980s, we elected a president, Ronald Reagan, who called for a return to the values of Calvin Coolidge and Dwight Eisenhower, and in the 1990s elected Bill Clinton, who wanted to revive the image of Jack Kennedy. The precursors were all presidents during previous bull markets. The extent of cultural innovation in the fifth wave is low; innovation occurs in the third wave, copying in the fifth. And, by the way, the oldies radio trend is about exhausted.

Why?

Because the fifth wave is about exhausted.

Hmm. I guess this explains why people don't really look back at the 1980s and 1990s with the fondness they have for the 1950s and 1960s. The 1980s were fun but somehow unable to measure up to the exuberance and spontaneity of the 1960s. Woodstock II drew a big crowd, but by 1960s standards, just the idea of a Woodstock reunion is an oxymoron.

Right. It's not a new idea or event. It's nostalgia.

I notice that in the second half of the 1990s, the Beatles have actually been one of the biggest money-making acts in show business.

Isn't that interesting? Here we have the popular musical stars of the 1960s topping process in social mood appearing for a rekindling of the mood in the late 1990s. In November 1995, the Beatles produced their anthology, a CD set and three-part television movie. A book version of the anthology is selling like crazy here in December 2000, their 1964 movie *A Hard Day's Night* is back in theaters, and as we finish this updated interview, their "#1 Hits" CD is #1 in national sales! So, the Beatles made it *to* the top, *at* the top, again. Still, Beatlemania II is a far cry from live performances drowned out by screaming teenage girls or watched by the biggest television audience in history, which was the scene in 1964-1965.

The difference fits your long-standing description of this fifth wave as a "hollow echo of the third."

Yep. In pop music as in the economy.

But it hasn't been a total rehash. We had plenty of new songs in the 1980s and 1990s, didn't we?

Songs, yes, but not styles. Unless you list rap as a style. Even then, some of the artists don't even make all of their own musical sounds. They take previously recorded music and then do what's called "sampling," then rap over it.

What seems to be lacking is inspiration and creativity and new horizons. Completely new sounds, new ideas, new approaches. It all relates to stuff that happened 30 to 50 years ago.

So don't look for anything new in the arts?

It depends on what you mean by "new." Bear markets are not times of great artistic innovation except in the intention to shock. So horror movies will present something new. In art, there will be the new but little of the artistic, because the point of art in a bear market is to shock. Take punk rock, for example. That was a new approach to popular music, and it was meant to shock. Whether you want to call it imaginative or creative is another matter. There are really two aspects: artistry and newness. Artistry survives the centuries; newness by itself doesn't. And bear market newness is often derivative, as its purpose is to annihilate something that already exists, not create something truly new.

Politics, Inclusionism and War

Have you used the insight of the market to anticipate outcomes for national leaders?

Sure, because the popularity of a country's leader is motivated by the same unconscious impulses that drive the stock market and the economy. A president's actual performance is irrelevant. Granted, this is a hard message for most people to accept. But *The Elliott Wave Theorist* has used this relationship to forecast the fates of three U.S. presidents when the conventional wisdom was predicting the opposite. In January 1987, when Reagan's presidency was being rocked by the Iran-Contra affair, EWT said that Ronald Reagan would exit as one of our "most loved presidents." In April 1991, when George Bush enjoyed a 91% approval rating, the highest for any president, EWT predicted that he would lose the next election. That latter forecast was as long a shot as there is in politics. Then, as Bill Clinton's reign began, we predicted that he would be pushed from office. It didn't happen, but he was impeached.

* * * * * * * * * * * * * * *

The Elliott Wave Theorist
March 29, 1991

In July 1990, with the Dow at 3000, George Bush was winning praise and high approval ratings. He was "a man for the season," riding "a huge current of political popularity." Just four months later, with the Dow below 2400, as reported in the November 30, 1990 issue of EWT, he was being bombed with derisive headlines. "Bush May Have Lost 1992 Already," "From Sizzle to Fizzle," "a quagmire of indecision and ineptitude which could take him the rest of the presidency to dig out of" typified the press reports. Here it is, exactly four months later once again, with the Dow back at 3000, and George Bush has a 91% approval rating, the highest in the history of the records, and the media love him again.

* * * * * * * * * * * * * * *

How did Clinton survive all those scandals?

Actually, anyone who doubts my socionomic thesis need only consider the amazing case of Bill Clinton. As Congress got ready to vote on his ouster, the bull market resumed. The higher the market went, the more feelings against him waned. His popularity remained high, and it saved him. It was the same reason that no one cared when Reagan faced the Iran-Contra scandal. The Lewinsky scandal and lies to the American public didn't hurt Clinton's popularity because the president's popularity reflects social mood, and its best meter, the stock averages, were still on their way to final all-time highs and record valuation in December 1998, the month of his impeachment by the House. That month, Clinton's approval rating was 73%, which turned out to be his all-time high. Public mood is the key to his resilience, and that comes from the unconscious part of the mind, not the part that weighs facts.

The lies and his behavior didn't matter?

Nope!

What about the next guy?

The next president, and maybe even one or two after that, should watch out. They will have to ride out the slide into a deflationary crash and depression. The party of the person who is in office during the worst of it will be devastated politically.

You apparently don't take sides.

No, my analysis is non-partisan.

Can you apply the rules of Elliott to political analysis?

The guideline of alternation seems to apply. It has a specific technical meaning in wave formation, but also pertains to social trends. For example, you might recall that Richard Nixon won re-election in a landslide in late 1972 at the peak of a bull market. Despite everyone's high hopes, he was hounded as a law-breaker and ultimately driven from office in August 1974 by the social mood reflected by the bear market. Bill Clinton took office with the market at a new all-time high amidst strong popularity, a *Time* "Man of the Year" cover, and high hopes for his performance. Like Nixon, he was hounded as a lawbreaker as the market corrected in 1994. Instead of Watergate, it was Whitewater. But one was a Republican and the other a Democrat. The *specifics* alternate. The essence repeats.

Back in 1989, when two-party politics appeared assured forever, you predicted a third party and a shake-up of the traditional parties.

Yes, because what normally happens in the type of period that is approaching is a polarization of opinion in all kinds of areas. It's not just that the left takes over or the right takes over. During bull markets such as in the 1950s and the 1980s, most people are centrists. In bear markets, you see extreme polarization. You get leftists and rightists on one axis, and authoritarians and champions of individual liberty on the other, battling it out for power.

Is there necessarily a direct relationship? Do the social dynamics that make investors buy or sell stocks also influence the electorate to choose one presidential candidate over the other?

Yes. The single best predictor of presidential popularity is the trend of the Dow Jones Industrial Average. The precision with which presidential popularity has tracked the Dow and its rate of change is remarkable. It usually also indicates whether an incumbent will win re-election.

Regardless of where they are?

Sure. For example, several world political leaders resigned or reached record low popularity readings in late 1990, when their countries' markets were down. In early 1991, George Bush and John Major governed the only countries in the world — the U.S. and England — in which a stock market average hit new all-time highs, so their popularity ratings were very strong. Meanwhile, Australia's Prime Minister Hawke and Finance Minister Keating and German Chancellor Helmut Kohl were way down in the polls, as their stock markets had only an anemic rebound. Now get this: West Germany was actually much better off economically than Britain. But popularity ratings do not primarily track the economy. They track social mood, which is more instantly reflected by the level, speed and direction of stock prices.

The market simply reflects the social mood, but once the trend is in place, can its performance reinforce what's going on in the political arena?

I used to think so, but I don't anymore. Mood is autonomous. The market is just a meter for it. In other words, it's easy to say that losing money in stocks makes people despair, but I think despair makes the market go down, so they lose money. It has to be this way, or stock trends would never end. So the trend toward happiness or despair causes voting patterns to change. It would happen even if there were no stock market.

Bear market politics seem more interesting.

Oh, yeah! That's when people tend to vote for more radical candidates. When the next general decline in world stock markets takes place, the popularity of all incumbents will suffer. If the markets fall as far as cycles suggest in the next few years, most incumbents will not win re-election. But don't confuse interesting politics with good fun. It's usually scary.

So by looking at what markets are doing, you have an objective, mathematical representation of the consciousness of the people at that time, and the consciousness of the people predicts in advance what's going to happen in the political realm.

I would say more precisely that the stock market is a mathematical representation of the *un*conscious shared mood of the people, and that unconscious mood drives social action in all kinds of arenas. Politics is just one of them.

What about the *results* of political decisions?

Well, you don't see all the results immediately. For instance, at a market low, you might get a revolution, an election of a military style leader, a coup, or whatever, but the ramifications of *that* come later, as they sometimes take a lot of time to develop.

So a government can effect change based on the old mood trend even if the mood that put it in place is past?

Oh, yes. Governments are almost always acting on the last trend, the one that is already well along or over entirely. For example, in the U.S., the stock market ended a 24-year bear market in 1859. But so much tension had developed that a few comparatively minor actions ignited the Civil War in 1861. The rising market reflected an improving mood, but the war, an expression of the old mood, didn't end until the market approached a high. Wars often end after mood has recovered, which, if you think about it, makes sense, too.

But aren't there instances in which the government can intervene in ways to throw the Wave Principle off? A lot of people say the Fed stepped in and bought futures after the crash of 1987, for instance. Isn't that an example of enlightened government action?

First, remember that the Fed did not prevent the 1987 crash. It happened. Many claim that the Fed averted further collapse, but in our opinion, it acted on the day the market was due to bottom anyway, the evidence being that *The Elliott Wave Theorist* said in print four days earlier that the two-week cycle was due to bottom on October 20, and the market bottomed that morning. Then there's what happened in 1929 when a consortium of bankers amassed a pool of money to halt the October decline. On the strength of that buying and the resulting euphoria, stocks soared, for one day. Then they fell even harder, utterly ignoring a second attempt at "organized support" on the 28th. History provides several examples of failed attempts to stop a market collapse.

The unprecedented popularity of Alan Greenspan suggests that most people are more focused on the more recent episode.

The Fed's apparent success in 1987 will make people, including Fed governors, confident that they can stop the next crash. But it won't work (more than briefly, anyway) because the wave of selling will be much bigger. When the Fed itself, then the professionals and soon afterward the public, realize that the Fed's attempt is failing, the overall panic will increase, at minimum negating any bullish effects of whatever actions it takes.

But there are no restrictions on the Fed, and, in recent years, especially in "crisis situations," we have seen there is no hesitancy to do whatever it takes to bail out troubled entities. Won't the Fed just lend its way out of the problem?

While it is true that the Fed has an unlimited power to offer credit, it cannot create liquidity, because it cannot *force* businesses and consumers to lend and borrow no matter how cheaply it offers credit. So deflation can happen regardless of the Fed's desires. As I see it, there are only two possibilities: (1) The Fed will act on the bottom day of a collapse and *appear* to have been effective, or (2) it will try to stem the tide early and fail. Either way, the market's ultimate destiny will be unaffected. Only people's thinking will be affected. Hope-filled bulls will hold on for the slaughter and irresolute bears will give up their positions. In other words, the main effect of this soothing news will be to produce a psychological deterrent to proper investment action.

The Fed has always been a focal point for the financial markets. In recent years, people's attention is absolutely riveted on every Fed meeting. Is this attention misplaced?

The obsession with the Fed's meetings is ludicrous. The Fed votes only to change its own rates, and it has always *followed* the rates set by the free market. In 1999 and 2000, when the Fed raised rates several times, it was repeatedly claimed everywhere that the Fed was conducting a "pre-emptive strike against inflation." But rates had been rising for months, and the Fed simply adjusted to the market, as always. We watch the market, which *leads* the Fed.

So the markets trump the central bankers?

If central banks really did control finance, gold's chart pattern of 1970-1980 wouldn't exist. Gold never would have enjoyed a historic bull market and reached $850 an ounce. If authorities could stop bear markets, then the Japanese market would not have fallen 60%. And it's not finished going down yet!

In the wake of an unexpected central bank action, have you ever had a wave pattern that skipped a beat or altered its course in any way?

Central bank action is never really unexpected because it's a product of the social mood, which permeates society. When you examine the charts, you can locate waves, but you can't locate central bank actions. Central bankers hope and panic and make decisions the same way the public does. Bankers are people, too, after all. They say, "We've got to react to this new condition. We've got to move money here. We've got to move money there." They are racing back and forth in rhythm with the market.

Politicians are the same way?

Sure. They react to markets; they don't move them. You'll find that a lot of political acts occur at predictable times, usually near the bottom of C waves and the top of fifth waves.

Since politics is so far behind the curve, why even talk about it?

If you're a trader or investor, there is no reason to talk about it at all! If you want to *anticipate political change*, which is something altogether different, the best way is to watch the stock market, which is the premier measure of a society's psychology.

In the end, people get to take their frustrations out on the politicians. At least there's that.

In the modern age, we're very lucky. In ancient times, when bear markets occurred and sovereigns had a lot of power, they went and chopped people up. But in modern days, it's the people that chop up the politicians. Except in war. That's when politicians go back to their roots.

Is there anything on the political scene that the waves are unclear about?

Always. What concerns me most is that while I know politics will become radical, I cannot tell which forces will ultimately win. The U.S. will surely become more authoritarian, because that's always the primary political force in a negative-mood trend. The U.S. has already been leaning this way, with its property seizure laws, anti-free speech laws, RICO, EPA levies, and gestapo-like attacks on private citizens by the FBI, ATF and DEA, welfarist business laws, OSHA impediments, demands for socialized medicine, you name it. Will it then become free again, by backlash? I don't know.

Women appear to be rising in dominance, as they did in the 1970s and 1940s. Although now it's not Rosie the Riveter but Sally the Senator.

That's because we're approaching a bear market. In every field, women gain dominance in bear market periods, and depending upon how the top is formed, the trend can begin a bit before or a bit after the price peak registered on the New York Stock Exchange.

It seems to be something that appears late in the cycle. When Rome went into decline, for instance, there was a similar phenomenon. Some historians have even blamed Rome's fall on the rise of women. These days some use it to say that Western civilization's main problem is that it's henpecked.

Well, I'm not saying that such things are causes. My position is different. The position you describe is one that implies it can be fixed. "If men would just change, or women would just change, then civilization would be saved." But changes in sexual roles are not the cause of things. They are a result of, or at least part and parcel of, the social dynamic reflected by Elliott waves.

Men can't get together and say 'Hey, let's stop being henpecked'?

No. At some level, they *want* to be henpecked. Men's role in this is just as important. In fact, one could argue that women rise in relative power because men abdicate it; they become docile and weak, so women fill the void. If men aren't getting the job done, which they do really well in bull markets, women take up the slack by assuming responsibility in areas that men have abandoned. So calling for change is just not going to work.

But is the timing right? It seems like this trend started long before this top. Didn't it start back in the '60s when Donna Reed, June Cleaver and Harriet Nelson went off the air?

Precisely! That's when the Grand Supercycle peaked out as measured in constant dollars and when it was almost entirely a man's world. You have to figure what the mix is in the overall picture. On a major trend basis, it's becoming increasingly a women's world. We had the feminist movement in the 1970s, more women heading into the work force and so on. I mean, maybe at the bottom we'll see another Joan of Arc or something. Can you imagine how submissive the Frenchmen of the time had to have been to allow England to take them over, then sit by and do nothing, or cooperate like weasels, until a female came along and challenged the English? And the men and women just weren't ready to be rescued yet. They both burned Joan for her trouble. Later on, men got socially recharged and took up the fight.

You have referred to the Clinton administration's effort to establish a government program to insure health care for all as a very major top signal. Why?

The Black Death occurred in the 1300s at the low of wave two in the Millennium degree advance, when one third of the population in Western Civilization died of disease. Historians have credited the Plague with inaugurating modern medicine.

The Plague exposed the inadequacy of the old "four humours" theory as well as cures based upon religion. So medical science was born at a time when health was considered a rare blessing. Today, personal health in the United States is considered a *natural condition*, an entitlement we're born with that only incompetent doctors could disrupt. The historically unprecedented number and size of malpractice awards bestowed upon customers of doctors by U.S. courts reflects that attitude among the population. In response to it, the leader of the world's most powerful government tried to decree "quality health care" a *right* of the entire population.

You see the change from the situation in the mid-14th century as a reflection of a long term journey from low to high?

Universal health care is such an extreme wish that it can only mean a top. It's not a mid-trend phenomenon. Medicare and Medicaid were launched at the major top of the mid-1960s, and this one is being floated now.

But universal health care didn't pass.

It nearly did. It had the support of 70% of the population for awhile. Besides, whether any such scheme is adopted or not, it is obvious that such social intentions are manifestations of an extreme *attitude* about "entitlements" to comfort and support that may not have existed in history except perhaps in the late Roman Empire.

Let's look deeper at the idea of inclusionism and exclusionism in bull and bear markets.

At the peak, there is a perceived brotherhood of men, nations, and indeed all living things, which is why there has been an environmental movement, in which trees are embraced as brothers. In bear markets, the trend changes, and the ultimate result is a psychology of "us vs. them."

So we will see a marked increase in factionalism during bear markets?

Yes, and the larger the bear market, the smaller the factional units. During the reduction process in the size of the social unit of allegiance, one's "in group" becomes smaller and smaller, moving from the universe to the world to the nation to the ethnic, religious, regional or sexual group to the city or feudal estate to the family to the individual. The trend halts at some point along that line that depends on the extent of the economic and psychological decline.

What's the stopping point for a large-degree decline?

In the Dark Ages, the feudal estate was the largest unit of allegiance in Europe. In times of starvation, such as in parts of Africa in recent times, even the family unit can disintegrate as babies are left to die while individuals fend for themselves.

Inclusionism is a sense of community and goodwill that gathers with a bull market, while exclusionism is the rise of factions and intolerance.

Right, at a peak, it's all "we;" everyone is a potential friend. At a bottom, it's all "they;" everyone is a potential enemy. When times are bad, intolerance for differences grows, and people build walls and fences to shut out those perceived to be different. When times are good, tolerance is greater and boundaries weaker.

Is inclusionism the same as collectivism?

Ironically, it appears to be the opposite. Bull markets reflect a trend toward inclusion in that more and more entities are given the nod of acceptance as individuals. Inclusionism is essentially well-wishing one's fellow man, which goes hand in hand with general increases in freedom. Collectivist notions are actually exclusionary in that they divide society into groups and give one group's possessions to another. The most extreme cases in fact occur at major bottoms. Hitler's takeover in Germany in 1933 was at a major bottom. 1949, the year of the communist takeover of China, was the exact year of the end of the constant-dollar corrective pattern that started in 1929. The 1940s also saw collectivism take over Eastern Europe. The disastrous five-year Cultural Revolution in China began in 1966, the year the bear market began. The aftershocks persisted throughout the bearish period of the 1970s. Those are classic bear market phenomena. In the U.S., most of our collectivist legislation came in the 1930s and 1940s during the Supercycle wave IV bear market and again in the late 1960s as the Grand Supercycle bear market began in constant dollars. Here in 2000, look at all of the worldwide examples we have of increasing freedom and inclusionism. Eastern Europe has been freed. Most of Southern China, even though the country is controlled by communists, has been freed up. The Eastern Bloc is approaching NATO membership.

Sometimes, though, a bear market and its exclusionist forces lead to increased freedom. The 1700s bear market led to the Revolutionary War, which was conducted to exclude the British from America, and the philosophy behind the formation of the government led to men in America being left free.

It was also a long term bottom for stocks. If acts or moments of extreme exclusionism are buying opportunities, is inclusionism bad?

It depends upon your perspective. The inclusionism itself is mostly healthy for living things. Unfortunately, an extreme in such feelings and actions, welcome as they are otherwise, is symptomatic of a major top, not a buying opportunity. The spectacle of communist governments relinquishing control and territory and admitting freedom is the opposite of the spectacle of Communists taking over countries. So if it was a buying opportunity for stocks when they were taking over countries, what is it when they give them up? The fall of communism reflected a general inclusionist good feeling that recalled 1967's Summer of Love and 1987's Harmonic Convergence celebration, both of which occurred at important market tops. This top is of much larger degree, and the nearly unprecedented global social harmony reflects that fact.

Does this inclusionism have any direct economic benefits?

The General Agreement on Tariffs and Trade took effect in January 1995. It cut tariffs worldwide an average of 33%, reduced agricultural subsidies, provided global patent protection, and set up large cooperating bureaucracies. It was passed with concessions and postponements on some issues because, as was widely trumpeted, "no one wanted it to fail." The key sentiment was *cooperation toward a friendly goal.* That is inclusionism at work.

You might be interested to know that GATT was founded in 1947, near the end of the last great bear market of 1929-1949. Agreements adopted by GATT resulted in trade liberalization throughout the bull market until 1969, right at the top. From 1970 forward, protectionist pressures resulted in less free trade through the end of the last meeting in 1979, right near the end of the bear market. GATT was reconvened in 1986, well into the new bull market, as the *Financial Times* of London put it, "to re-establish the credibility of GATT." The aim of this new round of talks was to re-establish the old free-trade trend, which they finally did in 1993, well into this bull market.

You've noted that fifth waves attempt to re-live the glory of the third wave but accomplish only a hollow echo. Can you find evidence of similar shortcomings in the most recent era of free trade?

The GATT accord fits well with this interpretation because it includes a number of restrictive provisions, accomplishing little more than a hollow echo of the third wave free-trade trend of the 1950s and 1960s, which was in turn a hollow echo of the flat-out laissez-faire environment of the third Supercycle wave in the late 1800s and early 1900s. So the character of the agreement is perfectly compatible with the long term trend. Our next trend will be toward *conflict* and *restriction* in world trade.

* * * * * * * * * * * * * * *

The Elliott Wave Financial Forecast
May 26, 2000

The late post-peak burst of positive social sentiment has carried into the political realm, as a major trade deal with Communist China was reached May 23. A vote by the U.S. House seals the granting of normal trade ties to China. The passage of this historic measure places another arrow on our chart [Figure 3-1] of Grand Supercycle milestones from *The Wave Principle of Human Social Behavior*. Will it be the last? We cannot say, but, if it is, it is interesting that these historic reconciliations followed the same geographic course, from Europe to China, as the progression of hostility shown for the bear market of the 1930s and 1940s. The trade ties that are now being restored originally ceased after the Communists took over China in 1949, where the final arrow in the last Supercycle degree *bear market* appears. Hopes today are as bright as they were faint in 1949. The vote is considered a huge victory for the "salivating" U.S. business community and its drive to gain access to "the expanding Chinese marketplace of 1.3 billion." According to USA Today, the measure marks the culmination of an "irresistible" 150-year-old "fantasy." In the past, these dreams have always been dashed. Our Elliott wave count for the Dow suggests that it will happen again. The goodwill represented by the "permanent" embrace of these two trade partners should fade as hostility develops with surprising speed.

Figure 3-1

* * * * * * * * * * * * * * *

Where does this unrest and the rising exclusionism eventually take us?

Trends become radicalized. Environmentalism, for instance, will follow an exclusionary path, adopt an "us vs. them" mentality, and become more hell-bent on destroying humans than on hugging trees. At the same time, a severe reaction to the movement will set in. The same will be true regarding every social question: immigration, welfare, you name it. Exclusion will gain the upper hand. In countless ways, persecution will wax. This is the likely direction of trend for the next dozen years and on a larger scale for as much as a century.

By 20th century standards at least, it's pretty quiet out there now.

Exactly. The current world scene is remarkably free of war-ring. We witnessed the warmest relationships between long-time archenemies the U.S. and Russia in at least forty years, and Russia and China in thirty years. Periods of peace generally coincide with the latter part of prolonged market uptrends, reflecting the effects of a positive social psychology, which is the engine of bull markets. During the later stages of bull markets, wars are nonexistent, brief, mild or contained. In U.S. history, all three fifth waves of Cycle degree have been peaceful.

Did you anticipate this side effect of the bull market?

In the October 1982 issue, a list of expectations for the coming decade included, "No international war for at least ten years."

Those ten years are well up.

So they are. What I am saying now is that the forces of social psychology will soon *no longer preclude war*. In fact, they will be trending toward it into the time of greatest risk: when the market is bottoming and shortly thereafter.

But haven't we had plenty of times when presidential popularity and/ or stocks fell and no war resulted?

Yes. The late 1970s are a good example. We didn't go to war, but Russia did. December 1979 is when the Russians marched into Afghanistan. Still, given all the forces currently at work, if stock prices are to fall as far as the Wave Principle suggests, then I deem it nearly certain that the U.S. will find itself embroiled in conflict. The global good feelings associated with the bull market will have evaporated by then.

The bull market was not a total love-in. What about the cold war? Isn't that an example of bull market hostilities?

Precisely. Bull market hostilities mean you don't fight. The Cold War is a phenomenon of a bull market. *Hot* wars happen in bear market trends.

There was a lot of fear, and there were war scares.

Right. And an Elliott wave analyst would have said, "Don't believe them." Now he says that as the market begins to fall, "If there appear to be *peace* agreements, don't believe them." Remember Neville Chamberlain's peace agreements with Hitler and Russia's countless broken guarantees in the 1940s. When the Grand Supercycle bear market begins, it will be a technical consideration overriding all others. Then, periods of peace will be temporary. What people initially think are short wars will prove to be just battles in a long period of conflict.

What does history say about the possible size of a major war?

The size and severity of each war reflect the degree of the associated bear market, and this one is going to be large.

Which wars were produced by which reversals?

In the past 200 years, even Cycle degree bear markets have produced significant wars such as the War of 1812, the Spanish-American War, World War I and Vietnam. However, bear markets of Supercycle degree or greater have produced the truly major wars. The bear market of 1720-1782/4 ended with the Revolutionary War. It was followed near the "wave two" low by the French Revolution and Napoleonic Wars. The bear market of 1837-1859 was followed immediately by the Civil War. The bear market of 1929-1932/49 resulted in World War II. The latter two produced far more U.S. casualties than any of the wars that occurred in the smaller Cycle degree bear markets. And, true to size, Millennium degree bear markets appear to produce prolonged periods of warring, such as occurred in the Dark Ages and into the "wave two" low thereafter.

The market bottomed in 1859, but the Civil War didn't even start until 1860.

As I've said already, the extreme in negative social mood often causes events to be set in motion that play out even as mood is reversing from its extreme. The lesson remains: mood change precedes and creates history. The timing is not precisely the same each time, but the relationship is there.

A lot of people consider the Kondratieff cycle *the* war engine. Does a given war's position within the K-wave affect how serious it is?

No. The Kondratieff cycle low of 1896 produced only the relatively minor Spanish-American war (in 1898), presenting powerful evidence that the Kondratieff cycle is *not* the determinant of a war's severity; the degree of the associated bear market, as interpreted under the Wave Principle, *is*.

* * * * * * * * * * * * * *

The Elliott Wave Theorist
December 25, 1989

> Various economists in past years have made a case that war is causally "bullish" for the economy (i.e., "let's have a war to get the economy moving"). The result of war is destruction, however, so that thesis is absurd. The process destroys assets; it doesn't create them.

* * * * * * * * * * * * * *

The implication is that war is likely to break out during the bear market. Since the next one will be a major war, shouldn't we have some idea of who it is we are to fight?

A scenario I presented in 1989 called for unrest in the Middle East to accelerate. That was written *before* any hint that the Gulf War was coming. That area of the world will undoubtedly continue to be a hotbed of conflict and probably one focus of our worries.

But things progressed after the Gulf War. The Prime Minister of Israel and the Chairman of the Palestine Liberation Organization shook hands on September 14, 1993, and several more historic agreements were reached between countries and religious factions that had torn the region through centuries of antagonism. Israel, Syria and all of Europe were talking about economic treaties that would bind the whole region.

Yes, it was quite different from the atmosphere at the bottom in 1981, when Egyptian president Anwar Sadat was gunned down by Muslim militants for signing a similar agreement with Israel. These treaties terminated a state of belligerence that has been in force since 1948, near the end of Cycle wave IV measured in constant dollars. "Children born today," said Israeli leader Yitzhak Rabin, "will never know war between us." Well, in recent months, these good feelings have dissipated. The Palestinians and the Israelis are at each other's throats again. The next major low in mood is due this decade. The mood *then* will sorely test the promise of the 1990s.

If there is war in the Middle East, it's not going to be like the Gulf War, when most of the world was united against one belligerent nation. Will it be more like the other big wars of this century? Will big nations take sides?

Yes. Exclusionism and polarity will be the overriding sentiments.

How do these things develop?

Take this line of thought. The former Soviet Union has lots of weapons and no money. Japan has no weapons and is heading into bankruptcy. A simple alliance with or purchase from a starving Russia could turn Japan into a military power virtually overnight. It may well be that the belligerent, some say racist, politician who penned the Japanese national bestseller, *The Japan That Can Say No [to the U.S.]*, who has been dismissed as an anomaly with less than one third of the country's support, will find himself even more popular as Japanese financial and social fortunes continue to collapse into depression. To many Japanese, the U.S. will make a convenient scapegoat, and the man who said it first, loudest and most angrily will be remembered and rewarded. That is how Hitler found himself in power when the depths of the Great Depression arrived in 1933, This is not a prediction. I'm just illustrating a way to think about the prospects.

Any other potential risks?

Well, with a downturn of the magnitude that is coming, we might see the return of religious militarism. The war in Bosnia has religious overtones. Most of the Middle East still thinks the West is the devil.

You took a timing position in *At the Crest of the Tidal Wave.*

Yes, I said that while conflicts should take place at the next stock market bottom of Supercycle degree, the next major international war, World War III if you will, is not likely to occur until wave (C) of the Grand Supercycle bottoms. That is likely to happen around mid-century ideally, although the wave label is the determinant, not any projected probable date.

As the one remaining super power, shouldn't the U.S. fare well in any war?

Watch out. First, you are projecting linearly. It is well to keep in mind that at the end of the last Grand Supercycle bear market, Great Britain lost the American colonies and accelerated its retrenchment back to the island from its former "sun never sets" position of world power. The peaking of a 200-year Grand Supercycle advance in U.S. progress is probably coinciding with the peak of U.S. influence as a world power. The United States will very likely be forced to remove a great deal of its military and commercial influence from the rest of the globe by the end of the Grand Supercycle bear market. History shows, though, that complete retrenchment can take a century, or even three. Second, might I point out that the U.S. could be the *dangerous* force this time? If an authoritarian government takes over, look out, world. I also think that Israel could end up acting nearly as badly as Nazi Germany. It's already socialist, has a huge military, and inflation has run rampant. The setup is similar. People may bristle at such ideas, but you have to think outside the box.

A Giant Leap Forward

Quite frankly, your appraisal on the state of affairs in the world is concise and illuminating, but it scares me.

It scared me too initially, when I first began to realize what the charts were saying about the likely course of events over the Grand Supercycle bear. However, putting my thoughts on paper has given me a frame of reference within which to judge events, and that in itself has a reassuring effect. Just think how panicked those people who have no inkling of what lies ahead will be as events unfold. They are the ones most likely to despair. Our forefathers survived crises. Let's live up to their courage.

What would cause you to change your mind on the big picture?

A return of valuations to lower levels, generally bearish market sentiment, and a completed bear market pattern.

There's nothing that could make you say you were wrong, it's time to turn and follow the uptrend?

I have little patience with questions such as "How high does the market have to go, or how long does it have to hold up, for you to turn bullish?" It is as if the sky were filled with clouds, you had concluded that rain was likely, and were asked, "How much darker do the clouds have to get before you'll decide it won't rain?" or "How long will the clouds have to remain for you to change your mind?" There is no such darkness level and no such time limit. The same thing was true in reverse in the late 1970s. "If the market breaks what level will you turn long term bearish?" I said then, "I'm not *going* to turn long term bearish. I may look wrong for awhile, but the signs are there and cannot be erased." There is no level at which a rising market can provide an excuse for a bullish opinion in today's historically bearish technical environment, nor is there a time limit on how long this environment can last before the bear comes out of hibernation.

Well, sometimes clouds go away without raining.

Let's not stretch the analogy too far! A comparable event in market analysis would be if companies tripled dividends on average while the public turned bearish on stocks while the pattern resolved into a "third of a third" acceleration while breadth expanded! If that were to happen, then the rain clouds would go away, and the market could keep going. You can bet on it if you want, but betting on it is not just an academic question. We're talking about whether you would agree to leave your priceless stamp collection out on the picnic table for two days despite a sky filled with billowing black clouds.

Let's grant that the market is extended. Can't it get much more extended?

Yes, but whether it does is irrelevant. The "greater fool theory" works great until the day it stops working, and then markets plummet. With each higher tick and every extra month, the risk of a collapse increases. If the peak price hasn't been seen, it's close, and the downside potential is so great that owning stocks is not an acceptable option, period. I'm so sure it's over that I'm putting two new books together. One is *View from the Top of the Grand Supercycle*, which reprints our best essays and also talks about my mistakes, and *Beautiful Pictures*, which displays the amazing Fibonacci relationships in the Supercycle from 1932 to the January high this year.

There has to be a bright spot. Can you leave us a glimmer of light for the future? Do you have any reason for optimism?

I am very optimistic that I can help people conserve money. A lot of people say "Hey Bob, you brought us good news for all these years, and now you bring us bad news." I object strenuously to that. Patterns of social behavior merely exist. The bad news happens not when you're warned but when you are caught on the wrong side of events. Misery and failure are created by trying to live in the old trend when a new one is in force. If you had stayed pessimistic throughout the 1950s and 1960s, you would have lost terrific opportunities. The same thing was true of the 1980s.

On the other side of the coin, if you had leveraged yourself to the hilt in 1968, you would have suffered tremendously. I think we are in a similar situation today. The "good news" is a warning that enables you to be on the right side of the trend.

Declines aren't all bad, either. When I speak of positive and negative trends in the stock market, I'm talking almost in the sense of poles on a magnet. It doesn't necessarily mean all good in one direction and all bad in the other. Some good things come out of the downside.

For instance...

Well, for one thing, sociologists have noted that in tough times, family ties grow stronger. Also, bear markets squeeze the excess out of the markets — everything from ill-advised debt assumption to dishonest accounting techniques. In bear markets, people tend to slow down and appreciate the more basic and, some say, more important things in life. Another plus is that every big decline sets the stage for the next great period of progress.

Will there be a new work ethic when the current house of cards comes crashing down? Or will society increase its demands for handouts?

I don't know. In the 1930s, a lot of people seemed rather docile and non-revolutionary standing in bread lines. But there were also socialist and communist demonstrations. A lot of people postulate that these days are different, that people have come to believe that their neighbors owe them a living. I don't know to what extent that is actually true in the depths of the American psyche. To the extent it is true, there is likely to be more unrest in the next fifteen years than in the 1930s. The degree of the coming bear market is higher, which supports the case for greater social unrest.

What if preparation could be done on a mass scale? Aren't there things that could be done to soften the downside of the cycle?

Perhaps there are things that *could* be done, but the real question is — and this question is sociological — *will* they be done? The answer is an unequivocal *no*. Einstein's comment, "God does not play dice with the universe," may have social implications as well. Society undergoes a pendulum-like swing, back and forth between prosperity and recession. It is part of mankind's nature. Therefore, there is nothing that will alter the tidal forces of social change. There appears to be no mechanism to get in the way of that motion — to stop it or reverse it. The alternative would be an absolutely flat-line society that never feels better or worse about itself. And, of course, history shows that there has never been such a thing. I don't think people are going to change.

What if the government changed, cut taxes by 70%, and took us back to a truly free market?

Again, the question is, *will* they? Do you see politicians becoming statesmen today and changing government so that we can avoid disaster? Not even close. They change when a crisis forces them to act, and that will come at the low, not here at the high.

Is there nothing that could get our political leaders to face reality? If they were aware of the Wave Principle and therefore ahead of the curve, they could institute public policies in time to do some good.

Only individuals can be induced to face reality. The fundamental problem with desiring "society" to face reality is that societies go through alternating patterns of facing and denying reality, and that cyclicality appears to be immutable. As far as public policy makers accepting the idea of the Wave Principle for any length of time, recall that *by definition, most participants in the markets and the economy must be unbelievers at the turns.* If our opinions were generally believed and respected, they would be wrong. How could it then be a top or bottom? Political leaders are immersed in the social mood and act as its puppets. It's that simple.

What about globalization and instantaneous communication — those are modern phenomena — isn't it possible they will help us escape the grasp of history and the Wave Principle?

No. Crowd behavior is rooted in psychology, which has its own pace of development regardless of whether communication speed has increased. Besides, it hasn't increased that much. In 1720, you would have known of a market move within minutes if you were at the exchange, and maybe an hour later if you were at work. Is it really much different today? Modern communications have simply enlarged the size of what three hundred years ago was a crowd in the town square.

How about New York Stock Exchange circuit breakers and all that high-tech stuff? That's all new. Don't you think that regardless of how bad it gets, we live in a more fluid world, one that can change much more rapidly. This time, can we get back into another bull trend faster?

No. Those are like "sticker insurance." They make you feel secure but don't mean anything.

I suppose the craze for foreign stocks is also a part of the problem rather than any kind of solution.

Of course. No crowd buys stocks of other countries intelligently. For decades, heavy foreign buying in the U.S. stock market has served as an excellent indicator of major tops. In the past several years, it is the U.S. investor who is the new "foreigner," and he has been pouring record amounts of money into the stock markets of other countries. To put this buying into perspective, consider that U.S. investors in fact sold Japanese stocks on balance for most of the 1980s, when riches were there to be had. Then as the peak was being approached, they acted as if they had seen the light and bought Japanese stocks in record amounts in 1989-1990 at the top. Similarly, the more recent pouring of funds into such overpriced markets as those of Mexico and South America are signals of a major long term top in those markets.

The scale of the coming stock market retrenchment indicates that it is going to have to correct a very serious error in social judgment. What do you think that breach of reason is?

Let me read something out of *Elliott Wave Principle*: "As this century progresses, it becomes clearer that in order to satisfy the demands of some individuals and groups for the output of others, man through the agency of the state, has begun to leech off that which he has created. He has not only mortgaged his present output, but he has mortgaged the output of future generations by eating the capital that took generations to accumulate." Today, over two decades after that was written, the U.S. public has a zero savings rate and has borrowed to the hilt, trying to make up for the shortfall that has resulted from decades of wealth destruction by government. When the depression hits, the average person's actual poverty will be revealed to him.

Are we looking toward a grim century ahead?

Yes, but with two major respites. The next decade or so is likely to be grim, but after that, we should have several very expansive decades. Then we'll have the grimmest decade probably mid century. Overall, it should be somewhat of a roller coaster ride of corrective and expansive forces, if my projections in *At the Crest* are right. Then it will be off to the races for humankind again.

You've said that the ultimate path of human progress is ever upward; it is merely interrupted by periodic setbacks. That's actually kind of optimistic.

It's not optimism; it's just a description of a net-beneficent reality. The fact that human behavior follows a sequence found in nature indicates that we're a part of nature, progressing in accordance with one of its principles for growing systems.

The Wave Principle.

Yes, three steps forward, two steps back.

A bipolar disorder?

Bipolar *order.*

O.K., I get it! But why does it have to be a look-but-don't-touch situation? If we learn it, why can't we influence the wave pattern?

Who's we? You and I? What would we do? No man can change nature's physical laws, but he can understand them and harness their power for his benefit. The same appears to be true of the laws of human social behavior.

It gave us the freedom to observe our own nature but not the means to fix it?

It gave *some* of us the opportunity to observe it, and those few of us can't change it.

So we collectively create out own miseries, and there's nothing we can do about it?

Well, don't forget that we create our own glories, too. Just look at the U.S. for the last 200 years. What a great time in history. What a great place to live!

I can also see that the Wave Principle increases our knowledge, at least for the individual who possesses it, if not for all society.

Exactly. With the Wave Principle, history is telescoped and the human mind can grasp the impelling socio-emotional pattern. Charts reveal in human social activities a continually repeating pattern that is typical of a progressive life form. That conceptual condensation is a powerful tool whose main practical values are in describing the past scientifically and in anticipating the tenor of the future. This kind of analysis can give you a panoramic view of the past, which by its very nature also implies certain things about the future.

You've been describing something that's far bigger than the money part of our lives. If the Wave Principle is as comprehensive as you make it out, isn't it even bigger than social forecasting? It must be deeply personal. We should be able not just to observe, but to take advantage of technical clues in our personal lives?

Without question, Elliott wave analysis is applicable in your personal and professional life. I've already told you about how it led me to recognize the onset of my professional bear market. But it also tells me now that my bear market is ending. Although I chart my public persona and business, which are *social* phenomena and thus in the realm of the Wave Principle, I have come to believe that every productive person moves through waves of progress and regress through his life. Try to plot yours and see where you are.

To possess history's road map, one need master the Wave Principle. Some people's basic objection to that is it's too simplistic to be true.

Most truths are simple and paradoxical, and so is this one.

If the Wave Principle is *the* answer, why aren't more people trying to nail it down?

The Principle says that the market moves in a way that to most people is counter-intuitive. Most people treat their mental defaults as if they were facts.

Will the bear market change things?

Oh, yes. I am quite certain that the Wave Principle will attract even greater interest when asset allocation models and fundamental stock selection techniques appear to stop working. Cyclic and pattern analysis goes in and out of style with major cycles in cultural trends.

You've said there are a lot of ways for a disciplined investor to get results. And a lot of really successful investors have done so, even though they ignore these deeper questions of natural law, culture and philosophy. Isn't the Wave Principle a complication?

Any method based on the market's behavior patterns will work if the goal is to make money trading as a business. But that doesn't interest me. I would have quit a long time ago if it were not for the Wave Principle's broader implications. Those and the aesthetics of the Wave Principle keep me involved. It is like watching an artist paint. The appreciation of that process in the actions of humanity are what the Wave Principle makes possible for the first time. It provides a framework within which to observe, reflect upon and enjoy the beauty of nature in the activity of man. And that is no small blessing.

SOURCES

The Actuarial Digest
The Aden Interviews
(American Association of Individual Investors) Journal
Atlanta Business Chronicle
The Atlanta Journal / The Atlanta Constitution
Atlanta Magazine
Barron's
Business Atlanta
The Business Journal
Business Week
Cable News Network (CNN)
Chicago Tribune
Commodity Traders Consumer Reports
Discover
Diversified Investor's Forecast
Dow Jones News Service
The Economist
The Elliott Wave Theorist
Financial Planning
The Financial Post (Canada)
Financial Security Alert
Financial World
Florida Dental Journal
Florida Today
Forbes
Forsyth County News
Fortune
Fulton County Daily Report
Futures
The (Gainesville, GA) Times
Gentleman's Quarterly
Georgia Trend
Gold and Silver Today
Grant's Interest Rate Observer
Hulbert Financial Digest

Intermarket
The International Currency Review
The International Herald Tribune
Investment Vision
Investors Guide
Investor's Hotline with Joe Bradley
Market Technicians Association Journal
Marketline (CSTA)
The Master Indicator
The (Memphis) *Commercial Appeal*
Mensa Bulletin
Money Maker
MoneyTalk (TV Show)
The National OTC Stock Journal
The (New York) *Daily News*
New York Post
The New York Times
Newsweek
Physicians Financial News
Power Talk with Anthony Robbins
Prodigy (on-line)
San Francisco Business Times
The Sound Money Investor
The Spectator
Successful Investing
Superstars of Investing
Technical Analysis of Stocks and Commodities
Technical Trends
The (New Orleans) *Times Picayune*
The Union Leader (Manchester, NH)
The Wall Street Journal
The Washington Post
Tim Hayes Investigative Report
USA Today
Wealth

NEW CLASSICS LIBRARY

Elliott Wave Principle
*A.J. Frost and
Robert R. Prechter Jr.*

Conquer the Crash
Robert R. Prechter, Jr.

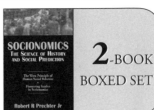

**2-BOOK
BOXED SET**

**Pioneering Studies in Socionomics
&
The Wave Principle of Human Social Behavior**
Robert R. Prechter, Jr.

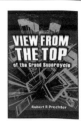

**View from the Top of
the Grand Supercycle**
Robert R. Prechter, Jr.

**Market Analysis for the
New Millennium**
*edited by
Robert R. Prechter, Jr.*

**At the Crest of the
Tidal Wave**
Robert R. Prechter, Jr.

**How to Forecast Gold &
Silver Using the Wave
Principle**
Robert R. Prechter, Jr.

**R.N. Elliott´s Market
Letters (1938-1946)**
*edited by
Robert R. Prechter, Jr.*

**Complete Elliott Wave
Writings of
A. Hamilton Bolton**
*edited by
Robert R. Prechter, Jr.*

**The Elliott Wave
Writings of A.J. Frost
and Richard Russell**
*edited by
Robert R. Prechter, Jr.*

**R.N. Elliott´s
Masterworks**
*edited by
Robert R. Prechter, Jr.*

Beautiful Pictures
Robert R. Prechter, Jr.

Available at
**www.elliottwave.com/books
Or call 800-336-1618** (inside
the U.S.) or **770-536-0309**
(outside the U.S.).

**New Classics Library
P.O. Box 1618
Gainesville, GA 30503 USA**

www.elliottwave.com/books